STENDHAL

A STUDY OF HIS NOVELS

STENDHAL

A STUDY OF HIS NOVELS

BY

F. W. J. HEMMINGS

OXFORD

AT THE CLARENDON PRESS

Oxford University Press, Ely House, London W. 1

GLASGOW NEW YORK TORONTO MELBOURNE WELLINGTON
CAPE TOWN SALISBURY IBADAN NAIROBI LUSAKA ADDIS ABABA
BOMBAY CALCUTTA MADRAS KARACHI LAHORE DACCA
KUALA LUMPUR HONG KONG

FIRST PUBLISHED 1964
REPRINTED LITHOGRAPHICALLY IN GREAT BRITAIN
FROM CORRECTED SHEETS OF THE FIRST EDITION
1966

CONTENTS

INTRODUCTION

VERY broadly, all novels, by whatever authors, may be considered to fall into one of two categories. There are those that draw their dramatic energy from the friction generated by the collision of a number of different characters, actuated by different interests and pursuing different aims; and there are those that solicit the reader's interest on behalf of a single hero detached, but not isolated, from the other characters who surround him, jostling, thwarting, or abetting him. The distinction will be clear, perhaps, if it is suggested that the *Iliad* provides the prototype of the one, the *Odyssey* of the other pattern. Keeping, for simplicity, to the French novel, we may find illustrations of the first category in *Les Liaisons dangereuses*, *Le Père Goriot*, *Germinal*, *Les Faux-Monnayeurs*, *Les Chemins de la Liberté*; of the second, in *Gil Blas*, *L'Éducation sentimentale*, *A la recherche du temps perdu*, *Jean-Christophe*, and *L'Étranger*. Such a collection of titles is bound to appear disparate: the only common element is the formula, which is social drama in the first case and the 'imaginary biography' in the second.

Now Stendhal's novels are very obviously cast in the mould of the imaginary biography, as the author himself realized quite clearly. 'Outre le génie, la grande différence entre Fielding et Dominique [Stendhal himself], c'est que Fielding décrit *à la fois* les sentiments et actions de *plusieurs* personnages, et Dominique d'*un seul*.' Stendhal then puts the question: 'Où mène la manière de Dominique? Je l'ignore. Est-ce un perfectionnement? Est-ce revenir à l'enfance de l'art, ou plutôt tomber dans le genre froid du personnage philosophique?'[1]

As a matter of fact, Fielding is not the best example that Stendhal might have chosen if he was looking for a novelist whose manner was directly opposed to his own: *Tom Jones* is as fair an example of the 'imaginary biography' as *Le Rouge et le Noir*. The success of such a type of narrative must be measured by the degree

---

[1] *Mélanges intimes et Marginalia*, ii. 230–1. References throughout are to the Divan edition of Stendhal's works. For details see Bibliography.

to which the narrator persuades the reader to identify himself, in part or in whole, with the hero.

Le poète comique me présente un jeune homme semblable à moi qui, par l'excès de ses bonnes qualités devient malheureux et qui par ces mêmes qualités devient heureux. Cela me procurant la vue du bonheur m'intéresse et me fait sourire. Tom Jones est un exemple. Plus le malheur du personnage avec qui je me suis identifié est grand, plus je réfléchis profondément pour trouver les moyens de m'en sortir, plus il m'intéresse.[2]

The reference to the 'comic poet' at the beginning and the flavour of the geometry text-book which clings to the passage as a whole betray the fact that, when he made these observations, Henri Beyle was still under the spell of the ideologists; the note was, in fact, written in 1804, shortly after his first reading of *Tom Jones*, and many years before it occurred to him to try his hand at writing novels.

However stiffly phrased, it is an important passage because it leads to the heart of the ambiguity embedded in the very term 'hero', applied to Stendhal's fiction. The 'imaginary biography' is a narrative constructed around a central character, conventionally called the hero. But this word also suggests a character possessed of superior, even superhuman qualities; at the very least, a figure compelling admiration. How did Stendhal intend his reader should regard his hero? with admiration or—as he implied in the fragment just quoted—with something less than admiration: with interest, which is a milder but closer sympathy? Is the character meant to be heroic as Corneille's Rodrigue is heroic, or is his role no more than that of the *hero of the novel*, like . . . Smollett's Roderick?

It is a question on which Stendhal's critics are sharply divided. Maurice Bardèche, for instance, argues eloquently in favour of the view that the hero in Stendhal is not merely the character standing at the centre of the narrative, but is also heroic in a moral, not to say mythical, sense. Stendhal, he says, was concerned to create 'the modern *beau idéal*; his aim is to vie with the sculptor of the Apollo or the Antinous. He seeks *the* hero of modern times . . . an image of perfection, the Apollo or the Antinous, the young god of a civilization that adolescents dream of.'[3] Francine Marill

---

[2] *Molière, Shakspeare, la Comédie et le Rire*, p. 280.
[3] *Stendhal romancier*, p. 68.

Albérès, on the other hand, suggests that the historic perspective alone is responsible for giving us the illusion that Stendhal's heroes were heroic.[4] They are so admirable as literary achievements that, with the passage of time, they have become admirable as specimens of a lofty humanism. They were not so intended originally and, properly read, these novels present us with young men as they are, not with the paragons sprung from a generous imagination. Idealized humanity is present in older works, in *La Princesse de Clèves*, in *La Nouvelle Héloïse*: Mme de Lafayette and Rousseau raised their characters above the norm in obedience to a literary convention which goes back to D'Urfé and Corneille. Stendhal drew his characters from reality; they were not invented to accord with the requirements of an exalted idealism.

In this debate, one point at least is clear. If the paramount need was for the reader to be able to identify himself with the hero, then it was necessary that the hero should be a little less than perfect. Stendhal might well have repeated, after Fielding: 'If thou dost delight in these models of perfection, there are books enow written to gratify thy taste; but, as we have not, in the course of our conversation, ever happened to meet with any such person, we have not chosen to introduce any such here.'[5] What Stendhal did write (to an aspirant lady novelist who had submitted him a manuscript) was this: 'Faites faire quelque petite gaucherie à votre héros, parce qu'enfin nous autres héros, nous faisons des gaucheries. Nous courons; un plat homme marche à grand'peine, et encore avec une canne; c'est pour cela qu'il ne tombe pas.'[6] If these sagacious words are placed alongside the lines already quoted about the young man 'qui par l'excès de ses bonnes qualités devient malheureux', then Stendhal's picture of the hero becomes a little clearer. Julien, Lucien, Fabrice, and the others will be endowed with qualities which, good in themselves, unfit them for the life that circumstances force them to live. There are stones in the hero's path to trip him up, puddles into which he will blunder; he will be bruised, mud-bespattered, and will cut a ludicrous figure at times; for he is a runner, heedless, and fares less well than the prudent pedestrian with his stick.

The qualities that Stendhal bestows on the heroes of his novels are the specific qualities of generous youth. Readiness to

[4] *Stendhal*, pp. 70–71.   [5] *Tom Jones*, book X, chap. i.
[6] *Correspondance*, ix. 31.

experiment and to adventure, a recklessness of the future, a contempt of caution. The tendency to judge others by one's own high standards of altruism, and to despise them unmercifully when they fall below these standards. A dread of ridicule which, exaggerated, turns into a foolish fear of appearing what one is—young and inexperienced. A dread, too, of the gilded cage and of all hostages given to fortune. Quick intelligence often rendered unavailing by intellectual presumption. Golden dreams—those that others have dreamed, those one dreams for oneself—preferred invariably to cast-iron reality: in a specific context, Juliet on her balcony rather than Juliet in bed.

The opposite to such a figure is the thick-set merchant in one of Molière's plays who complained of his cook's composing verses and ruining the roast, and threatened to consign every book in the house to the attics except a Plutarch heavy enough to serve as a collar-press. Stendhal evokes him in the *Vie de Henri Brulard*, simply in order to make clear what he hates, what he has always hated, what turns his stomach much as the smell of oysters indisposes a man who has eaten too many oysters. 'Tous les faits qui forment la vie de Chrysale sont remplacés chez moi par du romanesque. Je crois que cette tache dans mon téléscope a été utile pour mes personnages de roman, il y a une sorte de bassesse bourgeoise qu'ils ne peuvent avoir, et pour l'auteur ce serait parler le *chinois*, qu'il ne sait pas.'[7]

Not one of Stendhal's heroes but shares with Stendhal this inability to 'talk Chinese'. This is what makes them, to use Bourget's expression, 'ses sosies moraux', his spiritual doubles, and this is why Thibaudet (stating the obvious, as usual, rather well) observed that 'Henri Brulard remains the model for the heroes of Stendhal's four novels: Octave, Julien, Lucien, and Fabrice'.[8] But there is more. Most young men, as time goes on, learn to speak Chinese, and acquire, in the age of ripeness, a tolerable fluency: Chrysale's 'bassesse bourgeoise' lies in wait for most of us in our forties or fifties. But not for Stendhal who never reached middle age except in respect of arteries and eyesight. 'Ce défaut — mon horreur pour Chrysale — m'a peut-être maintenu jeune. Ce serait donc un heureux malheur, comme celui d'avoir eu peu de femmes...'[9]

[7] *Vie de Henri Brulard*, i. 134.
[8] Bourget, *Nouvelles pages de critique et de doctrine*, i. 31; Thibaudet, *Stendhal*, p. 96. [9] *Vie de Henri Brulard*, i. 272.

The moral axioms in accordance with which Stendhal declares his preferences among his characters, and the moral standards by which he hopes that we shall judge them, are evidently unusual, idiosyncratic, and, most of us would add, perverse. It is as much as anything because his moral assumptions work across the grain of our traditional way of thinking that he has been, on the whole, seldom properly understood in this country—either dismissed as a frivolous libertine, or else brazenly trumpeted by excited rebels. Considering him simply as a writer, we have the choice between pronouncing him to be negligible, and admitting that he makes nonsense of some of our carefully established canons: for our own novelists, those of his century at least, assume in the reader a close and loving acquaintance with 'Chinese'; and—to use a precise and familiar illustration—one fancies that if Stendhal had had to deal with a pair such as Mr. Knightley and Frank Churchill, he would have contrived, with his usual combination of impudence and irony, to enlist our sympathy for the latter and turn the former to ridicule. There is no doubt that Stendhal calls for a particular effort of the understanding if he is to be appreciated by Anglo-Saxon readers. But the effort should be made: there is no better antidote for a certain cultural insularity to which we are as prone today as we always have been. 'Oh! rien n'est ennuyeux', as one of Stendhal's mouthpieces remarks, 'comme l'Anglais qui se prend de colère parce que toute l'Europe n'est pas une servile copie de son Angleterre.'[1]

Since it was only during the last sixteen years of his life that Stendhal was writing novels—whereas he had been reading them since boyhood—it has seemed reasonable to start by suggesting what he might have learned from earlier writers and specifying how he reacted to those of his contemporaries whose fictional work he deigned to peruse. Some kind of an aesthetic of the novel, admittedly loose and fragmentary, emerges from Stendhal's miscellaneous reading and disjointed meditations over this preliminary period. Next we shall attempt a generalized 'portrait of the hero' in Stendhal's fiction; there are important differences, of course, from one novel to another, but enough similarities none the less to justify a broadly sketched composite picture. Thereafter we shall consider each of the four major works in turn, centring discussion on the protagonist but not confining ourselves to an

---

[1] *Lucien Leuwen*, ii. 149.

analysis of his role, behaviour, and motives, since such an analysis is of interest mainly as an approach to the more important business of evaluating the novel as a work of art. Throughout, we shall keep in mind the question from which we started: whether these four heroes, all of them or any of them, may be properly regarded as examples of an ideal humanity, their careers as specimens of an exemplary way of living. Generally speaking, criticism has been accustomed to view some of Stendhal's characters, in some respects, as figures proposed for our admiration (Octave de Malivert has been accounted heroic in his devotion to duty, Julien Sorel has been acclaimed for his indomitable will-power); while others have been decried as dilatory weaklings (Lucien Leuwen) or amiable drifters (Fabrice del Dongo). It has seemed to us doubtful whether Stendhal, had he been acquainted with these judgements, would have endorsed them without some ironical *arrière-pensée*; and to establish the case for a revision of opinion here we have drawn on the only available secure source of information about Stendhal's privately held values—his own pronouncements in his personal writings, in his diaries, letters, marginal scribblings, and autobiographies, and his heartfelt asides even in those works written for publication during his lifetime.

BIOGRAPHICAL NOTE

It will be indispensable on occasion to allude to this or that event in Stendhal's life; at the same time, since our approach is not primarily biographical, such allusions cannot be developed without interrupting the argument. For this reason it may be useful to have, set forth in as condensed a form as possible, the biographical data of which knowledge has to be assumed.

Henri Beyle (who adopted the pseudonym Stendhal for his third published book, *Rome, Naples et Florence en 1817*) was born at Grenoble on 23 January 1783. His father combined the practice of the law with an interest in farming: the family was comfortably off. Henri's childhood was darkened by the death of his mother when he was seven; he and his two younger sisters were brought up by an aunt, Séraphie Gagnon, whom Henri cordially detested, and by his father for whom he also developed a strong dislike. The rest of his mother's family, particularly his grandfather (a retired doctor) and great-aunt Élisabeth, constituted a cultivated and heart-warming 'second home' for the rebellious little orphan.

His education was entrusted first to private tutors, ecclesiastics suspected of disloyalty to the young Republic. Beyle's lifelong anti-clericalism is usually traced back to childhood resentment of his treatment at the hands of one of them (Abbé Raillane), and his democratic sympathies seem similarly to have originated in the need to oppose his father's political outlook which was deeply reactionary. At the age of thirteen he became a pupil at the École Centrale of Grenoble, a school of a new type, distinguished from older establishments by a broader syllabus which included such studies as philosophy and mathematics. Beyle developed a strong interest in the latter subject and, after winning first prize at school, was sent to Paris to sit the entrance examination of the École Polytechnique.

This was in 1799; he actually arrived in Paris the day following the *coup d'état* by which Napoleon established himself master of France. Whether through carelessness or through lack of interest, he omitted to present himself for examination. Some distant relatives, the Darus, took him under their wing; he was found a clerk's job in the War Office and then, a few months later (in May 1800), was dispatched to Italy. Thanks to his connexions, he was given the rank of second lieutenant of dragoons and attached to the staff of General Michaud. He learned a little Italian, took to frequenting the opera-house at Milan, fought a duel, and fell in love. The lady, Angela Pietragrua, was not conspicuously chaste, but Beyle was too inexperienced to voice his passion in her presence. (Eleven years later, on a fresh visit to Milan, he succeeded in making his declaration and Angela succeeded in making him happy—for a short while.)

He was invalided out of the army at the end of 1801 and for the next few years led a studious though impoverished life in Paris. He read the works of the ideologists, tried to learn English, and studied the great dramatists of the past in the hope that one day he might write a successful comedy. He became an enthusiastic theatre-goer, and eventually fell in love with a young actress, Mélanie Guilbert. He went to extraordinary and unnecessary lengths to triumph over her virtue: she had to wait until he had followed her down to Marseilles, where she had a professional engagement, before he consented to be her lover.

The visit to Marseilles lasted from July 1805 until May 1806; Beyle found employment there with a firm of exporters, but the work was dull and he was not sorry in the end to pay heed to the protests of his family and re-enter government service. Martial, the younger and flashier of the two brothers Daru, took him to Germany, and he was found an administrative post in the occupied province of Brunswick. He rose steadily in the ranks of the service and began to lead a brilliant society life. In 1809 he was sent on a mission to Vienna; about this time he became convinced that he was in love with the wife of his patron, Count Pierre Daru, but failed to convince her that she was in love with him. During the next two years his official duties kept him in Paris except for a four-month visit to Italy at the end of 1811. This period was the climax of his career in a worldly sense—he occupied a gratifyingly responsible post, he had plenty of money, he was well received wherever he went, Paris was a whirl of gaiety, and to the optimistic the fortunes of the Empire seemed founded on rock.

He saw the rock shattered the following year, when he was sent to Russia with dispatches for Napoleon, and arrived in good time to see Moscow burn and to participate in the disastrous retreat. Thereafter he was shuttled from Paris to Silesia, then down to his native Dauphiné to help organize resistance against the invader; he returned to Paris in 1814 only to witness the fall of the capital to the troops of the Allies. His career broken, he left France altogether (not troubling to return during the Hundred Days) and took up residence in Milan where living was cheaper and life was sweeter.

Here he might have stayed indefinitely—he had friends, leisure to write, and just about enough money to permit him the occasional trip away from base (thus in August 1817 he made the first of several journeys to England). Unfortunately, two developments combined to sour his *dolce vita* among the Milanese. He was smitten with a desperate passion for a proud beauty (Mathilde Dembowski) who would have nothing to do with him; and he fell under suspicion of being a spy—the Italian liberals, who were his friends, believing him to be a government agent, while the Austrian authorities who controlled Milan regarded him as a *carbonaro*. He returned to France in a suicidal frame of mind in 1821.

From then until 1830 he led a precarious existence in Paris, having an exiguous income and little prospect of official employment. The books he had published while living at Milan (the *Vies de Haydn, de Mozart et de Métastase*, the *Histoire de la peinture en Italie*, and *Rome, Naples et Florence en 1817*) had given him a certain reputation in literary circles but had brought him in little money. The works he brought out subsequently had varying fortunes: *De l'amour* (1822) did not sell at all, but his *Vie de Rossini* (1823) enjoyed a *succès d'actualité*; *Armance*, published anonymously in 1827, pleased no one but the author; on the other hand, the guide-book called *Promenades dans Rome* (1829) was widely read. Probably he owed his growing reputation as a man of ideas and a mordant wit to his pamphlets as much as anything: *Racine et Shakspeare*, the title given to two broadsides against the classicists (1823 and 1825), and *D'un nouveau complot contre les industriels*, a satire on the Saint-Simoniens (1825). Magazine editors in Paris and in London paid him irregularly for articles on current literary, artistic, and musical events.

He was made welcome in a number of different houses, notably those of the Comte de Tracy, the philosopher whose *Éléments de l'idéologie* he had so admired during his youth, Étienne Delécluze whose chambers in the Rue Chabanais were a meeting-ground for literary men of politically liberal opinions, and Cuvier the zoologist whose guests were mainly men of science. His reputation as a brilliant but dangerous talker dates from this period. And he succeeded, if not in consoling himself for the obduracy of Mathilde Dembowski (he never did this), at any rate in forgetting it temporarily in the arms of Clémentine Curial, the wife of a general whom Napoleon had created count. This flattering liaison lasted two years; but constancy was not the countess's *forte* and on his return from a trip across the Channel in 1826 Beyle found he had been supplanted. He took it hardly. An equally unfortunate but much shorter-lived liaison with Alberthe de Rubempré, a mistress of Eugène Delacroix, followed in 1829; and then, in 1830, began his long and chequered affair with an Italian girl living in Paris, Giulia di Rinieri, who took him completely aback by declaring her love for him. She was an attractive twenty-nine and unmarried, he was forty-seven and ugly. After he had a little hesitantly accepted her favours he proposed marriage, but her guardian politely declined the honour of allying his family with the Beyles.

At this time he was engaged in writing *Le Rouge et le Noir*, the proofs of which he was correcting when the July Revolution broke out. The change of dynasty in 1830 made it possible for him at last to solicit a government post with success: he was appointed French consul at Trieste at the end of the year, and was already in residence there when the novel was published. His stay at Trieste was brief, however: the Austrian authorities had good memories, and Metternich signified to the French government that the Court at Vienna would be better pleased with some other representative than this irreligious liberal. Beyle was transferred to a less well-paid post at Civitavecchia, in the Papal States. Though he disliked the job, he clung to it since it was a guarantee against penury in his old age, and consoled himself by paying frequent visits to nearby Rome and other cities of the Peninsula, and by writing voluminously. During these years he composed the *Souvenirs d'égotisme* (1832), *Lucien Leuwen* (1834–5), and the *Vie de Henri Brulard* (1835–6)—two autobiographical works and a novel, all of which remained unpublished until long after his death. In 1836 he was granted three months' leave and came to Paris; thanks to the protection of his patron Molé, then Foreign

Minister, the three months were extended to three years, during which time he composed and published the *Mémoires d'un touriste* (1838) and *La Chartreuse de Parme* (1839). Apart from a collection of short stories set in Renaissance Italy (issued in 1839 under the title of the longest of them, *L'Abbesse de Castro*), these were the last works of Stendhal to appear during his lifetime. He resumed his consular duties at Civitavecchia in August 1839; engaged in one last and mysterious amorous intrigue (the woman concerned may have been English, but has never been identified with complete certainty); and found that his health was beginning to give way. Various seizures gave him warning of the end; he put a brave face on the inevitable and wrote to his friend Fiore: 'Je trouve qu'il n'y a pas de ridicule à mourir dans la rue, quand on ne le fait pas exprès.' The witticism turned out to be prophetic: on 22 March 1842, walking down the Rue Neuve-des-Capucines in Paris (he had been granted sick-leave in October of the previous year), he was struck down by an attack of apoplexy and died, still unconscious, in the early hours of the following day.

I ⮞ THE RELUCTANT NOVELIST

On the morning of 16 October 1832 the French consul at Civitavecchia was standing on the Janiculum admiring the view over Rome. It was, as he tells us in the prefatory pages of his autobiography, one of those days when one is glad to be alive: the air was warm, a light breeze was blowing, there were no clouds in the blue sky except a few hanging over Mount Albano. His spirits were hardly dashed when the thought occurred to him: in three months' time I shall be fifty. Fifty! surely not! born 1783 . . . yes, fifty. Turning down the top of his white ducks, he noted the fact on the waistband in elliptical French: *J. vaisa voirla 5* (*je vais avoir la cinquantaine*, I shall be in my fifties).

Open Stendhal's books anywhere, read half a page, and half a dozen diverging avenues of thought propose themselves to you. A bureaucrat at the Ministry of Foreign Affairs in Paris, had it been given to him to read these confidences, might well have wondered why Monsieur Beyle, consul at Civitavecchia, had absented himself that day from his post to wander over the Seven Hills. A psychologist might speculate on the curious impulse that drove Stendhal to record so banal a thought before it slipped his mind; to record it, moreover, on his trouser-belt; and, as though it were a state secret, to record it in a sort of cryptogram calculated to foil the faceless spy who haunted his waking dreams and who was evidently not above scrutinizing trouser-belts. A moralist would look to see what further reflections this mournful reminder of mortality set in train. How have you spent your life, Monsieur Beyle? Stendhal's response is to name all the women with whom, at different times in these fifty years, he had been more or less violently in love, many of whom refused to listen to him, some of whom never knew the impression they had made, and all of whom would be totally forgotten today but for the chance that he 'crystallized' for them. But hardly a word of the books he had written, books which a few of these women and one in particular, the lady of Milan with a Polish name whose coldness condemned him to four years of abject misery, had inspired. 'A vrai dire,' he writes, 'je ne suis rien moins

que sûr d'avoir quelque talent pour me faire lire. Je trouve quelquefois beaucoup de plaisir à écrire, voilà tout.' *Le Rouge et le
Noir* had been published just two years before, but in this autobiographical essay called the *Vie de Henri Brulard* Stendhal
expressed the gravest doubts whether his novel would survive
till 1880, the date at which he thought it might be prudent to publish *Brulard*. If posthumous fame was to be his, was he even sure
he would owe it to this novel? Toying with the idea that there
might, after all, be a life beyond the grave, he decided he would not
fail to pay a visit to Montesquieu, and if Montesquieu told him
'Mon pauvre ami, vous n'avez pas eu de talent du tout', then,
writes Stendhal, 'j'en serais fâché mais nullement surpris'.[1] Mock
modesty? Surely not, in a work designed as an exercise in sincerity.
Besides, the anticipation of this ghostly interview is recorded twice
(the *Vie de Henri Brulard* having been inadequately revised). What
is curious is the choice of judge. The author of the *Lettres persanes*
barely rates as a novelist; but Stendhal admired him for his
economic handling of language: 'il ne m'ennuie jamais en allon-
geant ce que je comprends déjà';[2] and, once more, even at fifty
Stendhal was far from clear that novels, and his novels in particular,
had any sort of a future.

Stendhal's belittlement of his own fictional writings is of a piece
with his surprising reluctance to venture into this branch of literature. It is a remarkable fact that if Jane Austen, his contemporary,
had waited as long as he did before she started to write her novels,
none of them would have been written. Like Richardson and
Laurence Sterne, Stendhal was a middle-aged novelist, in the sense
that he turned to the novel only when youth was spent; but, different in this from *Pamela* and *Tristram Shandy*, his novels breathe
the spirit of youth, so that one may be smitten with a passion for
Stendhal at eighteen and, in rare cases, conserve that passion till
middle age, making it a matter of spiritual hygiene to re-read the
two masterpieces once a year. Had Stendhal blown out his brains
at the age of thirty-eight, as he seriously thought of doing (this was
when, heartsick, he left behind for ever Mathilde Dembowski
and Milan), every one of his novels and short stories would have
remained unwritten, and his name would be as little remembered
today as—shall we say—Ulric Guttinguer's.

---

[1] *Vie de Henri Brulard*, i. 7–8.
[2] *Voyage dans le Midi de la France*, p. 105.

Late though the idea came to him that the proper vehicle for self-expression might, for him, be prose fiction, literary ambitions of one sort or another had haunted him since his teens. In the mass of private jottings which chance has preserved from the period of the consulship in Civitavecchia is a note on this lifelong vocation; it is couched in Stendhal's customary private language, a mixture of bad English and telegraphic French. 'On me. — Quelle différence, his life in Civitavecchia and his life rue d'Angiviller, au café de Rouen! 1803 et 1835! Tout était pour l'esprit en 1803. Mais, au fond, la véritable occupation de l'âme était la même: to make chef-d'œuvre.'[3] In 1803, twenty years old, having already served a spell under the colours in Italy, Beyle was lodging—his memory did not play him false—in a room on the fifth floor of the Hôtel de Rouen, 153 rue d'Angivilliers: a street located at the north-east corner of the Louvre, and long since torn up and built over

> (la forme d'une ville
> Change plus vite, hélas, que le cœur d'un mortel).

Even then he was writing; and reading and dreaming; trying to write the play which would 'sink' Goldoni and cause people to name him in the same breath as Molière; and filling one exercise-book after another with extracts from the philosophers, with personal reflections, with ambitious resolutions; for in the France of 1803 it was as natural and pardonable in the young to be naïvely ambitious as, a generation later, it was for them to flaunt a tragic disillusionment. 'Quel est mon but?' he asked himself in a note dated 3 May 1803. 'D'être le plus grand poète possible.' And again: 'Quel est mon but? D'acquérir la réputation du plus grand poète français, non point par intrigue comme Voltaire, mais en la méritant véritablement.' And, a year or so later: 'J'ai eu ce bonheur d'être fixé de bonne heure, dès ma plus tendre enfance, d'aussi loin que je puisse me souvenir j'ai voulu être poète comique. Toutes les opérations de mon corps, de ma tête, et de mon âme, ont tendu là.'[4] While he was still a schoolboy at Grenoble he had tried his hand at dramatizing a story by Florian. Between 1801 and 1805 he started on no less than eight different plays, tragedies or comedies, one of them being a *Hamlet* in which Ophelia was to be made the daughter of Claudius, so that the protagonist became 'a lover who avenges his

---

[3] *Mélanges intimes et Marginalia*, ii. 277.
[4] *Pensées, Filosofia nova*, i. 123, 81, 312.

father by killing the father of his mistress': Shakespeare Corne-
lianized, or *Le Cid* played at the Globe. In 1806 Henri Beyle finally
abandoned his dilettante existence and re-entered the service of
the Emperor. His administrative duties, combining with a natural
hankering after foreign travel, took him into Germany, Austria,
Italy, and ultimately to Russia. The old literary ambitions were
largely choked by this sprouting careerism; fine uniforms, a full
purse, new horizons, even success, up to a point, in his love-
affairs, caused Stendhal to forget that, as he later expressed it, 'le
vrai métier de l'animal est d'écrire un roman dans un grenier'.[5]
Nevertheless, the vocation was still there, temporarily suppressed
but not extinguished. He took his manuscripts about with him on
his travels; *Letellier*, the play which was longest on the stocks
(from 1803 until 1821 if not later) without ever approaching completion, accompanied him wherever he went, and at Moscow, on
the last day of September 1812, having re-read all he had written,
Stendhal noted naïvely: 'Je trouve presque toutes ces scènes
bonnes. Mais il n'y a pas de place pour en mettre plus de la moitié.
En comédie on ne peut pas dessiner avec un trait noir comme on
fait dans le roman. En traitant ce sujet en roman, j'y décrirais le
caractère de Saint-Bernard en dix lignes; mais ici il faudrait le
faire conclure de ce qu'on voit...'[6] This is perhaps the first clear
sign, not simply of Stendhal's increasing misgivings about his apti-
tude for writing plays, but of a faint suspicion that prose fiction
was his proper bent, that his real profession was *writing novels in a
garret*.

It was years, however, before this suspicion grew into a conviction. In his thirties and early forties (that is, between 1814 and
1825) Stendhal published more work than in all the remainder of
his life. There were the lives of the musicians (Haydn and Mozart
in 1814, Rossini in 1823), the history of early Italian art (1817),
the first of the travel books, *Rome, Naples et Florence*, in the same
year and its expanded re-edition in 1824, the treatise on love, the
early squibs in the battle of the romantics versus the classics, a
sizeable political pamphlet, not to mention a string of articles
contributed, after his return to Paris from Milan in 1821, to

---

[5] A phrase found in two letters to Domenico Fiore, 1832 and 1834. *Correspondance*, viii. 37; ix. 186.

[6] *Théâtre*, iii. 248. *Letellier* was to be a satire on contemporary literary life
(thus anticipating the subject of Balzac's *Un Grand Homme de Province à Paris*).
Saint-Bernard was intended as a caricature of Chateaubriand.

various French and English periodicals. One cannot say that all this output represents simply Stendhal's apprenticeship to creative literature; the very first books admittedly were little better than compilations, and they were nearly all written out of no worthier compulsion than the desire to augment a shrunken income (though the expected profit rarely materialized); but these volumes have undeniable quality—*De l'Amour* is a unique work—and are not to be viewed in the same light as the pot-boilers which Balzac turned out pseudonymously before he judged himself ready to start on 'serious' fiction, with *Les Chouans*.

Balzac, moreover, from the beginning was writing mainly, if not entirely, novels—historical novels, humorous novels, *romans noirs*. The works, catalogued above, of what might be called Stendhal's middle period (as opposed to the works of his middle age) were none of them novels. True, Stendhal quickly saw how a discourse on, say, the idiosyncrasies of the Italian national character could be lightened and enlivened by the introduction of *anecdotes*; and these anecdotes were invariably well told, as well as being 'telling'. But it needed a reader of unusual perspicacity to see this as a specially significant feature: such a reader as his young friend the naturalist Victor Jacquemont, who in 1825, writing to Stendhal about his *Histoire de la Peinture en Italie*, complimented him on 'a few charming stories related in the first [volume], Bianca Capello, etc., etc. I call them charming, because that is what you excel at: narrative.' Jacquemont, disconcertingly, proceeds to augur from this a great future for Stendhal . . . as an historian.[7]

It was a forecast which Stendhal could not have failed to find flattering. Historians in the first decades of the nineteenth century enjoyed an unrivalled reputation not only as men of science but also as psychologists. Self-appointed tutor to his younger sister Pauline, Stendhal had been accustomed to fill the lengthy and frequent letters he sent her from Paris (he being in his early twenties, she in her teens) with daunting reading-lists, in which the classics, Racine, Molière, Virgil, Ariosto, figured principally, but also, not uncommonly, the historians; and not only the recognized masters, Montesquieu, Voltaire, Saint-Réal, but many minor practitioners: Vertot, the author of a history of the knights of Malta, Millot, the forgotten compiler of a history of France 'from Clovis to Louis XV', and Fontaine-Désodoard whose *Histoire de*

---

[7] *Cent-soixante-quatorze lettres à Stendhal*, ed. H. Martineau, i. 139.

la Révolution française preceded Thiers's and was buried by it. History has lessons to impart about human nature; and Pauline will also find it a subject 'quotable' in good society, though he trusted that this consideration would not provide the major incentive to her studies. This was in February 1803; Pauline was not quite seventeen. The following year he was urging her to study Shakespeare's tragedies, Hume's *History of Great Britain*, and grudgingly giving her permission to read an occasional *novel*. He himself, he acknowledged, glanced through one every month or so and found it an agreeable relaxation. 'Tu sens bien que, dans les romans l'aventure ne signifie rien: elle émeut et voilà tout; elle n'est bonne ensuite qu'à oublier. Ce dont il faut, au contraire, se rappeler [*sic*], ce sont les caractères...'[8]

These letters to Pauline, engaging as they are, occasionally show up young Henri Beyle as something of a prig. He had not himself been so disdainful of what the novelists could offer, when he was Pauline's age or a little younger. The *Vie de Henri Brulard*, which deals only with his life up to his eighteenth year, has some information to give us on this point. He had started, like Gustave Flaubert as a boy, by conceiving a boundless admiration for *Don Quixote*; its chance discovery he called 'peut-être la plus grande époque de ma vie'—without, unfortunately, specifying precisely why. His father, whom he presents in these memoirs, perhaps unfairly, as a forbiddingly gloomy domestic tyrant, was so scandalized by his son's chuckles that he threatened to confiscate the book; but his grandfather, a cultivated, indulgent old gentleman whom the boy adored, was 'charmé de mon enthousiasme pour Don Quichotte'.[9] Cervantes afforded him what is perhaps the most precious of boons for young readers, a 'prediction' (Stendhal's word) of the world of men they have yet to enter. Adult society encompasses the growing child, but at a distance; it eludes, thwarts, and baffles him at every turn. The rare novelist who without condescending to the child nevertheless stands apart from the adult conspiracy, translating its secret language and unveiling its mysteries, will become the trusted guide, to be remembered with gratitude by the grown man who has no longer need for 'predictions'.

There are, however, false prophets. A work which Stendhal remembered reading 'couché sur mon lit... après avoir eu soin de m'enfermer à clef, et dans des transports de bonheur et de volupté

[8] *Correspondance*, i. 233.   [9] *Vie de Henri Brulard*, i. 123, 125.

impossibles à décrire',[1] was Jean-Jacques Rousseau's *La Nouvelle Héloïse*. A few years after this first reading he decided that Rousseau had been a dangerous and even pernicious influence on his imaginative development, responsible for a prolonged bout of what has since been termed *bovarysme*: that is, the entertainment of sweet illusions fostered by a perfidiously optimistic literature. 'Nous nous formons nos types de bonheur d'après les romans. Parvenus à l'âge où nous devons être heureux d'après les romans, nous nous étonnons de deux choses: la première de ne pas éprouver du tout les sentiments auxquels nous nous attendions. La deuxième si nous les éprouvons, de ne pas les sentir comme ils sont peints dans les romans.' This reflection is dated 8 April 1803. On 21 November 1804 Stendhal added a note: 'Voilà l'histoire de ma vie, mon roman était les ouvrages de Rousseau.'[2] The gloss is expanded in a long letter to Pauline written at the same time.

Ne voyant personne chez mon grand-papa, je portai toute mon attention sur les ouvrages que je lisais: Jean-Jacques eut la préférence! Je me figurai les hommes d'après les impressions qu'il avait reçues de ceux avec qui il avait vécu. Par là, il fit sur moi ce que les Romains, dont il avait nourri sa jeunesse, avaient fait sur lui.[3]

Étonné de ne point trouver dans le monde ces hommes parfaits (en bien comme en mal) que j'y attendais, je crus que mon malheur m'avait fait tomber dans une société d'ennuyeux et de gens froids... Cette folie me donna quelques moments de la plus divine illusion,... mais, en général, elle me donna une existence mélancolique, j'étais misanthrope à force d'aimer les hommes, c'est-à-dire que je haïssais les hommes tels qu'ils sont, à force de chérir des êtres chimériques, tels que Saint-Preux, milord Édouard, etc., etc.[4]

In the same breath, Stendhal here denounces both the romantic novel and the personal novel, speaking from the standpoint of the young reader, avid for instruction, that he was. The one provides an embellished or antiquated picture which experience shows to be false; the other, equally misleading, presents an individual view as universally valid. Disillusion and reaction follow inevitably, and Henri urges his sister: 'cherche à voir *l'homme dans l'homme et non*

[1] Ibid. 232.   [2] *Pensées, Filsofia nova*, i. 84–85.
[3] Stendhal is referring to Rousseau's early reading of Plutarch's *Lives*.
[4] *Correspondance*, i. 286–7. The authoritative study of Rousseau's influence on Stendhal has been written by V. Brombert, 'Stendhal lecteur de Rousseau', *Revue des Sciences humaines*, fasc. 92 (1958), pp. 463–82.

plus dans les livres'[5]—advice not easily followed by a seventeen-year-old girl living a sheltered life in a provincial town.

The novels he read as a boy were oracles for him in another, special sense, about which he could not open himself to Pauline. In a dusty corner of his grandfather's library he lit on a heap of erotic romances which had been bought by his scapegrace uncle, Romain Gagnon. They were forbidden fruit which he devoured eagerly. 'Cette découverte fut décisive pour mon caractère... Je ne saurais exprimer la passion avec laquelle je lisais ces livres.' He mentions, as particularly influential, a work by Nerciat, *Félicia ou mes fredaines*, the pornographic odyssey of an adventuress. 'Je devins fou absolument, la possession d'une maîtresse réelle, alors l'objet de tous mes vœux, ne m'eût pas plongé dans un tel torrent de volupté.'[6] The pleasure was, as he admits elsewhere in *Brulard*, properly non-literary; but here again, novels were serving as predictions of a sort. 'Il y a un cérémonial dans l'amour; nos seuls maîtres en ce genre sont les romans que nous lisons.'[7] This opinion, which Stendhal consigned to paper when he was twenty, was confirmed by later experience. Discussing the painfully slow ripening of Julien Sorel's first love-affair, Stendhal observes that, had he and his mistress been Parisians, contemporary literature would have speeded up the process. 'A Paris, l'amour est fils des romans... Les romans leur auraient tracé le rôle à jouer, montré le modèle à imiter; et ce modèle, tôt ou tard, et quoique sans nul plaisir, et peut-être en rechignant, la vanité eût forcé Julien à le suivre.'[8] *Sans nul plaisir...* Novels may be indispensable guides to conduct, particularly in the mating season, but they rob the novice of the delights of discovery. Julien and Mme de Rênal are in the precise situation of Byron's Don Juan and Haldée on their Aegean island: 'No novels e'er had set their young hearts bleeding.' So much the better for them, in one way at least. 'Comme madame de Rênal n'avait jamais lu de romans, toutes les nuances de son bonheur étaient neuves pour elle. Aucune triste vérité ne venait la glacer...'[9]

---

[5] *Correspondance*, i. 218.   [6] *Vie de Henri Brulard*, i. 228-9.

[7] *Mélanges de Littérature*, ii. 31. The sentence occurs in a piece first published in 1909 with the title *Catéchisme d'un roué*.

[8] *Le Rouge et le Noir*, i. 66.

[9] Ibid. 140-1. Mme de Chasteller is in much the same case. 'Tout l'étonnait... dans la passion dont elle était victime...Elle n'avait pas même l'expérience des livres: on lui avait peint tous les romans, au Sacré-Cœur, comme des livres obscènes. Depuis son mariage, elle ne lisait presque pas de romans... les romans lui semblaient grossiers' (*Lucien Leuwen*, ii. 191).

Vicarious experience insures the ignorant against blunders, but the premium exacted is exorbitant: this is one aspect of the conflict between naturalness and worldliness, naïvety and vanity, a perennial object of Stendhal's analysis. He was moved to attribute the fresh spontaneity of young Italian girls partly at least to the fact that they were not novel-readers. 'Comme si le hasard avait décidé que tout ici concourrait à préserver le *naturel*, elles ne lisent pas de romans par la raison qu'il n'y en a pas. A Genève et en France, au contraire, on fait l'amour à seize ans, pour faire un roman, et l'on se demande à chaque démarche et presque à chaque larme: Ne suis-je pas bien comme Julie d'Etanges?'[1]

The adolescent looks to novels to initiate him into the life of the senses and the sentiments which lies immediately ahead; the young man—the young provincial coming up to the metropolis—the anxious young careerist—may look to them to instruct him in the difficult art of day-to-day social intercourse. Beyle, who had seen little of society at Grenoble, was more apt than many to make this demand of the novelists he read, and particularly of those whose works were currently appearing. This is why he studied with such care and critical attention Mme de Staël's first novel *Delphine*, published in 1802. She was already a much discussed celebrity and Stendhal lost no time in acquiring his copy. In March 1803 he asked his friend Édouard Mounier whether he did not agree 'qu'on pourrait tirer de ce roman beaucoup de pensées ingénieuses et même profondes sur la société de Paris'.[2] 'Ce livre est le manuel des jeunes femmes entrant dans le monde', he noted sagaciously in his diary. Mme de Staël 'a connu les lois de la société de salon, elle en a montré la cause et l'effet, en un mot l'esprit'. His final judgement is mixed. 'Le dernier volume de *Delphine* est absolument insupportable à vivre. Dans le premier volume, il y a quelque chose d'émouvant, dans tout le reste il n'y a de bon que la connaissance des lois de la société dans un salon.'[3] The later novel *Corinne* provided an admirable picture of the tedious social life (*mœurs*

---

[1] *De l'Amour*, ii. 196. Julie was the heroine of *La Nouvelle Héloïse*. One finds the same idea, that ignorance of fiction ensures that Italian girls remain unspoiled, developed at great length in *Rome, Naples et Florence*, i. 156–7.

[2] *Correspondance*, i. 118. Stendhal was in fact making extracts from *Delphine* at the time; they have been rediscovered and published by V. Del Litto ('Stendhal et Mme de Staël', pp. 117–26 in H. Martineau and F. Michel, *Nouvelles Soirées du Stendhal Club*). Cf. also H. Jacoubet, 'Dominique et Corinne', *Ausonia*, vol. iv (1939), pp. 57–60.

[3] *Journal*, ii. 17, 18, 21.

ennuyeuses) of the English upper classes, among whom the women-folk would be ashamed to be seen leaving a drawing-room at the same time as their husbands at the end of an evening.[4]

Mme de Staël was a woman of wide experience, perspicacious and intelligent. It was possible to profit from her novels, but of how few others could this be said! In November 1807 Henri Beyle thought it necessary once more to put his sister on her guard against the ordinary run of fiction writers. Explaining that he had himself spent the previous couple of days reading novels 'qui n'ont d'autre mérite que d'être écrits en anglais', he exclaims: 'Combien ces livres donnent une fausse idée de la société; on les croirait écrits par et pour les habitants de la lune. Je crains que tu n'aies formé plusieurs de tes opinions d'après *these damned books*.'[5] The remark reinforces the impression that the principal quality Stendhal sought in the novels he read in his early twenties was what we should now call realism; and he required realism not on aesthetic but on almost moral grounds: without it, he suspected he was being hoodwinked. He was, in other words, reading novels for the same reason as he read, at the same time, the ideologists: to discover the secrets of the psychological mechanism of social man. But was it not altogether utopian to expect realism in the novel? The very public for which the novelists catered would reject the depressing picture they would present if they aimed to copy their models faithfully. 'La vérité n'est que l'opposé de ce qu'ils disent, c'est tout simple. S'ils montraient le monde tel qu'il est, ils feraient horreur et, même sur les gens qui sont de leur avis, produiraient une impression de tristesse qu'on chercherait à éviter.'[6] Many years before he even envisaged writing novels himself, Stendhal stumbled here on a practical problem of aesthetics which was to exercise him and all the major nineteenth-century realists after him: how to reconcile the demands of truth with the equally imperative requirement that a work of art should exalt the spirit. Shakespeare and the French classical tragedians had solved the difficulty in different ways; was it possible to achieve the desired synthesis in the framework of this newer form?

There had been realists in the previous century; but the great watershed of the Revolution had rendered their portrayal of society outdated, though their observations on mankind were, of course,

eternally valid. Lesage was one such author. 'Lis *Gil Blas*' he
advised Pauline, 'si tu peux te procurer sans indécence ce livre
très indécent, mais vrai';[7] and again: 'le tableau le plus ressem-
blant de la nature humaine, telle qu'elle est au XVIIIᵉ siècle en
France, est encore le vieux *Gil Blas* de Lesage; réfléchis sur cet
excellent ouvrage.'[8] Excellent it might be, but still, the monarchical
society of the *ancien régime* was poles apart from revolutionary
and post-revolutionary France. Should one, in obedience to the
cosmopolitan tastes of the day, look abroad? Stendhal made the
acquaintance of Fielding in 1803, when he read *Tom Jones* in De
la Place's translation. The book aroused nothing but aversion on
this first reading. Stendhal was offended by the author's prolixity
and by his tone of bantering satire; he castigated him for the
inadequacy of his conversational passages and for the omission of
all descriptive passages; finally, he protested that Squire Western
and Partridge were not characters at all, but caricatures.[9] Stendhal
was ill when he read the book; hence perhaps his ill humour.
Having in 1810 re-read it in the original English, he completely
revised his opinion, and thereafter *Tom Jones* became a kind of
sacred text. But Fielding, like Lesage, though his honesty was
beyond reproach and his realism beyond cavil, wrote of a society
which had totally passed away. 'Ce roman est aux autres ce que
l'*Iliade* est aux poèmes épiques; seulement, ainsi qu'Achille et
Agamemnon, les personnages de Fielding nous semblent aujour-
d'hui trop primitifs. Les bonnes manières ont fait de notables
progrès, et veulent que chacun déguise un peu plus ses appétits
naturels.'[1] Stendhal does not seem to have opened any other of
Fielding's books, and as for Defoe, Smollett, and Sterne, if he looked
at them at all there is little trace in his private writings of any impression they may have made on him. *Tom Jones* was the only significant work, as far as he was concerned, to survive from the early
English realist school.

A French disciple of Sterne, Diderot, offered, in *Jacques le
Fataliste*, a novel which delighted him in 1805[2] and for which he
kept his affection at least until 1837. 'Il faut arracher six pages à
Jacques le Fataliste; mais, cette épuration accomplie, quel ouvrage

    [7] Letter printed on p. 89 of the first volume of the index (*Table alphabétique*)
to the Divan edition of the works.
    [8] *Correspondance*, ii. 91.   [9] *Pensées, Filosofia nova*, i. 226.
    [1] *Mémoires d'un Touriste*, i. 52.   [2] *Journal*, ii. 305.

de notre temps est comparable à celui-là?'³ It is not difficult to spot the qualities in Diderot's novel that attracted Stendhal: the audacious negligence of the composition, the ironic philosophy, the tireless play of ideas, the incidental comments on manners, the proliferation of anecdotes, above all, perhaps, the habit of haranguing and harassing the reader—these are all elements which can, without stretching comparisons, be observed in Stendhal's own fictional work.

There were few important or influential novelists of the preceding century whose works Stendhal failed to peruse at one point or another in his youth. He remembered being deep in Prévost's *Mémoires d'un homme de qualité* when the mail-coach rattled over the cobbled streets of his home town, bringing the news of the execution of Louis XVI. He knew *La Vie de Marianne, Les Amours du Chevalier de Faublas, Les Liaisons dangereuses. Werther*, read in 1805, made a profound impression. Goethe's other novels, *The Elective Affinities* and *Wilhelm Meister's Years of Apprenticeship*, both read five years later, were scarcely less appreciated. His friend Mlle Jules de la Bergerie (to whom we shall return later) disappointed him grievously by failing to respond as she should have to *The Elective Affinities*. 'Il faudrait, avec une tête française,' he observed, 'une âme à la Mozart (de la sensibilité la plus tendre et la plus profonde) pour goûter ce roman.'⁴ He presented a copy of the book to the current divinity, Mme Daru; what she thought of it he does not record. In his first published volume, the *Vies de Haydn, de Mozart et de Métastase*, he paid Goethe the curious compliment of attributing to him a long passage presumably of his own invention, since it cannot be found anywhere in *The Elective Affinities* from which it purports to derive; and later, he used the title of the German novel as a chapter-heading in *Le Rouge et le Noir*.

The most illuminating observations on a novelist that can be found in Stendhal's papers—in those at least which belong to the first decade of the century—were called forth by the notorious Restif de la Bretonne, whose prolific output Stendhal was sampling between 1804 and 1806. Restif is an author of the category expressively designated by the term *bas réalisme*; at the end of the century the enemies of naturalism, much to the indignation of the naturalists, professed to regard him as the true progenitor of the movement.

---

³ *Mémoires d'un Touriste*, i. 130.   ⁴ *Journal*, iii. 282.

Stendhal criticized his novels on three scores. Firstly, Restif infringes the laws of psychological realism, which Shakespeare, for instance, instinctively observed: 'il ne fait pas sortir les faits du caractère, chaque action manque de motif.' Secondly, he is, intellectually, thin gruel. 'La morale de Restif est indécise, il n'a point approfondi... Son style est étroit, les idées qu'il donne fatiguent toujours le même endroit de la tête, il ne fait pas jouir le lecteur de toutes ses facultés.' Finally, though his characters experience passion, they are none the less ignoble specimens of humanity, and this is an aesthetic fault, Stendhal maintains firmly. 'Il faut donc, lorsqu'on peint les passions, les montrer dans des êtres où tout ce qui ne tient pas à la passion soit parfait. Autrement le dégoût fera tomber le livre des mains du lecteur. Il faut peindre l'Apollon du Belvédère dans les bras de la Vénus de Médicis, dans les plus délicieux jardins des environs de Naples, et non un gros Hollandais sur sa Hollandaise dans un sale entresol.'[5] The problem posed by the marriage of truth and beauty is here seen under another aspect: the choice of subject clearly matters for Stendhal. That the subject should be noble was a doctrine adamantly held and one which he applied to all the arts indiscriminately; it certainly complicated the search for a viable form of realist art. A remark made about Constable, who was exhibiting in the Paris art-collection of 1825, is revelatory of Stendhal's position. Constable, he wrote, is 'vrai comme un miroir; mais je voudrais que le miroir fût placé vis-à-vis un site magnifique, comme l'entrée du val de la Grande-Chartreuse, près Grenoble, et non pas vis-à-vis une charrette de foin qui traverse à gué un canal d'eau dormante.'[6] Stendhal was by no means immune from the romantic virus. No doubt he would have made little of Seurat or Pissarro; and if Zola can be accused of misunderstanding him, the imagination quails to conceive how Stendhal would have reacted to L'Assommoir.[7]

In this inevitably abridged survey of Stendhal's reading of the novelists prior to the collapse of the First Empire and his

---

[5] *Journal*, iii. 8–9; *Pensées*, *Filosofia nova*, ii. 235.
[6] *Mélanges d'art*, p. 93.
[7] A review by Stendhal (published in the *New Monthly Magazine*, Dec. 1828) of an early novel of proletarian life (Raymond's *Le Maçon*) allows one to make a guess, however. Stendhal wrote: 'This work presents pictures which, though not of the most agreeable kind, are nevertheless true to nature. . . . The author of the *Maçon* has pourtrayed the vices of the lower orders of Paris, with a degree of fidelity . . . revolting to the French reader. . . .'

retirement to Milan, it will have been noticed that scarcely one of his contemporaries has been named. Except for Goethe and Mme de Staël, however, they were an untalented group: the novel was growing in popularity but its practitioners satisfied the increasing demand with the most pallid and trivial of products. There is a lively scene in Balzac's *La Muse du Département* (1843) in which two characters, Lousteau and Bianchon, having got hold of the disjointed sheets of an old-fashioned novel in which a printer's devil has wrapped up the proofs of Lousteau's latest story, amuse themselves by reading it aloud. 'Formerly,' comments Bianchon, 'readers required one thing only of a novel: that it should enthral them. Style? no one paid any attention to style, not even the author. Ideas counted for nothing; local colour was undreamed of.' The growth or rebirth of the serious novel was, as Balzac accurately implied, a very recent event of French literary history; and even under the Restoration, from 1815 to 1830, portents of this event were few and uncertain. Associating as we do the eighteen-twenties with the first ferment of Romanticism in France, it is hard for us to realize how stagnant, to an enlightened contemporary, the state of literature must have appeared for much of the time. When, the Austrian police having elbowed him out of Milan, Stendhal reluctantly returned home, he relieved his feelings by composing a brief sketch, *La France en 1821*, which he did not care to publish at the time but happily preserved among his papers. An American, imbued with a great respect for French culture, arrives from... Havana, and proceeds to question a Frenchman about the literary celebrities of the day. The Frenchman parries by quoting the names of five scientists: Laplace the astronomer, Humboldt the geographer, Fourier the physicist, Flourens the physiologist, and Cuvier the biologist; the period of the Restoration was in fact one in which France was temporarily in the vanguard of scientific advance. But as for men of letters, the Frenchman warns the American that there is nothing like the constellation of geniuses who were writing in Voltaire's day. The gentleman from Havana then puts the question: What books, chosen among the productions of the past twenty years, would you take with you if you were to be marooned on a desert island? Stendhal starts his list of authors with Pigault-Lebrun, 'le plus gai de nos romanciers', and a little incongruously adds in the next breath the name of De Tracy, 'le plus grand de nos philosophes, ou, pour mieux dire, le seul philosophe que nous ayons'. The American asks about poets: 'Après M. Béranger, qui avez-vous? — Je suis bien en peine de vous répondre, à vous qui lisez Byron, Moore, Crabbe, Walter Scott; mais, en y réfléchissant, je trouve M. Baour-Lormian' (the egregious author of a translation of *Gerusalemme liberata* who, after his task was accomplished, is alleged to have announced his intention of learning Italian). As an afterthought, Stendhal names Lamartine (whose *Premières Méditations* had been published the previous year).

> *L'Américain*: Ce jeune homme qui a été si prôné par les journaux *ultra*? Nous l'avons fait venir en Amérique; c'est fort joli; c'est Lord Byron peigné à la française. Après?
> *Moi*: Nous avons MM. Chênedollé, Edmond Géraut, Alfred de Vigny.
> *L'Américain*: Les titres de leurs ouvrages?
> *Moi*: Je les ignore; je les crois fort bons, mais je vous avoue que je ne les ai jamais lus.

There is some further talk about dramatists (Lemercier and Delavigne), after which Stendhal exclaims despondently: 'Vous voyez, mon cher ami, l'état de notre littérature, et cela quand nos voisins les Anglais ont huit ou dix poètes vivants, quand l'Italie a Monti, Foscolo, Manzoni, Pellico!' The polite American concludes consolingly: 'Oui, mais ces pays n'ont pas eu cinquante généraux célèbres et dix victoires par an. Vous voyez bien en noir, mon cher Européen; un peuple n'est jamais grand que dans un genre à la fois.'[8]

At the end of 1822, having come to an arrangement with the London publisher Henry Colburn, Stendhal began sending articles for anonymous publication in different British periodicals: the *New Monthly Magazine and Literary Journal*, the *London Magazine*, and later the *Athenaeum* in the year of its foundation. His contributions consisted partly at least in book-reviews; the novelists he is obliged to discuss are for the most part deservedly forgotten, or else remembered for other works than the novels they were producing at the time. (Thus, there is a long and amusing review of Hugo's horror novel *Han d'Islande* in the *New Monthly Magazine* for April 1823, characterized by the oddest mixture of eulogy and denigration; Vigny's novel of the wars of the Fronde, *Cinq-Mars*, is treated with the utmost asperity in the issue for July 1826.) The

---

[8] *Mélanges de politique*, i. 151–64.

fashionable authors about whom Stendhal has to write seriously
have such names as Salvandy and Picard, D'Arlincourt and Kéra-
try, Mme de Duras and Mme de Cubières. It was, in truth, a
barren period for the French novel. 'Romance-writing is almost a
dead letter in France at the present.'[9] In France ... Stendhal was
writing for the English market; but this is not enough to account
for the warmth with which he speaks of Scott every time he has
occasion to mention him in these articles. As a literary cosmopolitan,
Stendhal ranks beside Heine, Turgenev, Henry James, and André
Gide. In addition this was one of the periods when the French
mind was unusually open to suggestions from abroad. Stendhal was
certainly not alone among his countrymen in believing that if any
cure could be found for the asthenia afflicting French fiction it
would come from a careful study of the Waverley Novels. But he
was, probably, among the first to arrive at this conclusion.

He had discovered Scott while still at Milan: this we learn from
the deliciously improper letters he addressed from that city to his
crony the Baron Adolphe de Mareste, at the time director of the
passport branch of the Paris Prefecture of Police and unofficially
Stendhal's literary agent and chief liaison officer with the metropolis. On 18 July 1819 Stendhal told Mareste he had just come to
the end of *Quentin Durward* and *Old Mortality*. 'Le dernier demi-
volume d'*Old Mortality* ne vaut pas un f..., le reste est à côté de
Tom Jones, c'est-à-dire dans les nues.' But why, he asked, do all
modern novelists, Mme de Genlis, Miss Maria Edgeworth, and now
Sir Walter Scott, fight shy of an honest representation of sexual
love? 'C'est qu'ils ont assez d'esprit pour savoir que pour peindre
la passion, il faut l'avoir sentie.'[1] The unspoken extension of the
idea (Stendhal was then in the throes of his unhappy affair with
Métilde Dembowski) would be: I, passion-tost, what novels might
I not write, if I chose? ...

In the succeeding twelvemonth his admiration was verging on
idolatry. 'Aurait-on la bonne idée à Paris, de réimprimer les divins
romans de Walter Scott?' he asked Mareste. 'Je brûle de les lire.
Je n'en connais que deux ou trois. Quel peintre! Qu'est-ce que
Mme de Genlis auprès?' And six months after that: 'Ne trouvez-
vous pas Scott bien supérieur à Byron? — En 1890, l'on enseignera l'Histoire dans les collèges avec les pièces historiques de

9 *New Monthly Magazine*, vol. xii, p. 942 (June 1825).
1 *Correspondance*, v. 256.

Shakspeare, les romans de Scott, et ceux des cent ou deux cents mou-
tons qui vont l'imiter.' He commissioned Mareste to post to him the
latest titles published by Firmin-Didot, beginning with those he
had not read: *The Abbot*, *The Antiquary*, *Rob Roy*.... 'Je voudrais
quatre volumes de Scott chaque mois.'[2] The contemptuous allusion to the 'hundred or two hundred sheep' suggests that even at
this stage the thought never crossed Stendhal's mind to pay Scott
the compliment of direct imitation; and it is a fact that, at a period
when so many French writers of fiction—Vigny, Mérimée,
Balzac, Hugo—sacrificed to the fashion for historical novels, Stendhal held aloof. The imprint Scott made on his writings is visible
in subtler ways: it is clear, for instance, that the treatise *De
l'Amour*, composed between December 1819 and July 1820, when
his enthusiasm for Scott was at its peak, owes a perceptible debt to
the Waverley Novels.[3]

On his return to Paris Stendhal, according to his later reminiscences, used to engage Mareste in arguments about the real worth
of Scott's genius. If we are to believe him, his admiration was
already ebbing fast. 'Je soutenais qu'un grand tiers du mérite de
sir Walter Scott était dû à un secrétaire qui lui ébauchait les
descriptions de paysage en présence de la nature. Je le trouvais
comme je le trouve, faible en peinture de passion, en connaissance
du cœur humain.'[4] Was it simply that Stendhal, finding everyone
talking about Scott in France, was moved by the spirit of contradiction to find fault with both Scott and the majority opinion? Certainly in his articles for the London papers he reports faithfully on
the current vogue; but with a tinge of irony also. 'The only writer
since the restoration of the Bourbons, who has had a success really
popular, is Sir Walter Scott. Jeanie Deans, Flora M'Ivor, or the
sublime Rebecca, are better known at Toulouse, Dunkirk, Besançon, than the queens of France, Clotilda, or Mary de Medicis, or
than the personages of Voltaire's and Pigault Lebrun's novels.'[5]
However, the sources of this popularity are perhaps not of the
purest. Scott's toryism is a recommendation for many French
readers (it damned him in Stendhal's eyes and the question had

[2] Ibid. 346, 383, 384.
[3] The epigraph was taken from *The Pirate*. For further details see J. C.
Alciatore, '*The Bride of Lammermoor* et *De l'Amour*', *Le Divan*, no. 296 (1955),
pp. 221–30.
[4] *Souvenirs d'égotisme*, p. 157.
[5] *London Magazine*, new series, vol. i, p. 277 (Feb. 1825).

already led to an interesting disagreement with Byron[6]). Further,
Scott's prudent treatment of passion betrayed too tender a solici-
tude for the susceptibility of that important section of the public
whose crippling influence over the English novel Edmund Gosse,
at the end of the century, was still deploring: 'those timorous
circles of flaxen-haired girls, watched over by an Argus-eyed
mamma'. 'Walter Scott', wrote Stendhal, 'has stirred up all hearts.
In consequence of his painting *love*, the bugbear of all mammas, in
a cold and uninteresting manner, most mothers have permitted
their daughters to read his works. The circulation has consequently
extended all over the provinces, whilst Lord Byron is only relished
at Paris and Dijon.'[7] The most valuable by-product of Scott's
popularity was the interest in historical studies which his works
had aroused in circles where hitherto such pursuits had been
regarded as a narrow specialism. 'The Scotch novelist, notwithstanding the difference in some of his recent productions, is still
the author *à la mode* in France, to the literature of which he has
given a new colouring, at least as far as regards romances and history.'[8] Scott's influence has been comparable to that of Richardson
on eighteenth-century French literature (and Richardson, we must
remember, begot Rousseau). 'History is what we best know in
France; and yet for all the histories which have been written
within these ten years we are indebted to Sir Walter Scott. Had
not the Scottish Baronet given us his novels in prose, these histories would have been still unpublished.'[9] The tribute, coming
from Stendhal whose passion for history we have already noted,
is not negligible.

Stendhal's attitude to Scott, wherever we look, can only be
described as ambiguous. Since Richardson, as he says, no novelist
had so stirred the European reading-public, with the possible

---

[6] Stendhal had inserted a disobliging reference to Scott's toadyism in *Racine
et Shakspeare I* (footnote to chapter iii). Byron, in a polite letter dated from
Genoa, 29 May 1823, took him to task and vouched for Scott's personal character, even though he acknowledged he had no sympathy with his political views.
In his reply, Stendhal stood pat on his first position (see *CLXXIV lettres à
Stendhal*, i. 47–48 and Stendhal, *Correspondance*, vi. 46–47). The exchange of
views may be thought to illuminate a fundamental distinction between the
national temperaments represented by the two men: for Byron, an individual's
politics are his private affair; Stendhal claims they cannot be so regarded.

[7] *London Magazine*, loc. cit. 277–8.
[8] *New Monthly Magazine*, vol. xii, p. 556 (Dec. 1824).
[9] Ibid. vol. xxii, p. 583 (June 1828).

exception, as he forgets to say, of the 'gothic' novelists—but their methods were intolerably cheap, and they were totally ignorant of those 'laws of the human heart' which were Stendhal's constant preoccupation.[1] Scott had, admittedly, made certain concessions to an anaemic taste; but he had, equally, opened up new territory. His innovations were at least worthy of impartial study by a critic of novels, shortly to emerge as a novelist in his own right.

Chief among Scott's technical innovations was his use of natural description. The novel as practised in France in the eighteenth century had been (if we exclude the novel-by-letters) a judicious interweaving of narrative and dialogue. Readers had been surfeited of description by the fashionable prose fiction of an earlier age.

Were I to imitate the writers of romance [remarks Lesage on the point of introducing the most famous episode in his novel], I should give a pompous description of the Bishop's palace at Granada; I should expatiate on its architecture, vaunt the opulence of its furnishings, speak of the statues and pictures to be seen there; I should not spare the reader the least of the stories they represented; but I will be content to say that it equalled in magnificence the palace of our kings.[2]

Scott restored description to a place of honour by making it serve the purpose of transporting his reader in imagination to the scene in which the action was to be played out. The feature was analysed by Stendhal, on the whole appreciatively, in an odd corner of his study of Rossini which was published in November 1823. The digression occurs in the second chapter, and is introduced on the slightest of pretexts: a comparison between Rossini's use of instrumental orchestration to back up the singing parts, and Scott's use of descriptive passages to prepare the dialogue and narrative parts, a habit which Stendhal calls 'le moyen de l'art peut-être qui a valu les succès les plus étonnants à l'immortel auteur d'*Old Mortality*'. He instances, at length and with evident approval, the opening pages of *Ivanhoe*.

...L'homme de génie écossais n'a pas encore achevé de décrire cette forêt éclairée par les derniers rayons d'un soleil rasant, et les singuliers vêtements des deux personnages, peu nobles assurément, qu'il nous présente contre toutes les règles de la dignité, que nous nous sentons

---

[1] Ann Radcliffe, 'dame anglaise douée de toutes les perfections de son île, mais regardée comme hors d'état de peindre la *haine* et l'*amour*, même dans cette île' (preface to *La Duchesse de Palliano, Chroniques italiennes*, ii. 13).

[2] *Gil Blas*, book VII, chap. ii.

déjà comme touchés par avance de ce que ces deux personnages vont se dire. Lorsqu'ils parlent enfin, leurs moindres paroles ont un prix infini. Essayez par la pensée de commencer le chapitre et le roman par ce dialogue non préparé par la description, il aura perdu presque tout son effet.

Scott's descriptive passages are not, then, gratuitous adornment; they are functional and on the whole found only when the pace of the story has temporarily slackened (or before the story is under weigh), so that the reader has the necessary composure to savour them. This rule is occasionally broken—Stendhal found that certain dialogues in *Peveril of the Peak* were disagreeably broken up by description. But in general he endorsed Scott's use of description:

lorsqu'elle est bien placée, elle laisse l'âme dans un état d'émotion qui la prépare merveilleusement à se laisser toucher par le plus simple dialogue; et c'est à l'aide de ses admirables descriptions que Walter Scott a pu avoir l'audace d'être simple, abandonner le ton de rhéteur que Jean-Jacques et tant d'autres avaient mis à la mode dans le roman, et enfin oser risquer des dialogues aussi vrais que la nature.[3]

This unstinted praise for Scott's descriptive technique comes curiously from Stendhal; for of all those members of the Romantic generation in France who responded, to a greater or lesser extent, to the appeal of Scott, he alone in his fiction dispensed with the long descriptive passages which Balzac and in general the writers of historical novels composed with such gusto; and which became, later, part of the stock-in-trade of the realists. 'The external world' wrote Zola, 'scarcely exists [for Stendhal]. He pays no attention to the house in which his hero has grown up, nor to the horizon bounding his life.'[4] This judgement is undoubtedly too sweeping: there are descriptions of localities and dwelling-places to be found in Stendhal's novels—the pen-picture of Verrières in the opening pages of *Le Rouge et le Noir*, the main street of Königsberg described in *Le Rose et le Vert*, the account of the Norman village of Carville in *Lamiel*. But Stendhal liked to experiment with different openings. A characteristic note in his unfinished novel *Une Position sociale* runs: 'Au lieu de commencer le livre par la diable de description, selon la méthode de Walter Scott, on pourrait débuter par l'analyse suivante du caractère de la duchesse...'[5] In the body

---

[3] *Vie de Rossini*, i. 82–85.   [4] *Les Romanciers naturalistes*, p. 84.
[5] *Mélanges de littérature*, i. 152.

of a novel, Stendhal uses description soberly, though vividly when he does use it; an essay on 'landscape in *La Chartreuse de Parme*' turns out to be, in reality, an essay on the absence of landscape description in the book.[6] It is a feature of Stendhal's art which helps to give his writing its exquisitely archaic patina: neglect of external nature being a recognized characteristic of the classical period in French literature. It is also, of course, a sign of the writer with an almost exclusive interest in the human actors of a given scene. If the scene impresses itself on the sensibility of the actor, then the author will show it to us; not otherwise. How better could Stendhal have conveyed M. de Rênal's absorption in his jealous suspicions of his wife than to say no more, of the coming of the dawn which finds him still feverishly agitated, than this: 'Cet homme malheureux s'aperçut alors, à la pâleur de sa lampe, que le jour commençait à paraître'? That sentence is found in the 21st chapter of *Le Rouge et le Noir* (book I). In the 25th chapter Stendhal wants to present to us the seminary in which Julien is to spend the next few wretched months. He makes no attempt, properly speaking, to describe its appearance; instead, he devotes a page to recording Julien's emotions as he approaches and enters the building. 'Il vit de loin la croix de fer doré sur la porte; il approcha lentement; ses jambes semblaient se dérober sous lui. Voilà donc cet enfer sur la terre, dont je ne pourrai sortir!' Julien hears the hollow reverberation of the door-bell, endures the ten-minute wait, is confronted by the porter of hideous aspect: 'cette physionomie ne montrait pas le crime, mais plutôt cette insensibilité parfaite qui inspire bien plus de terreur à la jeunesse'. The porter's muteness; the crazy stairway, the slowly pivoting doors, the dark, low-ceilinged rooms with whitewashed walls and smoke-blackened pictures, the virtual absence of furniture, the utter silence—all this is shown, but in terms always of the mounting terror in Julien's panic-stricken soul. 'Il était atterré, son cœur battait violemment; il eût été heureux d'oser pleurer.' Such a passage may be contrasted with a dozen in Balzac: for instance, the description of the den inhabited by the solicitor Fraisier, in the 45th chapter of *Le Cousin Pons*. Balzac might have shown this rather similar interior through the eyes of Mme Cibot, who approaches it with much the same anxiety and

---

[6] P. Jourda, 'Le Paysage dans *la Chartreuse de Parme*', *Ausonia*, vol. vi (1941), pp. 12–28. The same might be said of P. Hazard's article, 'La Couleur dans *la Chartreuse de Parme*', *Le Divan*, no. 242 (1942), pp. 64–74.

superstitious dread as Julien the seminary. Instead, he gives the same neutrally angled description as Scott had popularized, a description designed to induce a certain emotional state in the reader, not to convey to the reader the particular emotional state of one of his characters.

It is typical of Stendhal's critical acuity that he was one of the first to observe and pay due tribute to Scott's innovation; and typical too of the keenness of his insight into his own creative temperament that he wasted no time in trying to imitate what was clearly contrary to his own nature. 'Écrire autre chose que l'analyse du cœur humain m'ennuie' he observed in the *Souvenirs d'égotisme*. 'Si le hasard m'avait donné un secrétaire, j'aurais été une autre espèce d'auteur.' The secretary would presumably have performed the function which Stendhal impertinently imagined Scott's secretary discharged for him, to go into the country and sketch out for him his descriptions of nature. In the same autobiographical work Stendhal includes a long account of the various *habitués* of De Tracy's *salon* which he had frequented in the late eighteen-twenties. At the end of this lively series of pen-portraits he notices that he has forgotten to tell his reader what the drawing-room looked like. 'Sir Walter Scott et ses imitateurs eussent sagement commencé par là, mais moi, j'abhorre la description matérielle. L'ennui de la faire m'empêche de faire des romans.'[7] In fact, he had already written two novels when he composed the *Souvenirs d'égotisme*; but Stendhal could never quite convince himself, in the teeth of contemporary practice, that his books did very well without descriptive passages: almost at the end of his life he was planning a revised edition of *La Chartreuse de Parme* in which 'bits of landscape description' should be introduced.[8]

Scott's formative influence on Stendhal was, in reality, slight. His importance in the history of Stendhal's literary evolution is that, by inciting him to meditate more deeply than ever before on the problems of the novel-writer—if only for the purpose of refutation—he allowed Stendhal to reach a provisional estimate of the direction his own novel should take. This can be seen clearly enough in an essay written, in fact, when *Armance* had already been published and when Stendhal was actively engaged in com-

---

[7] *Souvenirs d'égotisme*, pp. 160, 57. ·
[8] *Mélanges intimes et Marginalia*, ii. 371 (note dated 27 July 1840), and 382 (11 Feb. 1841).

posing *Le Rouge et le Noir*. 'Walter Scott et la Princesse de Clèves',[9] besides representing his most considered estimate of Scott, has the distinction of being one of the few sustained pieces of literary theory to be found in Stendhal's writings outside *Racine et Shakspeare*.

Initially the critic is concerned to weigh the relative merits of the historical and the psychological novel, regarded as being two extremes diametrically opposed to one another. But the distinction he makes is not so much a distinction of *genre* as of method—along the lines already indicated. 'Faut-il décrire les habits des personnages, le paysage au milieu duquel ils se trouvent, les formes de leur visage? ou bien fera-t-on mieux de peindre les passions et les divers sentiments qui agitent leurs âmes?' Stendhal makes it sound as though the choice lay, as perhaps it did, between material and spiritual art.

Undoubtedly the historical novel poses fewer problems to an author: 'L'habit et le collier de cuivre d'un serf du moyen âge sont plus faciles à décrire que les mouvements du cœur humain.' So much for *Ivanhoe*: by 1830 Scott has so far lost ground with Stendhal that he is being accused of facility, of all offences in the artistic calendar surely the most heinous. By 1840, Stendhal predicts, his reputation will have slumped to fifty per cent.

At this point in his essay Stendhal raises the far more fundamental question of realism in the novel or, more broadly, of truth in literature. His approach to the time-honoured mimetic theory of art has the virtue of novelty, and is formulated with that characteristic swashbuckling forthrightness which is always a signal, in Stendhal, of a cliché about to be cut to pieces. 'Tout ouvrage d'art est un *beau mensonge*: tous ceux qui ont écrit le savent bien. Rien de ridicule comme ce conseil donné par les gens du monde: *imitez la nature*. Eh! je le sais bien, morbleu! qu'il faut imiter la nature; mais jusqu'à quel point? voilà toute la question.' Where does one draw the line? The answer Stendhal offers seems oddly mean-spirited today; this is because, for a hundred years or more, we have become so thoroughly indoctrinated with the strange opinion that the Artist is a superior person (pending his dislodgement by the Scientist), that Stendhal's saner estimate of his position is bound to strike us as excessively diffident. Stendhal, who never put

---

[9] Published first in *Le National*, 19 Feb. 1830, it has been reprinted in *Mélanges de littérature*, iii. 305–11.

his own name to any of his writings, is closer in spirit to Turoldus than to 'Ego Hugo'. He took it for granted that literature is a dialogue between writer and reader, in which the reader has the last word; and so the solution which he here proposes to the question he has propounded is: Imitate nature . . . to the degree your reader will tolerate and in a manner calculated to content him.

Take Racine and Shakespeare (the eternal Punch and Judy of Stendhal's demonstrative *fantoccini*). Take two of their plays, having analogous themes: Iphigenia about to be offered as a human sacrifice by her father Agamemnon; Imogen, whose death has been ordered by Posthumus her husband. How utterly different *Iphigénie* and *Cymbeline*!

Ces grands poètes ont *imité la nature*; mais l'un voulait plaire à des gentilshommes campagnards, qui avaient encore la franchise rude et sévère, fruit des longues guerres de la rose rouge et de la rose blanche,[1] l'autre cherchait les applaudissements de ces courtisans polis, qui, suivant les mœurs établies par Lauzun et le marquis de Vardes, voulaient plaire au roi, et mériter le suffrage des dames. *Imitez la nature* est donc un conseil vide de sens. Jusqu'à quel point faut-il imiter la nature pour plaire au lecteur? Telle est la grande question.

Stendhal had no difficulty in showing how futile would be any attempt to imitate nature absolutely and directly; one would arrive at something like a shorthand transcript of all the proceedings at Aulis.

His difficulty is rather that, in good logic, he ought to be arguing for the best-seller and the box-office success; and that, in the case in point, Scott demonstrably manages very well to 'give pleasure to the reader'. So Stendhal is led to make a significant reservation—not, however, *ad hoc*, to justify his poor opinion of Scott, but basic, as it turns out, to his aesthetic doctrine. Scott *gives pleasure to the wrong readers*. 'L'art n'est donc qu'un beau mensonge; mais sir Walter Scott a été trop menteur. Il plairait davantage aux âmes élevées, qui, à la longue, décident de tout en littérature, si dans la peinture des passions il avait admis un plus *grand nombre de traits de nature*. Ses personnages passionnés semblent *avoir honte d'eux-mêmes...*,' etc.; the actual criticisms Stendhal makes of Scott

---

[1] Stendhal had long ago decided that Shakespeare's 'defects' were due to the uncultured audiences for which he wrote. 'Ce qui manque à Shakspeare et Alfieri, c'est de n'avoir pas eu à amuser des ennuyés rendus difficiles' (*Journal*, iii. 123; entry dated 4 Oct. 1806).

matter little here; they simply articulate more decisively the misgivings expressed in the early letters to Mareste. The great point
is that Stendhal's caveat involves the principle of writing, not for
the largest possible number, not for the 'average reader', but for a
limited public, composed of the *âmes élevées qui, à la longue, décident de tout en littérature*: of writing, in short, for an élite.
We have said that this principle is basic to Stendhal's doctrine.
It was formulated, in a rudimentary but quite comprehensive way,
many years before he wrote this essay on 'Walter Scott et *la Princesse de Clèves*'. On the last day of the year 1804 Stendhal went to
see Fabre d'Églantine's comedy *Le Philinte de Molière*. His diary
shows that he was delighted almost as much by the audience as by
the play. 'On applaudissait à chaque mot; le sourire, les mots que
j'entendais de tous côtés me prouvent qu'on le sent parfaitement.
Voilà vu ce public choisi et peu nombreux à qui il faut plaire; le
cercle part de là, se resserre peu à peu et finit par moi. Je pourrais
faire un ouvrage qui ne plairait qu'à moi et qui serait reconnu beau
en 2000.'[2] The germ of the notion of writing for an élite can be
traced in various other notes dating back to this period, when he
was in his twenty-first or twenty-second year. 'On peut travailler
pour plusieurs publics. Choisir mon public.' 'Il me faut déter-
miner à quel public je prétends plaire, me faire une idée nette de
ce public.' On one occasion he risks a brief characterization of the
ideal reader or spectator: 'un jeune homme de vingt-cinq ans,
ayant senti les passions'.[3] His mental image of this ideal reader
underwent modifications as he grew older. The *Histoire de la
Peinture en Italie* was dedicated (as later *La Chartreuse de Parme*)
'to the Happy Few,'[4] whom Stendhal takes care to define: that part
of the public not yet thirty-five years of age (Stendhal was then
thirty-four) and comfortably off (in the annual income-range of
2,000 to 20,000 francs).[5] 'Mon vrai public' he noted in the margin

[2] *Journal*, i. 279. On Stendhal's inexplicable enthusiasm for this rather poor
play, see G. Natoli, 'Stendhal e Fabre d'Églantine', pp. 192–214 in *Studi in
onore di P. P. Trompeo*, Naples, 1959.

[3] *Pensées, Filosofia nova*, i. 124; ii. 219; i. 27.

[4] Goldsmith appears to have been the source of this famous formula. The
Vicar of Wakefield relates that, having given some thought to the question
whether a widowed clergyman should remarry, 'I published some tracts upon
the subject myself, which, as they never sold, I have the consolation of thinking
were read only by the happy few'. See P. Hazard, 'The Happy Few', pp. 394–6
in *Mélanges... Edmond Huguet*, Paris, 1940.

[5] *Histoire de la Peinture en Italie*, i. 203 n. In March 1820 Stendhal sent three

of one of the scenes of his aborted play *Letellier*, 'est celui que je me forme idéalement'[6]—i.e. in his imagination. For another play, *Les Deux Hommes*, he projected at the end of 1803 a preface 'dans le genre de Sterne où je dis avec la plus grande franchise ce que je suis: Ce n'est point à la postérité que je veux plaire, c'est à mon siècle, et encore ce n'est pas à tout mon siècle, c'est à la partie la plus aimable, etc.'[7] Save in the special cases of his autobiographies, Stendhal did not consider that to write for posterity was sensible or even practicable; 'la *postérité*,' he commented elsewhere, 'mot vide de sens inventé pour consoler la médiocrité. Qui peut deviner ce que sera la postérité?'[8]

From youth to the threshold of middle age, Stendhal had been—unconsciously for most of the time—debating the form which creative activity should take for a man of his era, his experience, and his temperament. He was converted from the idea of writing for the stage, ultimately, by realizing that the enlightened, intelligent theatre-audience which he needed, and which he thought he had glimpsed in 1804, was dwindling rapidly, if it had not already disappeared. Where were the delicately cultivated members of that gilded society which flourished under Louis XV? 'Ce sont peut-être là les vrais spectateurs de la comédie,' he wrote in his diary (1810), and added in Shakespearian English: 'devoutly to be wished even at the cost of the lettres de cachet'.[9] Stendhal still continued half-heartedly, from time to time, to make sketches for plays and even to write a few scenes. In August 1816, for instance, he composed part of a comedy, probably thought of as an opera libretto, *Il Forestiere in Italia*, which was drawn straight from *Twelfth*

copies of this book to Thomas Moore with a covering note of which the first two sentences run: 'Les amis du charmant auteur de *Lalla Rookh* doivent sentir les arts. Ils font sans doute partie de ces *Happy Few*, pour lesquels seuls j'ai écrit, très fâché que le reste de la canaille humaine lise mes rêveries' (*Correspondance*, v. 314–15).

[6] *Théâtre*, iii. 35.

[7] V. Del Litto, *En marge des manuscrits de Stendhal. Compléments et fragments inédits*, p. 146.

[8] *Molière, Shakspeare, la Comédie et le Rire*, p. 231 n. The phrase frequently used by Stendhal: a book is a lottery-ticket for a lottery to be drawn in fifty (or a hundred) years' time (see *De l'Amour*, i. 103; *Souvenirs d'égotisme*, p. 88; *Vie de Henri Brulard*, ii. 8; and a letter to Mérimée dated 26 Dec. 1823: *Correspondance*, vi. 258) is not to be taken as a declaration of faith in posterity's verdict; on the contrary, Stendhal implied by it that the approval of posterity was as much a matter of chance as winning the lottery prize.

[9] *Journal*, iii. 358.

Night; with the difference that Malvolio, here a young Frenchman, the 'foreigner in Italy' of the title, was to see his wooing of Olivia crowned with success. At that time Stendhal had just completed his history of Italian art, or as much of it as was needed to make up the two volumes which his friend Louis Crozet, the civil engineer, arranged to have published in Paris. He dispatched to Crozet at the end of September of the same year a kind of programme of future literary activity which he headed: 'Reasons for not doing the third, fourth, fifth, and sixth volumes of the *Histoire de la Peinture en Italie*.' There were, it seems, two reasons. In the first place, as psychology progresses (and provided it is treated as an exact science there is every reason to suppose it will progress fast), so advances are bound to be made in the theory of aesthetics which will in a brief time render his present conjectures outdated: as nice an example as any, this, of the immense credit Stendhal was prepared to extend to science in its application to human affairs. His second reason for abandoning the profession of art historian is that, as he says: 'il est petit de passer sa vie *à dire comment les autres ont été grands*... Je n'ai que trop de regrets d'avoir passé deux ans à voir comment Raphaël a touché les cœurs'—especially since, in those two years, with his own heart prisoner of a wilful mistress (Angela Pietragrua) he should have been able to create some powerfully original work.

This work he still visualizes as that of a latter-day Molière. 'Depuis qu'à douze ans j'ai lu Destouches, je me suis destiné *to make comedies*. La peinture des caractères, l'adoration sentie du comique ont fait ma constante occupation.' (Destouches, it should be explained, was a contemporary of Marivaux who wrote edifying comedies which occasionally succeed in being amusing.) Now, at the age of thirty-four less three months, he plans to take up *Letellier* again and try and write a score of comedies over the next twenty years. After all, he can see where other playwrights—Molière and the rest of them—go wrong; if he can improve their works in his study, how can he fail to excel them as soon as he strikes out on his own? 'En tout temps, avec un copiste je me charge de faire une comédie en cinq actes en huit heures de temps, prises dans une seule journée.'[1] Stendhal's self-confidence borders on the perverse. *Letellier* had, after all, been on and off the boil since 1804—twelve years.

[1] *Correspondance*, iv. 380–4.

In the end the course of history as much as anything drove him to abandon the hopeless attempt to write a play.[2] Throughout the Restoration he watched excitedly the struggle to replace the classical tragedy, still, in the Napoleonic era, virtually unchallenged, by something different. On occasions he leapt into the fray. His position was that of a fervent Shakespearian.

Quand verrons-nous Talma, après avoir joué un jour *Andromaque*, nous montrer le lendemain le malheureux Macbeth entraîné au crime par l'ambition de sa femme?... On criera beaucoup; il y aura des pamphlets, des satires, peut-être même des coups de bâton de distribués dans quelque moment où le public, dans une profonde tranquillité politique, sera juge compétent en littérature. Mais enfin ce public, excédé des plats élèves du grand Racine, voudra voir *Hamlet* et *Othello*.[3]

What is most remarkable about this accurate prediction of the romantic revolution on the stage is that it should have been published as early as 1814, sixteen years before the *bataille d'Hernani*. The revolution when it came did not take quite the course Stendhal had expected. Racine was banished, but his place was taken by a bevy of newcomers who owed perhaps rather more to the melodrama of Pixérécourt than to the psychological realism of Shakespeare's plays.[4] This betrayal of his hopes finally cured Stendhal of his ambition to set the groundlings roaring. Like Musset at the same time, he concluded that there was simply no audience in Paris for the delicate character-portrayal which alone counted for him. His analysis of Alexandre Dumas's *Henri III et*

---

[2] The question is bound to occur to the reader, if it has not done so already: what inhibited Stendhal from finishing any of the plays he started on? Since it is marginal to our subject, we need do no more, perhaps, than refer him to the relevant chapter in Jean Prévost's book, and quote the remark this writer makes concerning *Les Deux Hommes*, to the effect that this play was 'slain by good intentions'.—'Il avait cru se préparer à créer la critique. Or, en pratiquant la critique, on n'apprend bien qu'à critiquer' (*La Création chez Stendhal*, p. 61).

[3] *Vies de Haydn, de Mozart et de Métastase*, p. 221.

[4] It was his 'fidelity to nature' that Stendhal chiefly prized in Shakespeare. 'Nous sourions de plaisir de voir dans Shakspeare la nature humaine telle que nous la sentons au-dedans de nous' (*Pensées, Filosofia nova*, i. 189). 'Mon admiration pour Shakspeare croît tous les jours. Cet homme-là n'ennuie jamais et est la plus parfaite image de la nature' (ibid. 227). 'Comme sa manière de peindre est large! c'est toute la nature... Ses personnages sont la nature même, ils sont sculptés, on les voit agir. Ceux des autres sont peints, et souvent sans relief...' (*Journal*, ii. 32). 'Shakspeare laissa aux objets de la nature leurs justes proportions; et c'est pour cela que sa statue colossale nous paraît tous les jours plus élevée' (*Histoire de la Peinture en Italie*, i. 123).

sa cour was not unfair—but certainly not rapturous. 'The best tragedies of Racine and Voltaire would appear cold next to such a piece as *Henry III*; but if Racine and Voltaire were now living, and would avail themselves of the freedom afforded by the imitation of Shakespeare, they would, of course, produce plays infinitely superior to that of M. Dumas.'[5] Victor Hugo's *Hernani* was shrugged off as a poor imitation of the *Two Gentlemen of Verona* 'et autres pièces de ce genre du divin Shakspeare'[6]—here Stendhal was being less than fair. He was away from France—discharging his consular duties first at Trieste, then at Civitavecchia—during the years in which the Romantic verse drama was consolidating its hold on the Parisian theatre-goers. Stendhal followed developments and drew his conclusions; they were finally embodied in an essay, forthrightly entitled 'La Comédie est impossible en 1836', which the *Revue de Paris* published in April of that year.[7]

Stendhal's thesis has a limpid simplicity. 'Depuis que la démocratie a peuplé les théâtres de gens grossiers, incapables de comprendre les choses fines, je regarde le roman comme la Comédie du XIXe siècle.' The novel is the only form of art in which *les choses fines*—delicate subtleties—are not misplaced: the novelist can count on at least a few readers who will appreciate them. But the playwright is not given a hearing unless he can satisfy his audience; the average quality of the audience sets strict limits on the degree of subtlety he can afford to risk; and since the advent to full political and economic power of the middle classes this average quality has steadily deteriorated.

La révolution de 1789 à 1835, en donnant l'idée d'aller au spectacle et l'argent pour payer à la porte à un grand nombre de Français incapables de sentir les choses fines, a créé le genre grossier et exagéré de M. V. Hugo, Alex. Dumas, etc. L'auteur comique est comme le citoyen de New York, il doit compter les suffrages et non les peser. — La majorité qui juge les pièces a donc changé, et changé en mal par la Révolution qui a donné le bon sens à la France.

C'est peut-être le seul mauvais effet produit par la Révolution. La société de Mme de Sévigné approuvait les sottises que La Bruyère dit sur la religion et le gouvernement, mais quel juge admirable pour une scène dans le genre de celle de Mme de Rênal avec son mari...

[5] *New Monthly Magazine*, vol. xxv, p. 496 (June 1829).
[6] *Correspondance*, vi, 286.
[7] It has been reprinted in *Mélanges de littérature*, iii. 417–44.

—a naïve reference, at the end here, to chapter xxi of the first book of *Le Rouge et le Noir*.

For Stendhal had, when he wrote 'La Comédie est impossible', already made his choice; he is concerned simply to justify it. 'Les contemporains de Mme de Sévigné n'avaient pas tous de l'esprit, sans doute; mais on trouvait chez eux l'intelligence des choses littéraires... Aujourd'hui la moitié de la bonne compagnie, qui a de belles voitures et des soirées, ne comprend rien aux choses d'esprit, ce qui ne veut pas dire, du tout, qu'elle manque d'esprit'—but that it applies its talents to getting on in the world instead of devoting them to admiring and enjoying the products of the intelligence and the imagination. It is evident that, even exiled in Italy, Stendhal had the clearest insight into the temper and trends of his age; and further, that his analysis is as valid as ever for the communities grouped around the North Atlantic coasts. The only difference is that the *belles voitures* run without horses and that there are rather more of them.

In Stendhal's tone there is no satirical wrath and little real indignation; in this he differs from some of those who came after him, notably Flaubert. Neither is he in the least stirred, apparently, by the dramatic potentialities inherent in the spectacle of this zestful new society of materialists; in this he differs from a few of his contemporaries, notably Balzac. Stendhal looks neither backward nor forward. There is, admittedly, a strain of nostalgic yearning for the 'good old days' of the *ancien régime*, but it should be said that his essay was originally designed as a preface to a new edition of a favourite work, De Brosses's *Lettres familières écrites d'Italie en 1739 et 1740*, a circumstance which legitimizes his adoption of the language of a *laudator temporis acti*.[8] He specifically disclaims, however, any wish to turn the clock back. As for the future, he prefers to shut his eyes to it. He foresees two equally unpleasant possibilities. The first, the Americanization of Europe, a recurrent nightmare for Stendhal. 'Rien ne se rapproche plus de notre position que la morose Amérique; elle seule peut nous éclairer un peu

[8] At the same time, it may be observed that Stendhal not infrequently speaks of the eighteenth century as though it were a vanished golden age. 'La France a été un pays charmant de 1715 à 1789. Depuis, il n'y a plus de société...' (letter dated from Erfurt, 29 Apr. 1813: *Correspondance*, iv. 130). In *Armance* the author slips in a reference to 'cet heureux dix-huitième siècle où il n'y avait rien à haïr' (p. 239). Cf. too the fragment 'Les Grands Seigneurs', written apparently in 1824 (*Mélanges de politique*, i. 180).

sur notre avenir.' The second was the proletarianization of society. 'Je voudrais, quant à moi, que le vulgaire fût heureux... mais je ne voudrais pas, pour tout au monde, vivre avec le vulgaire, et encore moins être obligé de lui faire la cour.' The age he lived in was uncomfortable enough, but it was the age into which he had been born, and there was no question of escaping from it; the problem was, how to come to terms with it.

Stendhal's novels can be viewed as being, by and large, a series of attempts to solve this problem; or, if solutions failed, a means to by-pass it. His normal procedure, as we shall see in the next chapter, is to set the problem to an imaginary *hero*, a central character young and resilient enough to wrestle with it or to overleap it. The novel was chosen rather than any other form because, firstly, it had attained in the hands of Sir Walter Scott a satisfactory status in the hierarchy of literature and because, secondly, no other form of writing could reach the kind of reader whose interest Stendhal aspired to capture: the 'happy few' were so few now that they could not be counted on to fill a theatre auditorium. The novel was chosen, but only after a long period of agonized hesitation. Stendhal's reluctance to turn to it was due partly to his distrust of a type of writing which he felt had served more often to mask than to unmask the blemishes of society; and partly to his ingrained respect for the comedy, the comedy of Molière, Regnard, Lesage, and Beaumarchais, which had served so well in the past to expose evils, puncture pretensions, and mend manners.

II · PATTERNS AND FORMULAE

STENDHAL published during his lifetime three completed
novels: *Armance* (1827), *Le Rouge et le Noir* (1830), and *La
Chartreuse de Parme* (1839), together with a few short stories
set for the most part in Renaissance Italy. The latter, with one
exception, appeared in the *Revue des Deux Mondes* between 1837
and 1839; after his death they were collected and brought out
under the general title *Chroniques italiennes*. But Stendhal's present
reputation as a novelist rests almost as much on those of his works
which were discovered in his papers and published posthumously.
The early editions of these texts were faulty and truncated, and it
cannot be said even now that we have completely satisfactory ver-
sions of them, since the state of illegibility and confusion they
were left in confronts the most devoted editor with a task of almost
insuperable difficulty. The most important of them is *Lucien
Leuwen*, composed at Civitavecchia in 1834–5. Stendhal originally
intended it should have three parts, each with a different geographical setting. He wrote the first two parts but nothing of the
third. The work as we have it exceeds the dimensions of an ordinary
novel; it is probable that Stendhal would have pruned it had he not
abandoned work on it to turn to the autobiographical *Vie de Henri
Brulard* which he never completed either. *Lamiel*, undoubtedly the
most tantalizing of his unfinished novels, was started in 1839; at
his death in 1843 Stendhal was still struggling with its protean
ramifications. Three other novels which progressed some way before
Stendhal threw up the pen were *Une Position sociale* (1832), *Le
Rose et le Vert* (1837), and *Féder ou le mari d'argent* (1839). In addition there are novels or short stories of which only the opening
few pages were ever written, like the fragment which has been
dubbed *Le Roman de Métilde* and which appears to have been
Stendhal's earliest attempt at prose fiction: jotted down at Milan
one day in 1819, it was intended, probably, for dispatch to Mme
Dembowski, to mollify her or to re-engage her attention. There are
a couple of other scraps of semi-autobiographical romance: *Le Lac*

de Genève (1831) and *Paul Sergar* (1832). The oddly entitled *A-Imagination* and *Don Pardo* (1838 and 1840) were promising experiments in novels centred on a morally debased hero; but they failed to hold Stendhal's interest for long. There are certain dreams which peter out and which could be compared to these stories which break off at the difficult point.

Finally, there were the short stories. The *Chroniques italiennes*, already mentioned, are all specimens of this form, save one, *L'Abbesse de Castro*, which is of the dimensions of a short novel. *Le Coffre et le revenant* was published in the *Revue de Paris* in May 1830: with its Spanish setting and macabre atmosphere it seems to have been the sole fruit of Stendhal's excursion to Barcelona the previous September. In the same journal and in the same year appeared *Le Philtre*, a modernization of one of Scarron's *Nouvelles tragiques*. One other story, *Mina de Vanghel*, was virtually completed at this time though it was not published until 1854. 1830 was, as it happened, a year of quite abnormally intense activity for Stendhal.[1]

Set down thus, the corpus of Stendhal's fictional work presents a superficial appearance of the wildest confusion: a tangle of false starts and loose ends above which tower two acknowledged masterpieces. In reality the work is astonishingly homogeneous; one can talk about the Stendhalian novel with more assurance than one can about the Flaubertian novel or even the Jamesian novel. From the start Stendhal instinctively adopted a basic form or pattern from which he rarely deviated, and never with any success (in the sense that he never succeeded in pushing very far a work which was conceived according to a different pattern).

This form, the 'imaginary biography' as we have already

---

[1] More precisely, this activity lasted from his return from Spain in Nov. 1829 until his departure for Trieste in Nov. 1830. *Vanina Vanini* (included in the *Chroniques italiennes*, inappropriately, since it has not an historical setting) appeared in the *Revue de Paris* in December 1829. A sketch, partly fictional, called *Philosophie transcendentale*, was written on 18 December. On Christmas Day he read *Le Coffre et le revenant* to Mérimée. He was working on *Mina de Vanghel* in December and January. On 17 Jan. work began in earnest on *Le Rouge et le Noir*; on 8 Apr. he signed the publisher's contract and in May he was correcting proofs. Meanwhile he had written *Le Philtre* (24–25 Jan.), the essay *Walter Scott et la Princesse de Clèves* examined in the previous chapter, and another on Lord Byron. He also found time to attend the first night of *Hernani*, 25 Feb., and spend a first night with a new mistress, Giulia di Rinieri (22 Mar.). Even at forty-seven Stendhal was, given the right conditions, as capable as Balzac of a demonic zest for life.

denoted it, ought logically, perhaps, to begin the hero's life where it is begun in *David Copperfield*, or even farther back, at the point Sterne chooses for the start of *Tristram Shandy*. In point of fact Stendhal normally picks up his hero at the uncertain frontier separating adolescence from adulthood. His early life is passed over with the greatest possible rapidity. We hear nothing at all of the childhood of Octave (the hero of *Armance*), Lucien Leuwen, or Féder. The opening sentences of the three novels in which they figure all give the same impression of the hero's being abruptly tipped into adult life, to sink or swim. 'A peine âgé de vingt ans, Octave venait de sortir de l'École polytechnique.' — 'Lucien Leuwen avait été chassé de l'École polytechnique pour s'être allé promener mal à propos, un jour qu'il était consigné.' — 'A dix-sept ans, Féder, un des jeunes gens les mieux faits de Marseille, fut chassé de la maison paternelle.' Of the boyhood of Julien Sorel and Fabrice del Dongo we are given the minimum of information necessary for an understanding of the subsequent action. The only novel in which Stendhal made a special study of the childhood of his protagonist was *Lamiel*, a fact which accounts for some of the peculiar interest which attaches to this, the last of his works.

The constant underplaying of infancy and boyhood in Stendhal's fictional biographies is most easily explained with reference to his own lonely and unhappy childhood, and to the fact that he never had any children of his own nor, apparently, felt the need for them. 'Je n'ai jamais conçu', he wrote to Pauline after her marriage which was childless, 'cette manie d'avoir des enfants, de jolies poupées qui deviennent des sots à faire fuir, à moins d'une éducation forte et originale, et qui a la patience de donner cette éducation?'[2] An isolated sally this, to which perhaps no great attention should be paid; there is general agreement that Stendhal, though he had little to do with children, was capable of a genuine affection for those he came to know. This seems to have been the case with the daughter of one of his mistresses, Mme Curial, a precociously intelligent and captivating little girl whose early death he felt keenly.[3] And there is the better documented story of how Beyle, then in his late fifties, used on visits to the Countess de Montijo to

---

[2] *Correspondance*, iii. 182.
[3] See François Michel's moving study of this episode: 'Bathilde Curial. Une enfant à travers l'œuvre de Stendhal', pp. 13–32 in *Nouvelles soirées du Stendhal Club*, Paris, 1950.

take Paquita and Eugenia, her two small daughters, on his knees and tell them exciting and no doubt apocryphal stories of Napoleon; the younger of the two, when later, having married Louis-Napoleon, she became herself empress, recalled to the end of her life the delight with which she and her sister hailed the arrival, once a week, of the old consul on leave from Italy.[4] Moreover, to return to the novels, it cannot be said that the child goes altogether by default. Apart from Lamiel, there are in *Le Rouge et le Noir* the three young sons of Mme de Rênal, admittedly slightly sketched but forming a happy family group; and the brief, sad appearance of Sandrino, Fabrice's child by Clélia, at the end of *La Chartreuse de Parme*. One must conclude that in this particular respect Stendhal's experience was limited, and that, wisely, he wrote as little as possible outside his experience.

On the other hand it is difficult to account for the peculiar relations between almost all Stendhal's heroes and their parents—their fathers in particular—without reference to Stendhal's relations with his. He claims in the *Vie de Henri Brulard* that he was in love with his mother (she died when he was seven), while as for his father, 'je ne désirais qu'une chose: ne pas me trouver auprès de lui. J'observai, avec remords, que je n'avais pas pour lui une *goutte* de tendresse ni d'affection. Je suis donc un monstre, me disais-je. Et pendant de longues années je n'ai pas trouvé de réponse à cette objection.' Had Chérubin Beyle any inkling of the aversion he aroused in his son? He might well have been appalled had he known. Nothing that even Stendhal can tell us shows him to have been anything other than a well-meaning, perhaps not very percipient father, proud of his son's precocious intelligence, but at a loss to deal with his occasional outbursts of rebelliousness, and ready enough at times to display an affection usually held in check by his aloof shyness. When Henri left home to continue his studies in Paris his father's eyes were filled with tears. Far from being affected, the sixteen-year-old boy's only thought was how ugly his father looked when he cried. Faithfully recording this moment in his memoirs, Stendhal begs us make allowances: 'Si le lecteur me prend en horreur qu'il daigne se souvenir des centaines de promenades forcées aux Granges avec ma tante Séraphie, des

---

[4] The enigmatic footnote at the end of chapter iii of *La Chartreuse de Parme*: 'Para V. P. y E. 15 x 38', has been deciphered as 'Para vosotras Paquita y Eugenia', with the date.

promenades où l'on me forçait, *pour me faire plaisir*. C'est cette hypocrisie qui m'irritait le plus...'[5] How different Proust's memories of being taken for walks by his parents and what a world separates Les Granges from the banks of the Loir at Illiers! What is perhaps more to the point, how different must have seemed to Stendhal the relations which Rousseau, in the opening pages of his *Confessions*, describes as existing between his father (also a widower) and himself in his childhood!

As we look at Stendhal's novels the importance of all this is seen to lie less in the lifelong antipathy which he felt for his father than in the 'remorse' he confesses to, the idea that this antipathy was unnatural, that he, Henri Beyle, was a 'monster' whom any decent man would 'regard with horror'. One of the last books he published, the *Mémoires d'un touriste*, is a partly fictitious account of various excursions into the south and west of France undertaken by Stendhal alone or in the company of Mérimée in 1836 and 1837. The supposed author, the Tourist, is conceived in much the same way as the hero of one of Stendhal's novels: he is, and yet is not, Stendhal himself. A middle-aged ironfounder, he summarizes his life-story in a page in the body of the work.[6] The same pattern of rebellion against parental authority is traced, the same note of remorse is struck: 'Moi, je craignais d'être un monstre, forcé de m'avouer que je n'adorais pas mon père.' The possibility is that Stendhal extended this 'monstrous' filial impiety to each of his heroes in order to convince himself that, far from being unnatural, it was normal. Did not Zeus rise against Kronos, as Kronos had revolted against Uranus?

In the novels proper not one of Stendhal's youthful protagonists has entirely happy relations with his father. The Marquis de Malivert is a nonentity, perhaps a nitwit. Octave de Malivert is far too gentlemanly even to imagine showing him anything but the purest respect; but he sees as little of him as possible, as Henri Beyle had, as far as possible, avoided his father's company. More fortunate than Henri, however, Octave is blessed with an understanding and devoted mother. Lucien and Fabrice similarly have mothers who sympathize with them and side with them; Julien alone is, like his creator, deprived of this natural source of affection and consolation

[5] *Vie de Henri Brulard*, ii. 45, 179.
[6] And more fully in an Introduction, not given in the *editio princeps*, but printed in the Michel Lévy edition (1854).

—hence, to some degree no doubt, his prickly defensive shell. Julien spent his childhood in an aggressively masculine household: his brothers are brutes, his father a sly, hard-fisted peasant. There are only two significant incidents in which old Sorel and his son are confronted. At the beginning of *Le Rouge et le Noir* Stendhal relates how the father, who is owner of a sawmill at Verrières, furious at seeing the boy immersed in his reading when he should have been attending to the machinery, knocks the book into the stream and all but dashes Julien off his perch into the threshing shafts and wheels. At the end, after Julien has been sentenced to death, his father visits him in prison.

Julien se sentit faible, il s'attendait aux reproches les plus désagréables. Pour achever de compléter sa pénible sensation, ce matin-là il éprouvait vivement le remords de ne pas aimer son père.

Le hasard nous a placés l'un près de l'autre sur la terre, se disait-il pendant que le porte-clefs arrangeait un peu le cachot, et nous nous sommes fait à peu près tout le mal possible. Il vient au moment de ma mort me donner le dernier coup.

Julien succeeds in recomposing himself only by playing on the old man's avarice; this restores to him his sense of superiority.[7]

In *Lucien Leuwen* Stendhal undertook a far more detailed and delicate analysis of disharmony between father and son. The elder Leuwen is, unlike the Marquis de Malivert, witty and highly intelligent. It is an open question whether he has any genuine affection for his son, or whether he takes an interest in his welfare merely because he knows that his wife cannot be happy unless Lucien is;[8] he seems, however, to grow more attached to his son as time goes on. As time goes on, however, Lucien's dislike of his father hardens, and simultaneously, like Julien in his cell, he is tormented by feelings of guilt.

Lucien avait un grand remords à propos de son père. Il n'avait pas d'amitié pour lui, c'est ce qu'il se reprochait souvent sinon comme un crime, du moins comme un manquement de cœur... Le *chasme* entre ces deux êtres était trop profond. Tout ce qui, à tort ou à raison, paraissait sublime, généreux, tendre à Lucien, toutes les choses desquelles il

---

[7] *Le Rouge et le Noir*, ii. 473–4.
[8] 'Vous ne pouvez vivre sans votre fils', he says to her, 'et moi sans vous' (*Lucien Leuwen*, ii. 303). After Lucien's affair with the Comte de Beausobre he tells him: 'Enfin, je t'aime, et ta mère te dira que jusqu'ici, pour employer une phrase des livres ascétiques, je l'aimais en toi' (ibid. 377–8).

pensait qu'il était noble de mourir pour elles, ou beau de vivre avec elles, étaient des sujets de bonne plaisanterie pour son père et une duperie à ses yeux.[9]

The passage catches a particular strain of the dissonance between the idealistic hero and the prosaic realists who surround him; but in addition Stendhal was thinking here of the gulf which always yawns between two generations, and which becomes impassable when, as was the case with the Leuwens, the father's outlook had been moulded in the closing years of the *ancien régime*.[1] In his other writings (notably in *Racine et Shakspeare*) this lack of attunement is studied in its cultural repercussions: they merely overlaid the spiritual rift between a pre-revolutionary and a post-revolutionary generation. Finally—and this gives a more universal significance to Stendhal's analysis of the relations between the elder and the younger Leuwen—the novel illustrates the situation of a sensitive young man struggling to free himself from the domination of an exceptionally brilliant and powerful father (the only father in Stendhal to whom these epithets could be applied). François Leuwen is not domineering, but he cannot resist managing his son's life. When his help is appealed for he refuses it, in his son's interests, of course, and when his son could well do without his meddling, he puts into action a tortuous plan for Lucien's 'happiness'. At the very end of the book Lucien revolts, leaves home, and takes rooms in an *hôtel garni*. 'Il se promena avec délices dans ce joli petit appartement, dont le plus beau meuble était cette idée: "Ici, je suis libre!... Ici, je serai... tout à fait à l'abri de la sollicitude paternelle, maternelle, sempiternelle!"'[2] For all their advantages of wealth and social position Octave and Lucien are in a way unluckier than Julien and Féder whose family ties are severed at the outset.

[9] *Lucien Leuwen*, iii. 285–7.

[1] In Constant's novel there exists between father and son exactly the same disharmony. 'Je trouvais dans mon père (says Adolphe) non pas un censeur, mais un observateur froid et caustique, qui souriait d'abord de pitié, et qui finissait bientôt la conversation avec impatience.' Stendhal had certainly read *Adolphe*, but with less admiration than one might expect. The appearance of the third edition was the occasion for a brief review in the *New Monthly Magazine*, Dec. 1824 (*Adolphe* is 'a romance which has more singularity than excellence in it'), and a grudging tribute in the *London Magazine*, Oct. 1825: 'There is a great deal of affectation in the book, but after all it *says something*, well or ill, which distinguishes it from most modern books.'

[2] *Lucien Leuwen*, iii. 372.

Fabrice del Dongo, of whom it is said that 'le caractère de son père avait dépouillé de tout charme les souvenirs de la première enfance',[3] is no exception to the general rule that the Stendhalian hero must be at loggerheads with his father. But in Fabrice's case this antagonism is to a certain degree legitimized in the reader's eyes by the suspicion discreetly sown by Stendhal that Fabrice's father is not that timorous tyrant the Marchese del Dongo, but a certain young lieutenant—subsequently a general—who entered Milan with the victorious French troops on 15 May 1796. Fabrice himself, however, never appears to suspect his possible illegitimacy; and when the news of the death of the Marchese del Dongo is brought to him in his prison cell, he, like Julien and Lucien, reproaches himself—though more mildly—for his unnatural insensibility. It is true that Fabrice weeps when the lines of his mother's letter, giving the information, are read out to him; but once the messengers have left him he checks his tears and asks himself: 'Suis-je hypocrite? il me semblait que je ne l'aimais point.'[4] Stendhal adds, this time, no commentary. It would have been clean contrary to his conception of Fabrice, the young sun-god, to have had him dipping into any shadowy introspective pool of self-reproach.

The theme of the hero's secret bastardy, boldly introduced into *La Chartreuse*, had been toyed with in *Le Rouge et le Noir*. In the brief hour of his social triumph, the Marquis de La Mole having secured him a commission in the hussars under the name of Sorel de la Vernaye, Julien is tempted to draw the conclusion that he is in reality 'le fils naturel de quelque grand seigneur exilé dans nos montagnes par le terrible Napoléon. A chaque instant cette idée lui semblait moins improbable... Ma haine pour mon père serait une preuve... Je ne serais plus un monstre!'[5] Stendhal seems to have taken pleasure in stimulating curiosity over Julien's parentage without ever satisfying it. Thus M. de La Mole, wishing to do Pirard, the director of the seminary, a favour, and hearing that Julien is spoken of as his favourite pupil, sends Julien 500 francs under the cover-name 'Paul Sorel'. This first gives Pirard the idea that Julien might be 'the natural son of some rich man', a supposition reinforced by various other small incidents. At the Hôtel de La Mole, when instructing Julien in his duties as secretary, Pirard is astonished at the young man's violent indignation when he

---

[3] *La Chartreuse de Parme*, i. 276.   [4] Ibid. ii. 212.
[5] *Le Rouge et le Noir*, ii. 386.

warns him against being suborned into disclosing the Marquis's secrets; the priest wonders whether to take this as a sign of left-handed descent from some touchy aristocrat. Later, the Chevalier de Beauvoisis, to justify the honour he has done Julien in fighting a duel with him, spreads the rumour that he is the illegitimate son of a friend of the Marquis de La Mole, and the Marquis, far from denying the story, gives Pirard to understand that there may be something in it.[6] Perhaps all these carefully scattered hints demonstrate little more than the author's ineradicable love of mystification: a transference to the novel of the delight he took, in private life, in hoaxing his friends.[7] Much more important, if we are to understand the direction Stendhal's imagination was taking in this case, is Julien's own account of himself as a kind of foundling, 'une sorte d'enfant trouvé, haï de mon père, de mes frères, de toute ma famille'; a foundling, it may be added, for ever vainly in search of his *true father*. 'J'ai été haï de mon père depuis le berceau; c'était un de mes grands malheurs; mais je ne me plaindrai plus du hasard, j'ai retrouvé un père en vous, monsieur.'[8] These strange words are addressed to Pirard, who is, however, only one of the many father-substitutes Julien finds on his path. The first is the old army surgeon, already dead when the narrative opens, who lends him books and tells him stories about Napoleon. The local priest at Verrières, Chélan, is another, and even the Marquis de La Mole, at certain moments, appears cast for the part. So too Fabrice, another hapless Telemachus; his cheated filial affection is likewise centred on a priest, the Abbé Blanès.[9] The normal mode of address from a cleric to a layman, 'my son', encourages, of course, the fiction of paternity.

Properly, the only true foundling is Lamiel, adopted from a foundlings' home and spoken of among the villagers of Carville as 'the devil's daughter'—a paternity cheerfully acknowledged by Lamiel herself: 'le diable mon père saura me maintenir en gaieté.'[1] The theme of the hero of uncertain birth is of course as old as

---

[6] *Le Rouge et le Noir*, i. 376; ii. 17, 91.

[7] An example: Mme Ancelot's account in her memoirs of how Beyle, on the first occasion he attended one of her *soirées*, posed as contractor to the Government for the supply of nightcaps to members of the armed forces, and for the duration of his visit talked volubly about the manufacture of these necessary articles. (*Les Salons de Paris: Foyers éteints*, Paris, 1858, pp. 67–68.)

[8] *Le Rouge et le Noir*, i. 60; ii. 24.

[9] 'L'abbé Blanès était son véritable père' (*La Chartreuse de Parme*, i. 279).

[1] *Lamiel*, p. 51.

fiction itself; Stendhal's only innovation—a significant one—was to suppress the customary resolution of the mystery in the conclusion. Tom Jones is discovered at the last to be Allworthy's nephew. All the troubles of Don Alphonse are ended when his foster-father discloses that he is the legitimate son of Don César de Leyva (*Gil Blas*). If Marivaux had finished *La Vie de Marianne*, undoubtedly Marianne would have verified what she constantly suspects, that the parents she lost as a baby were of gentle birth. Scott does not disdain the gambit either. He used it in his first novel, *Waverley*, and in others of the series: the hero of *The Abbot* (one of the books which, it will be remembered, Stendhal asked Mareste to procure for him) is a young man of doubtful parentage who finally emerges as heir to the ancient house of Avenel.

Stendhal's main purpose in weaving this rather hackneyed theme into the pattern of his novel was probably to set in relief the spiritual isolation of his hero. He starts from nowhere, no one has responsibility for him, he has as little feeling of responsibility for others as Camus's Outsider,[2] though he has—and this is as marked a characteristic as any—an exacerbated sense of his responsibility towards himself. Like another existentialist hero, Orestes in Sartre's first play, he may feel unattached and weightless like a floating ball of gossamer, and experience the need to 'engage' himself (this is to some extent the case, at any rate, with Octave de Malivert and Lucien Leuwen; but the only central figure in a story by Stendhal who is truly 'engaged' in Sartre's meaning is Missirilli in *Vanina Vanini*). More commonly, the hero is seen in search of emotional rather than political engagement.

Here he rejoins his creator who in his autobiography made the shocking admission: 'L'amour a toujours été pour moi la plus grande des affaires, ou plutôt la seule.'[3] One reason why love loomed so large was that he could never take it lightly. He had the ambition to be, and sometimes succeeded in passing as, 'un homme à bonnes fortunes', a devil with women, but in reality he was the most hesitant, the least bold and adroit of men when his heart was truly engaged. Facile conquests held few attractions for him; what was fascinating was what was fearful, and twice in the *Vie de Henri*

---

[2] Meursault's affinity with Stendhal's heroes has been pointed out more than once, and the parallel between *L'Étranger* and *Le Rouge et le Noir* has been traced in detail by L. Lesage, 'Albert Camus and Stendhal', *French Review*, vol. xxiii (1950), pp. 474–7.

[3] *Vie de Henri Brulard*, ii. 38.

Brulard we find him referring to woman by an apparently deroga-
tory, in reality devotional, formula, as a 'terrifying animal': 'cet
animal terrible, si redouté, mais si exclusivement adoré, une femme
comme il faut et jolie', 'cet animal terrible: une femme aimable,
juge du mérite des hommes'.[4] Certain sayings in other books can
be linked to these, such as that 'toutes les grandes passions sont
craintives et superstitieuses', that 'les plaisirs de l'amour sont toujours en proportion de la crainte', and above all, this: 'L'amour
est une fleur délicieuse, mais il faut avoir le courage d'aller la
cueillir sur les bords d'un précipice affreux.'[5] Passion darkening
into terror, ardour freezing into timidity, this was the special form
which love took for Stendhal and which it takes for each of his
heroes: the form which it not infrequently takes in a highly imaginative, introspective adolescent.

'C'était un jeune homme bien né, et qui avait encore besoin de
prendre sur lui, pour avoir du courage avec les femmes qu'il
aimait.' This sentence might come from almost any of Stendhal's
novels (*Le Rouge et le Noir* only is excluded by the epithet 'bien
né'). In fact it is used to describe the hero of an insignificant story,
Le Philtre.[6] The dread of passion besets every hero, except, once
more, Julien, too much the Roman or too much the egotist even to
entertain the thought that he might one day be caught in this trap
of self-alienation. In his first novel Stendhal chose a queer, extravagant expression of the fear of falling in love. A disability has rendered Octave incapable of complete sexual experience: this can be
regarded as a limiting case of the reluctance to surrender to passion. Such an interpretation of Octave's impotence receives some
corroboration from various references in the course of the novel to
an oath 'never to love', taken when he was sixteen. 'Lui', writes
Stendhal, 'qui tant de fois s'était fait des serments contre l'amour,
que l'on peut dire que la haine de cette passion était la grande
affaire de sa vie...'[7] Octave is then anti-sexual rather than asexual:
a Hippolytus as Euripides saw him, not as Racine did. He is
genuinely unaware that he is falling in love with Armance. 'Il
s'était fait les serments les plus forts contre cette passion, et comme
il manquait de pénétration et non pas de caractère, il eût probablement tenu ses serments.' It needs Mme d'Aumale's frivolously

---

[4] *Vie de Henri Brulard*, ii. 70, 108.
[5] *Vie de Rossini*, i. 315; *De l'Amour*, ii. 166, 15–16.
[6] *Romans et nouvelles*, ii. 57.   [7] *Armance*, p. 68.

mischievous insinuations to reveal the truth to him: and this revelation, when it comes, overwhelms and horrifies him. 'Il avait donc eu la faiblesse de violer les serments qu'il s'était faits tant de fois! Un instant avait renversé l'ouvrage de toute sa vie.'[8] There follows a night of bitter self-reproach and, next morning, the brutal rupture with Armance. The reader, to whom Stendhal's sense of decency forbade an outright disclosure of the secret of Octave's infirmity, is bound to suppose that, for reasons never divulged, Octave had taken a vow of eternal celibacy. The supposition is, if anything, reinforced by his renunciation of the vow during the illness ensuing on the wound he receives in his duel. He expects to die, and since he will not be called on to prove himself, may safely indulge in a little dalliance.

Need it be emphasized how characteristic such a syndrome is of a certain stage in adolescence? Stendhal returned to the theme, treating it, however, more soberly and realistically, in *Lucien Leuwen*, where his hero can be construed as a deromanticized version of Octave. Lucien has abjured love, but at least Stendhal tells us why; the puerility of his hero's reasoning makes Lucien human and convincing. He cannot feel enough contempt for his cousin Edgar 'qui fait dépendre son bonheur, et bien plus son estime pour lui-même, des opinions d'une jeune femme qui a passé toute sa matinée à discuter chez Victorine le mérite d'une robe, ou à se moquer d'un homme de mérite comme Monge, parce qu'il a l'air commun!'[9] When, notwithstanding this precocious misogyny, Lucien realizes he is falling in love, his mood of horrified self-censure repeats, in an attenuated form, Octave's sleepless night of agony.

'Aurais-je la sottise d'être amoureux' se dit-il enfin à demi haut; et il s'arrêta comme frappé de la foudre, au milieu de la rue. Heureusement, à minuit, il n'y avait là personne pour observer sa mine et se moquer de lui.

Le soupçon d'aimer l'avait pénétré de honte, il se sentit dégradé. 'Je serais donc comme Edgar, se dit-il. Il faut que j'aie l'âme naturellement bien petite et bien faible! L'éducation a pu la soutenir quelque temps, mais le fond reparaît dans les occasions singulières et dans les positions imprévues. Quoi! pendant que toute la jeunesse de France prend parti

---

[8] Ibid. 93–94, 165.
[9] *Lucien Leuwen*, i. 117. 'Victorine' stands, obviously, for any fashionable dressmaker. Monge was one of those responsible for founding the École polytechnique in 1794—hence, no doubt, Lucien's veneration.

pour de si grands intérêts, toute ma vie se passera à regarder deux beaux yeux, comme les héros ridicules de Corneille!'

Who, these days, can waste time on women? only dodderers in retirement. 'Mais moi! à mon âge! quel est le jeune homme qui ose seulement parler d'un attachement sérieux pour une femme?'[1] This patriotic talk is a pathetic subterfuge: Lucien is, when he is being honest with himself, tolerably cynical about political issues—he was living in a period when civic idealism was at a discount, when all the great causes had temporarily retreated into limbo. He is trying, simply, to rationalize his sexual terror. Stendhal suggests as much in a comment on his hero, when a week later his last doubts about the state he is in are dispelled.

Ce républicain, cet homme d'action, qui aimait l'exercice du cheval comme une préparation au combat, n'avait jamais songé à l'amour que comme à un précipice dangereux et méprisé, où il était sûr de ne pas tomber. D'ailleurs, il croyait cette passion extrêmement rare, partout ailleurs qu'au théâtre. Il s'était étonné de tout ce qui lui arrivait, comme l'oiseau sauvage qui s'engage dans un filet et que l'on met en cage; ainsi que ce captif effrayé, il ne savait que se heurter la tête avec furie contre les barreaux de sa cage.[2]

Whatever the temperament and antecedents of the hero, if he falls in love (and all invariably do, with the possible exception, once more, of Julien, who discovers himself *to have been in love* and so eludes the common fate), then at a given point this terror envelops him: fear of the unknown, fear of losing control of his destiny, of his over-prized identity, of becoming the toy of an implacable divinity[3] of whom the woman he loves—did he but realize it—is only an unconscious and innocent instrument. No hero is temperamentally more removed from Lucien, earnest, strenuous, and the soul of honour, than Féder, frivolous, cynical, ambitious, or than Fabrice, uncomplicated, lovable, childlike; but each is touched by the wings of this terror. Féder resembles Lucien in that he too 'tremblait de s'engager dans une passion, et il n'y a pas de doute que, s'il eût été certain de finir par aimer passionnément Valentine,

---

[1] *Lucien Leuwen*, i. 274–5.   [2] Ibid. 278–9.
[3] 'Vous m'inspirez de la terreur', says Lucien to Mme de Chasteller during their first walk together in the Forest of Bureviller. 'A peine rentrée dans les salons de Nancy, vous redeviendrez pour moi cette divinité implacable et sévère.' *Lucien Leuwen*, ii. 39. The latent masochism in such a passage is almost too obvious to need pointing out.

il eût quitté Paris à l'instant'. Stendhal had used almost the same words about the hero of *Armance*: 'Un mot qui lui eût dénoncé qu'un jour il pourrait avoir de l'amour pour mademoiselle de Zohiloff, lui eût fait quitter Paris à l'instant.'[4] Octave also says: 'Armance m'a toujours fait peur. Je ne l'ai jamais approchée sans sentir que je paraissais devant le maître de ma destinée'; while in the later novel, Stendhal wrote: 'Valentine inspirait à Féder une sorte de terreur, qu'à la vérité il ne s'avouait pas encore à lui-même.'[5] Féder's 'terror' is, however, rather differently rooted from either Octave's or Lucien's. He has already experienced one violent passion—for an actress whom he married but who luckily died; Stendhal relates the circumstances in a prologue to his novel. He has, then, already bruised himself rolling down that vertiginous precipice of which Lucien is so wary: his object is to avoid a second fall.

Il avait peur de son âme, il se rappelait toutes les étranges folies qu'il avait faites pour sa femme, et en vérité il n'en voyait pas le pourquoi. Le souvenir qui lui était resté n'était autre que celui d'une petite fille d'un caractère fort gai et qui adorait les chiffons venus de Paris. Au surplus, il ne lui restait aucun souvenir distinct et détaillé des sentiments qui l'avaient agité pendant tout le temps qu'il avait été amoureux. Il se voyait seulement accomplissant d'étranges folies; mais il ne se rappelait plus les raisons qu'il se donnait à lui-même pour les faire. L'amour lui inspirait donc un sentiment de terreur fort prononcé...[6]

Fabrice, on the other hand, is, for a large part of the period covered in *La Chartreuse de Parme*, a stranger to love. At intervals he even condescends to allow himself to be troubled by his inability to experience the emotion. 'La nature' he sighs, 'm'a privé de cette sorte de folie sublime.'[7] Octave was unable to love for physiological reasons, Lucien shunned love as an ignoble distraction, Féder's attitude was that of the burnt child fearing the fire, and finally Fabrice regards it as his personal fate to remain a bondsman to Artemis. The great Racinian theme, tremulously discernible in all Stendhal's fictional work, rises most clearly to the surface in *La Chartreuse*, with Mosca a mature and jealous Theseus, Gina Sanseverina an obvious Phaedra nourishing an unutterable,

---

[4] *Romans et nouvelles*, ii. 224; *Armance*, pp. 68–69.
[5] Ibid., p. 308; *Romans et nouvelles*, ii. 174–5.
[6] Ibid., 262–3.
[7] *La Chartreuse de Parme*, i. 258.

semi-incestuous passion, and Clélia Conti playing a discreet Aricia to Fabrice's Hippolytus.

At Bologna, sharing his time between the complaisant little actress Marietta and the study of astronomy, Fabrice has leisure to reflect, with the limpid nonchalance which characterizes his occasional bursts of self-analysis, on this supposed frigidity of his. Is love no more than a healthy animal appetite, to be satisfied as and when its pangs make themselves felt? In that case, what were Shakespeare and Tasso raving about when they created Othello and Tancred? Or could it be that he, Fabrice, is differently constituted from other men? Do they possess a faculty which nature has denied him? As if to prove to himself that this is not so, he feigns a passion for the noted singer Fausta, in the hope that he will end by contracting it; but after various incautious pranks, which include kidnapping the diva's official protector and forcing him to fight a duel, Fabrice remains reluctantly convinced 'que sa destinée le condamnait à ne jamais connaître la partie noble et intellectuelle de l'amour'.[8]

His destiny has no such inhuman design. The story of Fabrice serves merely to illustrate the epigram of the younger Crébillon: *Après avoir eu beaucoup d'affaires, on n'en est quelquefois pas encore à sa première passion.* A compassionate glance from Clélia, as he is led to his prison cell, is enough to kindle the fire and change his life. It is as simple as waking after sleep.

La duchesse d'A... [his mistress at Naples] et la Marietta lui faisaient l'effet maintenant de deux jeunes colombes dont tout le charme serait dans la faiblesse et dans l'innocence, tandis que l'image sublime de Clélia Conti, en s'emparant de toute son âme, allait jusqu'à lui donner de la terreur. Il sentait trop bien que l'éternel bonheur de sa vie allait le forcer de compter avec la fille du gouverneur, et qu'il était en son pouvoir de faire de lui le plus malheureux des hommes.[9]

Clear-sightedly, Fabrice has struck through to the essential source of this terror: the lover finds himself paralysed, the hero's liberty is forfeit, all now depends not on himself but on another, a remote, impregnable, inviolable spirit with a life apart, an alien will lurking withdrawn behind large soft eyes, manifesting itself in the modulations of a quiet contralto voice.

But fear dissolves shortly in peaceful unison. The spirit smiles,

---

[8] *La Chartreuse de Parme*, i. 419.   [9] Ibid. ii. 150.

consoles, and reassures. However frequently and painfully he experienced it himself, Stendhal could never bring himself to describe unreciprocated love (just as Proust could never bring himself to describe it reciprocated). Once the hour has struck, his lovers are spiritually at one, and the remainder of the novel is concerned simply with the removal or circumvention of the obstacles that prevent their final union—unless the obstacles prove insurmountable, in which case death or a nunnery provide refuge. It has frequently been argued from this that Stendhal's novels are cases of wish-fulfilment or compensation:[1] Mme de Rênal listens to Julien Sorel as Mme Daru had refused to listen to Henri Beyle; Bathilde shyly returns Lucien's love as Mathilde had harshly declined to return Stendhal's; Clémentine Curial's wanton treachery is softened into Clélia Conti's reluctant betrayal when she accepts Crescenzi's hand though her heart is for Fabrice. Speculations of this sort are more fascinating than illuminating, even though no one would deny the profound and obsessive subjectivity of Stendhal's work. Only it is perhaps more important to see that the immediately established harmony between hero and heroine corresponds to an inner need in the creator to colour his vision of an ignoble world made tolerable for the elect by their secret, inseverable unity.

For this is how Stendhal sees his lovers: as two beings from another sphere, encountering one another by a fortunate chance, and engaging in a dialogue couched in a tongue the profane cannot understand. There is a strange passage, in Stendhal's first novel, on the heroine's trick of gazing a little more intently than good manners allow at those in whose company she finds herself. Some amusement and some offence is caused thereby among the friends of Mme de Bonnivet in whose house Armance occupies an ambiguous position, niece and lady-companion at the same time. Mme de Malivert, as a woman of rather finer sensibility, defends her impatiently against her detractors, saying of the girl's look that 'c'est ainsi... que deux anges exilés parmi les hommes, et obligés

[1] According to Léon Blum, who started this particular hare, Stendhal 'goûtait une sorte de revanche à recommencer la vie sans cesse sur nouveaux frais' (*Stendhal et le beylisme*, p. 80). Cf. also Brombert (article entitled 'Stendhal: creation and self-knowledge', *Romanic Review*, 1952, and the chapter 'La Victoire imaginaire' in his *Stendhal et la voie oblique*); Hoog, *Littérature en Silésie*, pp. 136 et seq.; Starobinski, *L'Œil vivant*, pp. 214–15; Claude Roy, *L'Homme en question*, pp. 106–7; &c.

de se cacher sous des formes mortelles, se regarderaient entre eux pour se reconnaître'.[2] On Mme de Malivert's lips such a comparison is high-flown, but not out of character. It is a shock to find it used, with all its solemn, sacred overtones, by Stendhal himself in his capacity as narrator, in a later novel. Lucien Leuwen, meeting Mme de Chasteller at a ball, is inspired, we are told, to adopt in conversation with her 'cette nuance de familiarité délicate qui convient à deux âmes de même portée, lorsqu'elles se rencontrent et se reconnaissent au milieu des masques de cet ignoble bal masqué qu'on appelle le monde. Ainsi des anges se parleraient qui, partis du ciel pour quelque mission, se rencontreraient, par hasard, ici-bas.'[3]

The metaphor of the lovers discovering one another in a masked ball derives from *Romeo and Juliet*; there is nothing astonishing in this, it was one of Stendhal's favourite plays. The simile of the two angels meeting on earth is stock romantic cliché, and it would be wrong, no doubt, to look for a specific literary 'source'. Were one to do so, the works one would search would be those stamped with the approval of that 'Société des Bonnes Lettres' which Stendhal never mentions without scorn: poetry in which mystical fervour and gentlemanly high-mindedness contrived to blend with a discreet eroticism. Alfred de Vigny was the arch-exponent of this type of writing—not, of course, the Vigny of *La Mort du Loup* and the other anthology pieces, but of the 'mysteries', *Le Déluge*, *Éloa*. Stendhal, whose characteristic manner approaches the cold blue steel of Mérimée's prose, could and did vary it so that occasionally it shows traces of the suspect softness of this particular vein of base metal; between him and Vigny (despite the outrageous review with which he saluted the appearance of *Éloa* in 1824[4]) there may have been a closer affinity than is commonly admitted. Towards the end of the *Vie de Henri Brulard* Stendhal, trying to describe the rapt and trance-like state into which he fell during his first few months in Paris, resorts to quotation from Vigny's preface to his play

[2] *Armance*, p. 61.

[3] *Lucien Leuwen*, i. 306.

[4] '. . . Incredible amalgam of absurdity and profaneness . . . horrible and delirious rhapsody . . . impossible to read a hundred lines of this poem without yawning, and two hundred without falling into the most profound sleep' (*New Monthly Magazine*, vol. xii, pp. 557–8: Dec. 1824). Stendhal concluded rather cheaply by suggesting that *Éloa* (which describes how one of Christ's tears, changed into an angel, descends into hell to redeem Satan) was written when Vigny was drunk on *lachryma christi*.

Chatterton: 'J'étais plongé dans des extases involontaires, dans des rêveries interminables, dans des inventions infinies...', and adds: 'Oserai-je le dire? Mais peut-être c'est faux, *j'étais un poète*... Il ne me manquait que l'audace d'écrire, qu'une *cheminée* par laquelle le *génie* pût s'échapper.'[5] It was no falsehood, even though Stendhal was scarcely able even to write an alexandrine without some glaring error in prosody. The poetry emerges in the novels, not at all exceptionally; it is a poetry of situation primarily, where the scene of his imagining works so powerfully on Stendhal's sensibility that his habitual prosaic dryness is utterly swamped and the expression soars, briefly, into rhapsody; unless, indeed, the tension is such that language fails entirely, 'le sujet surmonte le disant', as he used to say.[6] The sensitive reader will discover in Stendhal a kind of eloquence which is his silence.

The particular situation illustrated from *Lucien Leuwen*, the angelic colloquy in the 'ignoble masked ball', can be matched with others in different novels.

Le soir, quand ils étaient aux deux extrémités opposées de l'immense salon où madame de Bonnivet réunissait ce qu'il y avait alors de plus remarquable et de plus influent à Paris, si Octave avait à répondre à une question, il se servait de tel mot qu'Armance venait d'employer, et elle voyait que le plaisir de répéter ce mot lui faisait oublier l'intérêt qu'il pouvait prendre à ce qu'il disait. Sans projet il s'établissait ainsi pour eux au milieu de la société la plus agréable et la plus animée, non pas une conversation particulière, mais comme une sorte d'écho qui, sans rien exprimer bien distinctement, semblait parler d'amitié parfaite et de sympathie sans bornes.[7]

The tone of the mood is given by the serene trust in each other that radiates from Armance and Octave. It is very different in a corresponding scene in *La Chartreuse de Parme*. Again, Stendhal arranges for his lovers to meet in a large and brilliant social gathering. Fabrice is a free man, cleared at last of the murder charge that had hung over him. But Clélia, after surrendering to him for one brief moment in his prison cell, has placated her father by accepting in marriage a wealthy snob, the Marchese Crescenzi; she has,

---

[5] *Vie de Henri Brulard*, ii. 192–3, 193–4.
[6] 'Car la parole est toujours réprimée, / Quand le sujet surmonte le disant': last two lines of a poem said to have been improvised by Francis I before the tomb of Petrarch's Laura, at Avignon. Stendhal probably read them in De Brosses, *Lettres familières écrites d'Italie*, where the poem is quoted in full.
[7] *Armance*, p. 239.

moreover, vowed solemnly never to look at Fabrice again. Both she and Fabrice are present at the court reception against their will: Clélia because her husband's vanity will not hear of her staying away, Fabrice because he has been warned that it might be regarded as a piece of affectation were he to be absent. Clélia does not expect to see Fabrice and Fabrice hopes, by leaving early, to avoid Clélia. But he is detained and is still there when the Crescenzis are announced. Annoyance makes him flush with anger, but the strains of an aria of Cimarosa transform his mood into one of soft, even tearful melancholy (by a process often analysed by Stendhal: music dissolves the harsh pain of the sorrower, substituting a kind of gentle nostalgic regret[8]). At a certain moment the creaking of a chair nearby makes him turn his eyes. It is Clélia who, not recognizing her lover, so greatly have grief and fasting altered him, happened to take this seat three paces from his. The eyes of each, swimming with tears, meet, and their union is once more sealed, without a word having been spoken.

So summarized, this inexpressibly moving scene might be thought more sentimental than truly pathetic; but in the reading no such impression is received, thanks to the pace of the purely factual narrative. Constantly the temperature is lowered by side-long glances at the courtiers: the pompous Crescenzi, an unnamed debtor of his whom he compels to relinquish a seat of honour in favour of his wife, a Father Superior whom Fabrice engages in a theological discussion. All the everyday intrigue and speculation simmer on, all the normal currents of envy and vanity continue to flow; Stendhal does not even forget to insert a deflationary reference to the atrocious playing of a Mozart symphony. He is, as everywhere in *La Chartreuse*, doing his job inimitably: moving us in the same way as poetry can, or music, but by borrowing none of the trappings of poetry or music. His art is rigorously that of the story-teller. His style, negligently prosaic, agile and stripped for speed, algebraic in its precision and disdain of colour, codifies the situation

---

[8] 'Pourquoi la musique est-elle si douce au malheur? C'est que, d'une manière obscure, et qui n'effarouche point l'amour-propre, elle fait croire à la douce pitié. Cet art change la douleur sèche du malheureux en douleur regrettante; il peint les hommes moins durs, il fait couler les larmes, il rappelle le bonheur passé, que le malheureux croyait impossible' (*Histoire de la peinture en Italie*, ii. 172 n.). Other passages in which this theory is enunciated are to be found in the *Vies de Haydn, de Mozart et de Métastase*, pp. 163–5, and *Vie de Rossini*, ii. 152–3.

as exhaustively as a series of letters and figures the state of play in a game of chess. The rest is up to the reader: if he has not learned or cannot intuit the chess of the emotions, the chapter will be devoid of significance. This is why Stendhal means all or nothing, according to the reader.

Whether in the ball-room at Nancy, in Mme de Bonnivet's drawing-room, or in the reception-room in the Prince's palace at Parma, the presence of the Others is indispensable to the pattern and completes the formula. Stendhal could not have written *Daphnis and Chloe* or *Paul et Virginie*. His lovers are invariably members of a given society, to which is allotted the role of disturbing, baulking, or checking their idyll. The prototype here was, as Stendhal suspected, *Tom Jones*, a book very much in his mind in 1832 when he started writing *Une Position sociale*. He never got farther than the opening chapters of this work, which are devoted to tracing the birth and slow growth of intimacy between the French ambassador's wife at Rome, the Duchess de Vaussaye, and the hero Roizand, a member of his staff. Much of the interest of *Une Position sociale* lies in the various plans for its continuation which are found at the end of the manuscript. Stendhal saw that his next step must be to break away from the analysis of the affair between hero and heroine and allow the *others* to intervene. 'La duchesse a bien une espèce de duel avec Roizand, comme Tom Jones avec Sophie. Les personnages voisins entrent dans ce duel…' Such subsidiary characters 'changent ainsi, *par force*, la route que leur passion tendait à faire parcourir aux deux amants. Ainsi, mistress Fitzpatrick, lady Bellaston, influent *par force* sur le sort de Tom Jones…'[9]

It is of some interest that Stendhal should pick here on the diversionary sexual adventures of Fielding's hero rather than any other of the innumerable events and circumstances which temporarily separate him from Sophia Western. The inclusion of subsidiary or pseudo-heroines is normal in Stendhal: the Rebecca–Rowena motif, if we may appropriate Harry Levin's useful term, is visible everywhere. Often the function of the pseudo-heroine is purely sexual: she intones the siren-song of the senses, temporarily drowning the deeper spiritual call of the angelic companion. This simple scheme was to serve Balzac admirably in *Le Lys dans la vallée*; Stendhal used it discreetly in his first novel, by the introduction

[9] *Mélanges de littérature*, i. 152, 153.

of the coquettish Mme d'Aumale who excites Armance's jealousy, and in *Lucien Leuwen*, where the hero starts a flirtation with Mme d'Hocquincourt, partly to bolster his self-confidence so badly shaken by Mme de Chasteller's coldness. In *Le Rouge et le Noir* Mathilde is cast for the part of this secondary heroine, as is made clear by Julien's rejection of her at the end; but the theme has become subtly modified in this novel which is in nearly every way exceptional in Stendhal's work. For Julien's relations with Mme de Rênal are of course not of the same sort as Octave's with Armance or Lucien's with Mme de Chasteller: the chatelaine of Vergy has left him, as Stendhal puts it, 'nothing more to desire'. Nevertheless, there clings to Mme de Rênal a certain shy innocence, a certain moral elevation which gives her, in spite of her fault, kinship with Bathilde de Chasteller, Armance de Zohiloff, and Fielding's Sophia. At all events, her appeal for Julien is of a totally different order from that of the girl with whom he deceives her. By alternately refusing herself and yielding, Mathilde de La Mole succeeds in irritating his senses in a way that Mme de Rênal had never managed or indeed wished to do. It is in this sense that, *mutatis mutandis*, Mathilde may be considered the Molly Seagrim to Julien's Tom Jones.

In *La Chartreuse de Parme*, though the pattern of the hero set between two women is superficially the same, Stendhal has again varied the formula. The Duchess Sanseverina is, in the first place, in love with Fabrice who can feel for her nothing stronger than affection. Secondly, she is a powerful and ruthless spirit. She is an eagle to Clélia's dove, and this alters the whole emphasis of the novel. There is perhaps some analogy here with the situation in *Féder* where Rosalinde, a strong-willed, older woman, passionately devoted to the hero and his interests, seems to have been intended to suffer jealousy and to revenge herself on Féder and Valentine in much the same way as Gina on Fabrice and Clélia.

However differently the theme of the pseudo-heroine is handled, its function in the economy of the novel is invariable: to furnish the essential distraction, the impediment without which the course of true love would run all too smoothly. It is, however, only one impediment among many, all deriving directly or indirectly from conflicts between the interests of society and those of the individual. The ultimate catastrophe is always traceable to the fundamental antagonism between the social order and the lovers' claims on one another. Shakespeare's use of the enmity between Montagues and Capulets, a particular aspect of the political situation at Verona, to turn the wheels of tragedy, is precisely analogous to Stendhal's way of proceeding.

Reversing the terms of the optimistic proverb, Stendhal illustrated rather how little the world loves a lover. Consider the sardonic comment he wrote on one of the few periods of unalloyed happiness accorded to Armance and Octave:

Ces jours sans nuage passèrent rapidement. Ces cœurs bien jeunes encore étaient loin de se dire qu'ils jouissaient d'un des bonheurs les plus rares que l'on puisse rencontrer ici-bas; ils croyaient au contraire avoir encore bien des choses à désirer. Sans expérience, ils ne voyaient pas que ces moments fortunés ne pouvaient être que de bien courte durée. Tout au plus ce bonheur tout de sentiment et auquel la vanité et l'ambition ne fournissaient rien, eût-il pu subsister au sein de quelque famille pauvre et ne voyant personne. Mais ils vivaient dans le grand monde, ils n'avaient que vingt ans, ils passaient leur vie ensemble, et pour comble d'imprudence on pouvait deviner qu'ils étaient heureux, et ils avaient l'air de fort peu songer à la société. Elle devait se venger.[1]

Society takes its revenge, ultimately, by compelling the two to marry. A curious form for catastrophe to take, but of course, given Octave's infirmity, connubial contentment is out of the question, and besides, Stendhal was as convinced as his heroine that marriage was the grave of love.[2] The marriage of Octave and Armance is short-lived; Octave commits suicide and Armance takes the veil.

At Nancy, Lucien's daily visits to Bathilde de Chasteller stir up a storm of resentment in which their affair finally founders. The lady is the wealthiest young widow in the province, and Lucien, a Parisian, is upsetting the pretentions of half a dozen eligible bachelors (whom she would never have looked at . . . but that is beside the point). Lucien himself, with his father's millions behind him, is an obvious 'catch', and provincial dames with marriageable

---

[1] *Armance*, pp. 240–1.
[2] 'Étrange effet du mariage, tel que l'a fait le XIXᵉ siècle! L'ennui de la vie matrimoniale fait périr l'amour sûrement, quand l'amour a précédé le mariage' (*Le Rouge et le Noir*, i. 274). Marriage was 'un lien qui fait le malheur de la grande moitié des personnes qui y sont engagées' (*Pages d'Italie*, p. 98). The letters Stendhal wrote to Pauline, a little before she became Mme Périer-Lagrange, are full of cautions against expecting passion to survive marriage (see especially *Correspondance*, ii. 236–8). Stendhal is known to have twice made official proposals of marriage; on both occasions his offers were declined by the interested parties.

daughters seethe with suppressed indignation. Those who are quite indifferent to the matrimonial dispositions of Mme de Chasteller or of Lucien Leuwen are as likely as not chewing over some real or imagined slight put on them by this cocksure cavalry lieutenant. A group of young hotheads form a conspiracy to rid their town of Lucien by fighting a succession of duels with him. The local doctor, Du Poirier, who enjoys considerable moral authority over the reactionary landowners of the district, dissuades them by arguing that if Lucien is killed, Mme de Chasteller will not remain at Nancy. He promises a surer way of driving off the interloper. His plan, odious and fantastically improbable, involves staging a false pregnancy while Bathilde is confined to bed with a minor indisposition, and concealing Lucien somewhere in the house so that he can be confronted with a wet-nurse and a babe in arms. Du Poirier triumphs and Lucien retires in headlong flight to Paris.[3]

The closest equivalent in Stendhal's fiction to the Romeo-and-Juliet situation is the Italian story, *L'Abbesse de Castro*. The two lovers, Hélène di Campireali and Jules Branciforte, are separated by the difference in fortune and status of their families: the elder Branciforte had been a mere soldier of fortune. The killing of Hélène's brother Fabio by Jules corresponds to the dispatch of Juliet's kinsman Tybalt by Romeo. But whereas Shakespeare's lovers marry in prudent haste, Stendhal's are persuaded by their own scruples into imprudent delay, by which society profits to force a wedge between them. First, Jules respects Hélène's innocence at a moment when she would have offered him no resistance, an act of generosity of which he later bitterly repents. Then Hélène, instead of acceding to his demand that she should absent herself from the convent to which her family has sent her, long enough for them to marry, imparts the whole story to her mother who takes prompt measures to frustrate the plan. Jules fails in a desperate attempt to deliver her by force of arms, and Hélène remains immured in the convent of Castro, 'et l'on pourrait

---

[3] The incident is so objectionable, on the score both of taste and verisimilitude, that it is extremely doubtful whether Stendhal would have retained it had he worked at the novel long enough to fit it for publication. He planned a somewhat similar development in the unfinished novel *Le Rose et le Vert*, the heroine of which, wishing to test the genuineness of her suitor's passion, pretends she has had a child. Though he does not withdraw his offer of marriage, the atmosphere is poisoned, and the lovers part. The force of the incident here is quite different, however, since in *Le Rose et le Vert* the initiative comes from Mina herself, not from a representative of the hostile 'outside world'.

terminer ici son histoire', writes Stendhal: 'ce serait bien pour elle, et peut-être aussi pour le lecteur. Nous allons, en effet, assister à la longue dégradation d'une âme noble et généreuse. Les mesures prudentes et les mensonges de la civilisation, qui désormais vont l'obséder de toutes parts, remplaceront les mouvements sincères des passions énergiques et naturelles.'[4] The Signora di Campireali is the principal agent of this 'civilization'. Her ambition (duly achieved) is to see her daughter abbess. Rich and influential, she is able to ensure that Jules is shipped off to Flanders. She forges letters purporting to have been written by him to Hélène, and carefully worded to trace a gradually declining passion.[5] Under this treatment the baser side of Hélène's nature gains control: she becomes vain, vindictive, and in the last resort depraved, embarking, out of mere wanton curiosity, on an affair with a handsome prelate. Her pregnancy, and the birth of a child, are at first kept secret; but the secret leaks. The abbess and the bishop are both sentenced to life imprisonment, and at this juncture in her affairs, news is brought to Hélène in her dungeon of Jules's return to Italy. She writes him a farewell letter and stabs herself.

The obvious pathos that can be wrung out of a clash between the demands of an insensitive society and the hero's private dream of happiness is perhaps sufficient to explain why Stendhal's novel so consistently gravitates towards this theme. But the heroic individual may have other aspirations just as cruelly baulked. The idyll (if that is the right word) of Mme de Rênal and Julien at Verrières ends in a flurry of whispered scandal and anonymous letters. Chélan, the parish priest, arranges that Julien should be admitted as a theology student to the seminary of Besançon; Mme de Rênal herself, afraid not for her reputation but of jeopardizing her husband's

---

[4] *Chroniques italiennes*, i. 138-9.

[5] A detail possibly borrowed by Balzac, when he relates how Rosalie de Watteville destroys confidence between Albert Savaron and the Italian duchess he hopes to marry, by sending her letters in Albert's handwriting indicating a cooling of his affections: the results of these manœuvres are disastrous to all three characters. *L'Abbesse de Castro* appeared in *La Revue des Deux Mondes* in 1839, *Albert Savarus* was published in 1842. In a paper called 'Balzac influencé par Stendhal' (*Le Divan*, no. 256 (1945), pp. 185-90), René Martineau advanced an unconvincing hypothesis that *Albert Savarus* was 'a kind of parody' of *La Chartreuse de Parme*. Henri Martineau wrote a pendent to this article under the same title (*Le Divan*, no. 257 (1946), p. 266), pointing out in *Albert Savarus* an indisputable borrowing from Stendhal's *Promenades dans Rome*. Balzac's full indebtedness to Stendhal has still to be reckoned up by an expert literary accountant. It is likely to prove astonishingly heavy.

life should he be compelled to fight a duel in defence of her honour,
urges Julien to fall in with Chélan's plan. Stendhal tells us nothing
of Julien's state of mind; but his passion for his gentle mistress
seems to have waned, he is ambitious, Besançon is a great city for
the village boy, and certainly he could not have spent all his life
vegetating at Verrières. The attack which society mounts against
the independent individual is, in *Le Rouge et le Noir*, insidious and
not at first apparent; it is, further, already engaged at the start and
is prolonged almost to the end of the novel. Society forces the
humbly born young man to think primarily if not exclusively of his
private wants, the first of which is a bare livelihood. 'Et moi,' cries
Julien, 'jeté au dernier rang par une Providence marâtre, moi à qui
elle a donné un cœur noble et pas mille francs de rente, c'est-à-dire
pas de pain, *exactement parlant pas de pain...*'[6] To earn his daily
bread, and at the same time to show himself the equal of those to
whom this, and much else besides, is given gratis, absorbs Julien's
energies; he has no time for happiness, and never knows it truly
until he has launched his defiant counter-attack against society.
Then, when he is locked away, quietly waiting for the law to make
its futile gesture of eliminating him, he is granted a glimpse of the
happiness which he had been cheated of before he could enjoy it.
'Autrefois,' he tells Mme de Rênal in his cell, 'quand j'aurais pu
être si heureux pendant nos promenades dans les bois de Vergy,
une ambition fougueuse entraînait mon âme dans les pays imagi-
naires. Au lieu de serrer contre mon cœur ce bras charmant qui
était si près de mes lèvres, l'avenir m'enlevait à toi; j'étais aux
innombrables combats que j'aurais à soutenir pour bâtir une fortune colossale... Non, je serais mort sans connaître le bonheur, si
vous n'étiez venue me voir dans cette prison.'[7] The deepest wound
in Julien's nature, his ambition, cauterized only when at the end a
rash deed lays his 'colossal fortune' in ruins, is inflicted by society:
by the post-revolutionary bourgeois society, that is, of Stendhal's
time, which challenged the young man of energy to rise by his own
efforts, to carve out a career for himself, a society which called
pushfulness a merit and ruthlessness the crowning virtue.

The underlying pattern of Stendhal's novel—the dry stick, to
use his own metaphor, on which the crystals of imagination were
deposited in various ways—shows a very young man, almost without a past, often with the vaguest of family antecedents, launched

---

[6] *Le Rouge et le Noir*, ii. 172–3.   [7] Ibid. 488.

into a particular circle of contemporary society. Sooner or later he will meet with an emotional revelation. Eventually he will disappear: abruptly, with the clang of the guillotine knife, or gently, withdrawing into his charterhouse. *Lucien Leuwen* alone might, if Stendhal had written the last part in accordance with his plan, have proved a true *Bildungsroman*, with the hero finally marrying his first love, having gained from experience the little it can offer, worldly wisdom, self-control, the power of judging men and handling women. The fact that Stendhal did not finish *Lucien Leuwen* is perhaps in itself proof that his aim was not to write case-histories of educations, intellectual, sentimental, or social.[8] Eugène de Rastignac survives to become prime minister, Frédéric Moreau outlives himself to see Mme Arnoux's grey hairs, but Stendhal's heroes are counted among those whom the gods love.

Stendhal's works, if they are not novels of apprenticeship, are, or are intended as, *predictions*. The middle-aged writer always saw the boy he once was, reading in a locked bedroom, asking of the novelist: what will it all be like? But, remembering too how badly he had been led astray by many of the novelists he had read with such avidity, Stendhal was scrupulous to tell the truth. 'The truth, however harsh!' was the epigraph chosen for *Le Rouge et le Noir*: 'La vérité, l'âpre vérité!' The novel is a mirror, as he reminded the reader in the preface to *Armance*, twice in the text of *Le Rouge et le Noir*, and in two of the three different prefaces projected for *Lucien Leuwen*. The point he makes every time about the mirror is that it cannot lie. If the camera had been invented, Stendhal would have claimed that his art was photographic. Wrongly, of course, but it is the intention that counts in this case: to avoid misleading the reader, always to respect his innocence, never to build on his guilelessness. Long before he started writing novels, Stendhal deduced this inflexible rule from his study of painting. 'En exagérant le moins du monde, en faisant du style autre chose qu'un miroir limpide, on produit un moment d'engouement, mais sujet à de fâcheux retours... [Le lecteur] chasse le jugement tout fait qu'on voulait lui donner, la paresse l'empêche d'en former un autre; et le héros, comme le panégyriste, vont se confondre dans le même oubli.'[9] This counsel of understatement gains in savour from

---

[8] 'Tout roman de Stendhal est l'histoire d'une éducation' (Bardèche, *Stendhal romancier*, p. 199). But there is no sense in educating the young and then killing them off. [9] *Histoire de la peinture en Italie*, i. 122.

having been proffered in the golden age of Romantic hyperbole. Almost at the end of his life, in the celebrated letter to Balzac concerning *La Chartreuse de Parme*, Stendhal said in effect the same thing when he wrote that he did not want to excite the reader by artificial means;[1] the reader, when he thought back to Count Mosca, ought to feel that there was nothing to be discounted in what Stendhal had written.

Stendhal's attitude to the question of realism was, as has already been suggested, conditioned by considerations more moral than aesthetic; or, to put it another way, he had come to the conclusion that honesty was the best policy, even for the artist. But realism could also be justified on purely aesthetic grounds. He outlined a defence along these lines in an interesting passage occurring in one of the appendixes printed at the end of the first posthumous edition of *Racine et Shakspeare*. Lamartine had made, in a letter to Mareste, certain objections to Stendhal's arguments in this work, and in particular had attacked the assumption that realism should be the artist's watchword: 'Il a oublié que l'imitation de la nature n'était pas le seul but des arts, mais que le *beau* était, avant tout, le principe et la fin de toutes les créations de l'esprit.' Stendhal answered Lamartine in the following words:

> Quoique j'estime beaucoup les peintres qui font du *beau idéal*, tels que Raphaël et le Corrège, cependant je suis loin de mépriser ces peintres que j'appellerais volontiers *peintres-miroirs*, ces gens qui, comme Guaspre-Poussin, reproduisent exactement la nature, ainsi que le ferait un miroir... Reproduire exactement la nature, sans art, comme un miroir, c'est le mérite de beaucoup de Hollandais, et ce n'est pas un petit mérite; je le trouve surtout délicieux dans le paysage. On se sent tout à coup plongé dans une rêverie profonde, comme à la vue des bois et de *leur vaste silence*. On songe avec profondeur à ses plus chères illusions; on les trouve moins improbables; bientôt on en jouit comme de réalités. On parle à ce qu'on aime, on ose l'interroger, on écoute ses réponses. Voilà les sentiments que me donne une promenade solitaire dans une véritable forêt.

This apologia for realism is very different from any the realists proper were to advance, whether painters or writers; Stendhal was, as usual, outside all camps. The point he is making is that, for a man endowed with imagination, the art even of unimaginative

---

[1] Stendhal used a highly indecent metaphor to express this idea: *Correspondance*, x. 282-3.

painters who are faithful imitators provides a pretext and an occasion for imaginative embroidery. 'La nature a des aspects singuliers, des contrastes sublimes; ils peuvent rester inconnus au *miroir* qui les reproduit, sans en avoir la conscience. Qu'importe! si j'en ai la touchante volupté.'[2] Ultimately, Stendhal is implying that the excellence of a work of art is only in part attributable to the talent of the artist; some of the credit must go to the man who contemplates it.

What is here advanced in respect of painting is elsewhere applied to the novel; there were no compartments in Stendhal's aesthetic theory. In *De l'Amour* he speaks of 'la rêverie' as being 'le vrai plaisir du roman' and adds: 'Cette rêverie est innotable. La noter, c'est la tuer...'[3] He means, of course, the reverie the novelist induces in the reader. It will be infallibly extinguished if the author is so ill-advised as to use the novel for didactic purposes: political argument, in particular, is as misplaced in the novel as a pistol-shot at a concert.

Prendre garde que l'homme de parti ne cache l'homme passionné. L'homme de parti sera bien froid dans cinquante ans, il en faut seulement ce qui sera intéressant quand le procès sera jugé. — Jamais de réflexion philosophique sur le fond des choses qui, réveillant l'esprit, le jugement, la méfiance froide et philosophique du lecteur, empêche *net* l'émotion. Or, qu'est-ce qu'un roman sans émotion? — Non, rien qui fasse penser, mais au contraire quelque chose qui dispose à l'émotion qui est le moyen de force du roman.[4]

His novel, then, was to be evocative rather than instructive, passionate rather than reflective, emotional rather than intellectual.

One might add that in that case its appeal was bound to be personal rather than universal, directed as it was to the sensibility which is variable in kind rather than to the intelligence which is variable only in degree. Hence the famous dictum: 'Un roman est comme un archet, la caisse du violon *qui rend les sons*, c'est l'âme du lecteur';[5] a saying which is meaningful only in the context of an unusual reliance on the reader's response. And Stendhal was, as we have seen, prepared to accord unlimited confidence to the reader, provided he was a reader after Stendhal's own heart, one of the 'happy few'.

---

[2] *Racine et Shakspeare*, pp. 347–8.   [3] *De l'Amour*, i. 72.
[4] *Mélanges intimes et Marginalia*, ii. 221, 243, 258. These were all notes made during the writing of *Lucien Leuwen*.   [5] *Vie de Henri Brulard*, i. 227.

III ✦ NARCISSUS

L ITERARY history differs from other branches of history in that, of the events and facts it brings to light, not all serve its purpose (which is to provide the means for a truer understanding and a heightened appreciation of literary masterpieces), while some even defeat that purpose. In the latter category belongs the well-known story of how Stendhal came to write *Armance*. A fashionable novelist, Mme de Duras, was rumoured in 1825 to have composed or to be composing a novel or a short story the hero of which was sexually impotent. The theme was an improbably scabrous one to be used by a titled lady in the starchy society of the Restoration, but two earlier works by the Duchesse de Duras had given her a certain reputation for audacity: the first described the passion of a well-born young man for a negress, and the second an equally unconventional affair between a daughter of the aristocracy and a man of no birth at all—as it might be, her gamekeeper. Mme de Duras, in fact, specialized in describing love-affairs which were socially impossible, so that there was nothing intrinsically unlikely in her choosing to write about a love-affair which was doomed by nature itself to disaster.

Apart from the fact that it was entitled *Olivier ou le secret*, little more was known, for over a century, about Mme de Duras's third and last work of fiction (the lady died in 1828 and Stendhal wrote her a handsome obituary notice in the *New Monthly Magazine*). Then one of her descendants, rummaging through the family archives, discovered the manuscript, which had been scribbled on the backs of letters addressed to her. There is a heroine, a widowed countess, in love with a childhood friend, Olivier de Sancerre. Seeing him jealous of one of her suitors to the point of calling him out and wounding him, she deduces delightedly that the next step will be a proposal. But she is disappointed. Olivier withdraws from her society, devoured by a secret melancholy, and finally commits suicide. He never has the courage to admit why he may not aspire to her hand. The reader, if the work ever had a reader, might just have guessed.[1]

But most probably Mme de Duras, judging her *Olivier* unfit for publication, contented herself with discreet readings to select circles. Someone, however, was indiscreet and a certain Hyacinthe Thabaud, well known in the world of letters under his pseudonym Henri de Latouche, conceived the idea of publishing a novel with the same title, *Olivier*, in which the same theme would be exploited. In order to ensure a *succès de scandale*, Latouche had his work published anonymously and in a volume of dimensions and typographical disposition similar to those of Mme de Duras's previous novels. The joke was perhaps not in the best of taste, but it seems to have amused Stendhal, who lent his support to the deception by reviewing *Olivier* in the *New Monthly* and attributing it without compunction to the good duchess.

Latouche's *Olivier* was published at the end of 1825 or early in 1826. At the end of January 1826 Stendhal began writing *Armance*. Originally he had intended to give his hero the same name, Olivier; this, he hoped, would indicate to his readers, without putting him to the disagreeable necessity of specifying it, what disability the young man suffered from; it was Mérimée who persuaded him (we cannot tell why) to alter the name to Octave. But though the novel rests on the same situation, it is not a copy of Latouche's book.[2] By the time it was ready for publication, in August 1827, the reading public had forgotten the *Olivier* scandal, or had grown tired of it; and *Armance* was ignored. Stendhal had put himself in the position of a man who caps a joke twenty minutes too late.

Armance has undoubtedly suffered from the circumstances attending its birth. Nineteenth-century critics, lacking the 'key'— not knowing, in other words, why Octave is so loth to marry Armance—tended to pass the book over as an incomprehensible and displeasing abortion. Auguste Bussière, who in the year following Stendhal's death published an extensive and remarkably shrewd

---

[1] These details, and a few more, are given in Luppé, 'Autour de l'*Armance* de Stendhal...', *Le Divan*, no. 250 (1944), pp. 263–8.

[2] 'Pas un épisode, pas une idée, pas un sentiment de commun entre *Armance* et *Olivier*, œuvres aussi différentes de style et de manière qu'il est possible.' H. Martineau, 'Stendhal et H. de Latouche', *Le Divan*, no. 174 (1931), pp. 467–8. A useful summary of Latouche's *Olivier* may be read in E. Henriot, *Livres et portraits*, 3e série, pp. 196–7.

analysis of his character, his turn of mind, and his literary achievement, had more reservations to make about *Armance* than about
any other of his books: it was the only one in which the author had
succeeded in boring his reader from beginning to end. The story
was unintelligible, the characters incoherent: 'on croirait se promener dans une maison de fous.'[3] (Forty years later, also writing,
like Bussière, in the *Revue des Deux Mondes*, Vogüé was to make
an almost identical remark about Dostoevsky's newly translated
novels.) In his turn Sainte-Beuve, who in any case rated Stendhal's fiction well below his other writings, described *Armance* as
'énigmatique par le fond et sans vérité dans le détail', while the
hero, 'capricieux, inapplicable et ne sachant que faire souffrir ceux
dont il s'était fait aimer, ne réussit qu'à être odieux et impatientant
pour le lecteur'.[4] Édouard Rod, writing towards the end of the
century, spoke much more appreciatively of the novel but gave no
sign of understanding Octave's predicament. The publication of
certain variants Stendhal hoped to introduce into a second edition
of the novel, with a view to making the situation clearer, and more
particularly the release of the text of Stendhal's letter to Mérimée
of 23 December 1826, with its discussion of the characters of various
impotents known to history (including Swift), have removed the
causes of perplexity; every critic and reader today knows what
Armance is about; or thinks he knows. The risk the novel now runs
is of being regarded primarily as a case-book of a particular psychological disorder. If this is what it is, then it is not a work of literature, but a fictional appendix to a treatise on psycho-pathology, and
the literary critic has no special authority to pronounce on its
value. Is it necessary to add that literary critics, a meddlesome race,
have not scrupled to do so?[5]

The other vexatious aspect of the story of its genesis is that
Armance has tended to be tacitly regarded as a work hurriedly
thrown together in response to a supposed public demand; as
though in our day a young novelist, having failed to get in first
with *Lucky Jim*, decided to write the second, or at least the third,
satire on the English provincial university. *Armance* is a great deal
less feeble than that. Infertile though its heroine was doomed to

---

[3] *Revue des Deux Mondes*, nouvelle série, vol. i (1843), p. 291.
[4] *Causeries du lundi*, ix. 327, 328.
[5] Gide being the principal offender: see his preface to the Champion edition
of *Armance*, reprinted in *Incidences*.

remain, the book that is called after her carries in its womb the embryos of those later works of Stendhal whose greatness is not disputed; and besides, it is clearly not an *œuvre de circonstance*: it connects, at many points, with some of the most deep-rooted of the author's preoccupations, personal, political, and artistic.

Aldous Huxley maintained that *Armance* 'if not one of the best, is certainly the queerest of all Stendhal's writings: the queerest and, for me at any rate, one of the most richly suggestive'.[6] His essay—which has in fact less to do with *Armance* than with the drawbacks of social permissiveness in matters of sexual *mores*—is entitled 'Obstacle Race'. Taken at the lowest level, as a piece of narrative engineering, *Armance* is just that, a more or less ingeniously contrived obstacle course. Huxley could not have known—and the fact has, perhaps, never been observed—that the basic plot of Stendhal's first novel is identical with that of the one and only comedy of his that was left in something like a state of completion. *Les Deux Hommes* was composed in 1803–4; it deals with the love of two cousins, frowned on by most of the other characters but favoured by one, a situation ultimately resolved by the removal of all obstacles and the marriage of the two young people. This scenario fits *Armance* pretty exactly. *Les Deux Hommes* would have been a kind of obstacle race, and Stendhal in fact remarked hopefully about his play: 'En s'intéressant vivement à l'amour de Charles et d'Adèle, le spectateur prendra intérêt à tous les obstacles qui surviendront à leur union, ces obstacles doivent aller *crescendo*.'[7]

The 'obstacles' did not, however, need to be very numerous, since a play, *ceteris paribus*, requires fewer incidents than a novel. In *Armance* the perpetual emergence of 'obstacles' constitutes the entire narrative framework, and a synopsis of the plot would read like a catalogue of misunderstandings, explanations, estrangements, reconciliations, offences given and pardoned, in an endless seesaw. Octave and Armance, both free from entanglements, are so obviously suited to one another from the beginning that the reader finds himself wondering how the author's ingenuity will stretch to deferring the inevitable marriage until the last chapter. In the later stages he has to resort to the introduction of fresh characters to blight the lovers' intimacy, and even to worn devices such as forged letters; but earlier, the· 'obstacles' are of a more tolerable

[6] *Music at Night*, p. 157. [7] *Théâtre*, ii. 80.

sort, arising as they do from certain over-delicate misapprehensions on the part of one or other of the two central characters.

The first such misapprehension occurs early on, when Armance mistakenly thinks Octave's head has been turned by the stroke of political fortune which has made him a man of wealth. Octave is distressed that his cousin should so misjudge him, and even more distressed that she should studiously deny him all opportunity of vindicating himself in a private conversation. 'Octave voyait *un obstacle* qui le séparait du bonheur...' By dint of patient manœuvring, he obtains the interview he needs. Armance is so touched that he should set such value on her good opinion that she bursts into tears and has to withdraw, not merely in confusion, but in despair: for has she not betrayed to her cousin that her feelings for him are more tender than is proper? 'Ô Dieu! après une telle honte comment oser reparaître devant lui?...Il faut élever *une barrière éternelle* entre Octave et moi.'[8] She faces him again with the story that she has a secret suitor to whom she hopes to be married; this, Stendhal tells us, is a 'heroic resolve', designed simply to hide from Octave the real reason for her fit of weeping—she was, she pretends, overwrought at the time because the projected marriage was on the point of falling through. In order that this false avowal should have no embarrassing consequences, she has to beg Octave to breathe no word about it either to his mother or to the aunt who is her guardian. It apparently never crosses Armance's mind—or Stendhal's—that for a young girl anxious above all to keep the good opinion of her cousin, this is a wildly incongruous course to take. For what esteem could Octave be expected to retain for an unmarried girl who coolly declares she is manœuvring to win a husband, and keeping her closest relatives in the dark about the whole affair?

When it is glibly advanced that Stendhal is a master of psychological motivation, one important reservation must be made: though he excelled in imagining how, in a given situation, his characters would feel, act, and speak, he was strangely devoid of the inventive power necessary to move them easily and naturally from one situation to the next. We have seen how he told Pauline, as early as 1804, that 'dans les romans l'aventure ne signifie rien', that importance should be attached only to the characters.[9] Be

---

[8] *Armance*, pp. 56, 84, 86. The italics are ours.
[9] See above, p. 6.

that as it may, there can be no novel without a 'story', and the
novelist in whom the elementary story-teller cannot be stirred to
life has a difficult time.

Some malignant fairy must have denied Stendhal the special
sort of imagination in which Scheherazade was supreme. This can
be admitted without any fear of belittling him: the novel is a form
which may start from the 'good yarn', but soon transcends it.
Undoubtedly, however, the fairy's evil spell resulted for Stendhal
in endless anxiety and frustration. To observe this best, we need
to digress briefly from *Armance* and consider such fictional works
as have come down to us together with their 'log-book', so to
speak.

Lucien Leuwen was not planned in advance because, as Stendhal
said, 'faire le plan d'avance me glace, parce qu'ensuite c'est la
mémoire qui doit agir, et non le cœur. L'appel à la mémoire me
glace...'[1] But, having no plan, and only the most tenuous of plots,
Stendhal found himself, in *Lucien Leuwen*, continually grinding to
a standstill, introducing more and more characters and not knowing in the least how to employ them. He had not had this trouble
with *Le Rouge et le Noir*, since there he had used a story drawn
from real life, and needed merely to modify it in certain respects
and fill it out. Similarly, in *La Chartreuse de Parme* his plot was
provided for him by a string of anecdotes discovered in an Italian
chronicle of doubtful authenticity. When, instead of having the
general lines of a plot laid down for him, he undertook, as in
Lucien Leuwen, to invent them, his struggles are almost painful to
watch. Having finished, after a fashion, the first part, which is set
in Nancy, he confessed himself 'diablement embarrassé pour
l'intrigue de la seconde partie à Paris'; eight months later he complained: 'Je ne puis mettre de *haute portée* ou d'esprit dans le
dialogue tant que je songe au fond. De là l'avantage de travailler
sur un conte tout fait, comme Julien Sorel. Je n'arrive à un peu de
brillant qu'en corrigeant pour la quatrième fois, après avoir oublié
le fond.'[2] *Lucien Leuwen* was left unfinished: apart from the missing
third section, there are blank chapters in the second. *Lamiel*
similarly, and *Une Position sociale*, were novels the plots of which
Stendhal flattered himself he could invent; they were both unfinished, and the manuscripts show how at a given point, once the

---

[1] *Mélanges intimes et Marginalia*, ii. 254.
[2] Ibid. 66–67, 271.

first impetus had exhausted itself, Stendhal's imagination ran
vainly hither and thither, experimenting with innumerable possible developments, unable to settle for any one in preference to
all the others; until finally inspiration dried up altogether and he
turned aside in disgust, promising himself he would return to the
story later . . . a promise only too seldom kept.

The most comforting conclusion he could reach regarding this
strange and, one would have thought, all-inhibiting deficiency in
his creative equipment, was that plot-invention and character
analysis were two distinct operations of the mind which in his case
could not be conducted simultaneously. 'Inventer les faits et voir
les beaux développements: deux mouvements *contraires* de l'esprit
de Dominique. Il invente en septembre, en janvier il a oublié et
peut peindre les détails comme s'il volait l'histoire à quelque vieux
bouquin.'[3] To understand all the allusions in this cryptic note (it
derives from the *dossier* of *Une Position sociale* and is dated 25 June
1833), one needs to know that while he was at Marseilles, in
September 1829, Stendhal was visited by what he called the 'idea of
Julien': it was then that he sketched out, in all likelihood, the
scenario of the novel, *Le Rouge et le Noir*, which he did not actually
start writing until *January* 1830. It appears, then, that Stendhal
needed to wait until the hour of illumination or 'invention' was
sufficiently distant for him to consider himself detached from it,
to the point, as he puts it, of having *forgotten* it. Once this vital
pause had been admitted, once the critical distance had been
reached, he could pick up the sketch and proceed to the elaboration,
the internal development, the psychological enrichment of situation and character which was the only part of novel writing that
interested him and appealed to him.

It may be supposed that this process was followed in the composition of *Armance*. We have Stendhal's own word for it that it
was written in two short bursts separated by a six-month interval,
three of the six months being occupied, incidentally, in a trip to
England. He conveys this information in one of those notes, at
once the delight and the despair of Beyle's biographers—so much
is said, and so much left unsaid. 'Travaillé à Olivier du 31 janvier

---

[3] *Mélanges de littérature*, i. 156. 'Dominique' was the name by which Stendhal
habitually referred to himself in his personal memoranda. It has been suggested
that he adopted it as a compliment to *Domenico* Cimarosa; another possibility
is that he derived it from the word *domino* in the sense of 'mask'.

au 8 février 1826. Je quitte cet ouvrage par la nécessaire impuiss. of making. Repris comme remède le 19 septembre 1826, terminé le 10 octobre. Reste à le traduire en style non offensant pour les demi-Buttalaqua.'[4] Some of these phrases are relatively easy to interpret. 'Olivier', as we have seen, was the name Stendhal originally intended to give to his hero; it stands here for the book, just as *Le Rouge et le Noir* was normally referred to by its author as 'Julien'. The 'demi-Buttalaqua' are presumably the tribe which Stendhal elsewhere calls 'les demi-sots', who make up the greater part of the critics and the educated public. Not complete fools, but not conspicuously intelligent either: half-and-halfs. When Stendhal says he resumed work as a remedial measure, we must understand that he had hoped to conjure the despair into which he had been plunged by Clémentine Curial's infidelity. His stock with her had been falling steadily since the previous October (1825); on his return from England he realized that his inconstant mistress would have positively no more truck with him, and his thoughts turned, not for the first time, to suicide.

The only truly enigmatic sentence in the note is: 'Je quitte cet ouvrage par la nécessaire impuiss[ance] of making.' Had Stendhal, in those nine days in the winter of 1826, written the opening chapters of the work, and then stalled 'by the inevitable inability to compose'? Or had he merely used the time to sketch out the main outlines of the plot and characters, and left things to simmer quietly in his unconscious until the necessary interval had elapsed between 'invention' and 'elaboration'? We are inclined to the second hypothesis, on the evidence of two briefer notes. In the first Stendhal writes: 'Je fis apparemment le premier jet de ceci en février 1826': 'le premier jet', the first sketch, or rough draft, is not the term which would be applied to the abandoned beginning of a novel. Then, on 5 July 1828 (after publication date), Stendhal noted: 'Je déchire l'original fait en neuf jours'—if 'the original' were the initial chapters, why should Stendhal tear these up and not the later chapters as well? It can hardly be doubted that the 'original fait en neuf jours' which he so regrettably destroyed was either an outline plan, with ideas for incidents, character sketches, and perhaps a few notes on *salon* society,

---

[4] *Mélanges intimes et Marginalia*, ii. 71. The note is one of the many concerning *Armance* which have been transcribed from an author's copy, bequeathed to his friend Donato Bucci, and hence referred to as the 'Bucci *Armance*'.

the comportment of impotents, &c.; or it was an early complete draft, subsequently worked over, enlarged, and revised. In either case it is clear that Stendhal made two bites of this particular cherry.

The disadvantage of his mode of composition is apparent from the most cursory examination of the narrative structure of *Armance*, which is surely as creaking and crazy an edifice as any in fiction. One would judge Stendhal to be quite incapable of what the merest tyro manages without effort: to conduct his reader gently from place to place along well-defined paths. He is for ever turning down lanes that lead to brick walls over which the reader and he have to clamber in a fatiguing and ungainly scramble, only to find themselves, after a short stroll, once more confronted with some other forbidding *obstacle*. We have already seen this sort of thing happen once, when an early discord between Octave and Armance is resolved at the cost of a serious infringement of elementary psycho-logical verisimilitude. Now, Armance having told Octave of an imminent marriage which has no more reality than her fears that he might have interpreted her emotional storm as an admission of love, Octave tells Armance that he has made up his mind not to marry before he is twenty-six. Since he is only twenty, Armance tells herself she can look forward to six years of tranquil 'friend-ship', and six years, at her age, is a lifetime. Casting around des-perately for some means of disturbing the unruffled and stagnant waters of their mutual satisfaction, Stendhal invokes Octave's mother, Mme de Malivert, whose role hitherto has been passive. Suddenly she conceives a violent desire to see Armance become her daughter-in-law, and communicates this plan not to Octave (which would be natural) but to Armance. When the embarrassed girl implores her not to think of such a thing, the older woman, with remarkable unscrupulousness, informs Armance that she has it from her son's lips that he is secretly in love with her. Had Mme de Malivert been a feather-brained or impulsive woman, or one delighting in intrigue for its own sake, the perpetration of this lie, to 'help things along', would be intelligible, if inexcusable, as being 'in character'; but she is a steady, sensible, inactive, and retiring person. It is not she, but Stendhal, who needs to 'help things along', and Stendhal himself, who qualifies her intervention as a 'singular decision', saw clearly enough how inadmissible this development was. It was, no doubt, the best that occurred to him.

It achieves, however, nothing at all: amounting to no more than a sudden gust of wind which puffs the two vessels round, then falls. Armance is raised 'to the summit of felicity' at hearing that Octave is in love with her, but thinks no more than previously of permitting him to become her husband. Here Stendhal is once more in the saddle: his Armance is exactly the cool, grave young puritan one knows so well, taking pleasure in the closest intellectual companionship with the young man whose mind and moral qualities she admires, but resolute in keeping the bridal chamber locked against him; ready, moreover, to disguise her own timidity by pretending to herself that she is applying the lessons of the great masters of disabused wisdom.[5]

Meanwhile Octave, who has noticed her demure elation, mistakes its cause, thinking it due to the approach of the marriage of which she had told him; she does not dream of disillusioning him either: 'ce mariage prétendu avec un inconnu que je préfère est ma seule défense contre un bonheur qui nous perdrait tous deux...' Not until the novel is two thirds through does Stendhal permit her to retract the story: 'Je ne me suis permis dans toute ma vie que ce seul mensonge, et je vous supplie de me le pardonner. Je n'ai vu que ce moyen de résister à un projet qu'avait inspiré à madame de Malivert l'excès de sa prévention pour moi. Jamais je ne serai sa fille, mais jamais je n'aimerai personne plus que je ne vous aime...'[6] Did Stendhal observe that, even as his heroine was owning to one lie, he involved her in another? for the story of the mysterious suitor had been thought up some time before Armance learned of Mme de Malivert's plans for a match between her and Octave. Stendhal, quite simply, forgot: at this stage he is lost in the ramifications of his own narrative, the penalty he paid, perhaps, for his odd method of composition. An even more remarkable instance of negligence: in chapter xxv he makes it appear that Octave has so completely forgotten Armance's disavowal of the unknown suitor (made in chapter xxiii) that he indulges in speculations about the identity of this future husband; he suspects it may be the Chevalier de Bonnivet; and later still, when an engagement to Armance is virtually forced on him, he asks her: 'Est-il possible...

---

[5] 'Ne dit-on pas que le mariage est le tombeau de l'amour, qu'il peut y avoir des mariages agréables, mais qu'il n'en est aucun de délicieux?' (*Armance*, p. 133). 'Il y a de bons mariages, mais il n'y en a point de délicieux' (La Rochefoucauld, 113th maxim).

[6] *Armance*, pp. 138, 220.

que vous n'aimiez pas le chevalier de Bonnivet et qu'il ne soit pas
cet époux mystérieux dont vous m'aviez parlé autrefois?'[7]

The final catastrophe is perhaps not, as we sardonically suggested earlier, that Octave marries his Armance, but that he marries
her doubting her integrity, suspecting her affection for him to be
a pretence. This, the last misunderstanding of all, and the most
tragic since it is never dispelled, is brought about by the agency of
a forged letter.[8] One French critic has called this development
Hardyesque;[9] in reference, doubtless, to all that turns, in *Tess*, on
the circumstance that a letter is pushed by mischance under a door-
mat and so is never discovered by its intended recipient. But there
is, in *Armance*, no 'President of the Immortals' to validate such a
cruel miscarriage. Instead, there is Octave's uncle, the mischievous
Commandeur de Soubirane, who dislikes Armance, and dislikes
even more the idea that his nephew should be marrying her. He
discovers that the affianced pair exchange letters by leaving them
at the foot of a certain orange-tree which has sentimental associa-
tions for them, and accordingly causes a letter to be written in
imitation of Armance's handwriting and placed in the orange-tree
box. This forgery is addressed to Armance's closest friend, Méry
de Tersan. Octave finds it as he is visiting the improvised post box
in order to deposit there a letter which has cost him infinite anguish
to write: in it he had made an honest declaration of the famous
secret, never fully disclosed in the novel—that, to use a polite peri-
phrasis coined by an earlier critic, he has a 'natural disqualification
for efficient marriage'.[1] He reads the letter that Soubirane has
planted; its general tenor is that Armance is marrying him simply
because such a marriage seems 'a reasonable and advantageous
arrangement', but that in her heart she would prefer a more amusing husband. In horror and despair he tears up his own letter,
though honour compels him to go through with the marriage.
However little one may wish to cavil, two objections at least present
themselves: why did Octave, who is the soul of delicacy, read a letter

---

[7] *Armance*, p. 270.

[8] It is, as we have seen, by forged letters that the Signora di Campireali
persuades her daughter that Jules Branciforte has forsaken her (*L'Abbesse de
Castro*). A forged letter (purporting to come from the Duchess Sanseverina) is
the means whereby Fabrice is decoyed across the frontier and arrested (*La
Chartreuse de Parme*).

[9] H. Jacoubet, *Les Romans de Stendhal*, p. 94.

[1] H. B. Samuel, 'Stendhal the compleat intellectual', *Fortnightly Review*,
vol. xciv (1913), p. 76.

which was not addressed to him? and why did it not occur to him that there was something strange in Armance's leaving a letter for a third person—and such a letter!—where he was most likely to find it?

Whither do these observations tend? *Armance* was the novel of Stendhal's apprenticeship. We have been submitting it to the kind of needling criticism from which certain other 'first novels', like *Madame Bovary* or *Sense and Sensibility*, would emerge triumphant; but before writing *Madame Bovary*, Flaubert had tried his hand, for twenty years, at fictional experiments—the *Mémoires d'un fou, Novembre*, an early version of *L'Éducation sentimentale*—which he had kept under lock and key, while Jane Austen similarly had served a fifteen-year apprenticeship, busying herself with the early drafts of the masterpieces of her maturity. Stendhal, a late starter, had not had the time to learn the elementary principles of his craft. Further, it must be owned that the craft of fiction can very well tolerate violations of its elementary principles—provided there is compensation. In *Armance* Stendhal flouts, time after time, the rules of verisimilitude; but are there not implausibilities as gross in *A la recherche du temps perdu*? We may grant, with Stendhal, that art is but a splendid lie; we must conclude that Stendhal had a poor head for concocting and sustaining lies. His art may, none the less, contain splendid truths. The Primitives are not to be condemned out of hand for ignoring the rules of perspective.

The defects of narrative composition that we have noted are probably hardly apparent to the ordinary reader, such is the insidious charm that emanates from the pages of the book, and wafts him into that state of reverie which Stendhal declared was the peculiar property of the novel. Certainly, to sense this charm requires on the reader's part more co-operative effort than he is called on to provide when he opens Stendhal's later works; but the charm is as real, and quite distinctive. Typical though the general pattern of *Armance* is of his work as a whole, Stendhal broached in it certain themes, ventured on certain problems, to which he never subsequently reverted.

It is the only novel, if we except the unfinished *Le Rose et le Vert*, in which the undertow of action is provided by marriage: marriage considered both as a potential personal experience and as a social arrangement. There is some question of marriage between Mathilde and Julien in *Le Rouge et le Noir*; but it is sprung on both of them by the accident of Mathilde's pregnancy and cuts clean across the expected line of Julien's ascent to high ecclesiastical office. Ostensibly, both hero and heroine in *Armance* are, whatever else they may do, bound to marry; if not one another, still, marry they must; whatever their personal inclinations, society expects at least that of them. In fact, their inclinations are against marriage: Octave's reasons we know about, Armance's we have touched on. She has considerable scruples about entering into a union which would be socially and financially so advantageous to her. Stendhal removes the grounds for these scruples by allowing her, not too tardily, to inherit a comfortable fortune;[2] but this event 'touched her little', we are told; by this time she has other worries: she suspects Octave of having transferred his affections to Mme d'Aumale. Her jealousy may be no more than a pretext: fundamentally, Armance wants Octave as her companion, not her husband. At a period when they have no secrets from one another, when they have attained 'that unlimited trust in one another which constitutes perhaps the most sweet charm of love', Octave forgets himself for a moment and dares to brush her cheek with his lips. Scarlet with indignation she threatens never to come out again without an attendant; several days elapse before she forgives him. Her frigidity matches his incapability.

One of Stendhal's latest critics—a woman, happily—suggests it might perhaps be considered regrettable that Armance did not offer herself to Octave before marriage. If he is suffering from nothing worse than a lack of self-confidence, such a mark of trust might have cured him.[3] It might, of course, have killed him that much earlier; and in any case, such a solution, almost inevitable in the middle of the twentieth century, would have been almost inconceivable in the early nineteenth century. (Mathilde de La Mole is an 'exception', as Stendhal carefully insists in the very pages of *Le Rouge et le Noir*.) Mme Albérès's speculation is pertinent none the less. An excessively guarded chastity may chill the

---

[2] 'Elle avait trois oncles au service de Russie; ces jeunes gens périrent par le suicide durant les troubles de ce pays', &c. (*Armance*, p. 254). Future editors of *Armance* may care to note that this is almost certainly an allusion to the suppression of the Decabrist conspiracy in December 1825, an event which appears to have impressed Stendhal: he alludes to it again in *Lucien Leuwen* ('Nous sommes tombés dans la même erreur que ces pauvres seigneurs russes en 1826...': iii. 64).

[3] F. M. Albérès, *Le Naturel chez Stendhal*, p. 339.

most 'normal' young man. It was not simply for the sake of departing from his nominal source that Stendhal replaced the young widow, who had been the heroine of Latouche's *Olivier*, by this virgin of terrifying purity, Armance.

As a treatment of courtship, therefore, the novel has its limitations, but if Octave were whole and Armance no more than shy, they would not perhaps behave very differently for most of the time. Their great concern is to persuade themselves that their love (or friendship, as they prefer to call it) rests on a solid basis of mutual respect and esteem. Octave is conducting a searching examination of the purity of his motives, Armance of hers, and their deepest joys are occasioned by the removal of some probably baseless fear that their integrity had come under suspicion. This no doubt accounts for the occasional after-flavour of Jane Austen in *Armance*; as far as can be known, the resemblance is fortuitous, there being no evidence that Stendhal ever looked at her works. Nevertheless an English reader who had never sampled *Armance* would not be altogether misled if he were told that the novel was a rather darker *Persuasion*, the situation between the lovers being, in a sense, reversed; for whereas at the outset of *Persuasion* Anne Elliot and Wentworth appear hopelessly estranged, this rift being gradually mended in the course of the narrative and healed at its conclusion, Armance and Octave are continually being driven asunder, and when finally the marriage takes place, Octave has perhaps a worse opinion of his bride than he had at any earlier stage. But the two pairs of lovers have this in common, that there can never be any question of passion blinding them to whatever moral failings they may detect in the beloved; on the contrary, the supposed moral superiority of their partners is almost a sufficient, and certainly a principal, basis for love. We are in a different hemisphere altogether from that inhabited by Manon Lescaut and the Chevalier des Grieux.

As we have noted, it is generally accepted that Stendhal invented the plot—such as it is—of *Armance*, just as it is generally recognized that he did not put himself to this trouble over *Le Rouge et le Noir* and *La Chartreuse de Parme*. Nevertheless, at the back of his mind there very possibly lurked the situation used by Rossini in his opera *La Pietra del paragone* (*The Touchstone*). At least one can say (going simply on what Stendhal himself had written about *La Pietra del paragone* in his *Vie de Rossini*) that librettist and novelist develop the same theme, and develop it not dissimilarly. This theme is the grounding of love on mutual esteem. Rossini's choice of title is explained by the fact that his hero, Count Asdrubal, having come into a large inheritance (just as Octave, at the beginning of *Armance*, finds himself unexpectedly enriched by the passing of the Bill of Indemnity), '*essaie* comme avec une *pierre de touche* le cœur des amis et même des maîtresses qui lui sont arrivés en même temps que la fortune', among whom is to be reckoned the Marchesa Clarissa with whom he is in love but who perhaps 'n'aime en lui que sa brillante fortune et son grand état de maison'. Speaking of Clarissa, Stendhal comments: 'Il s'agit d'un amour non plus contrarié par l'obstacle vulgaire d'un père ou d'un tuteur, mais par la crainte, bien autrement cruelle, de paraître aux yeux de ce qu'on aime n'avoir qu'une âme vile et commune... Toutes les amies possibles auraient dit à Clarice: Épousez, épousez bien vite, n'importe par quel moyen, et vous serez aimée ensuite si vous pouvez.'[4]

Throughout *Armance*, Mlle de Zohiloff is haunted by the dread that Octave should think his family fortune and position in society attract her more than his personal merits. And not only Octave: the *others* too, those worthy dowagers, unchallengeable arbiters of opinion. Armance is sure that to marry the Vicomte de Malivert would cost her her reputation. 'Je passerais dans le monde pour une dame de compagnie qui a séduit le fils de la maison. J'entends d'ici ce que diraient madame la duchesse d'Ancre et même les femmes les plus respectables... Elles peuvent tout dire sur mon compte, elles seront crues. Ciel! dans quel abîme de honte elles peuvent me précipiter! Et Octave pourrait un jour m'ôter son estime, car je n'ai aucun moyen de défense.' Is it right that a free spirit should be so much at the mercy of the judgements of society? The idea occurs to her that, once married, they might escape from Paris into the country. 'Le monde nous oublierait bien vite. — Oui; mais moi, je n'oublierais pas qu'il est un lieu sur la terre où je suis méprisée, et méprisée par les âmes les plus nobles.'[5]

One of the afflictions of woman's estate is that there can be no self-esteem without the esteem of others. 'Sois belle si tu peux, sage si tu veux; mais sois considérée, il le faut.' Stendhal had been sufficiently impressed with the good sense of Beaumarchais's faintly flippant maxim to quote it in *De l'amour*, having used it

[4] *Vie de Rossini*, i. 124, 128.   [5] *Armance*, pp. 133–5.

earlier in a letter to Pauline stuffed with sage admonishments.[6]
That Armance should rate so important the 'consideration' of
Octave is thus only natural; less expected, and more moving, is
Octave's need for Armance's approval. He believes he has innocently forfeited it at the famous *soirée* of Mme de Bonnivet's when
he makes his first appearance as a man of substance. Armance
alone in the company avoids congratulating him on his new fortune, and Armance alone, therefore, earns his respect. But he fancies
she must have misconstrued his *hauteur* towards the buzzing syco-
phants, when he overhears a remark she makes to her bosom friend
Méry de Tersan: 'Que veux-tu? Il est comme tous les autres! Une
âme que je croyais si belle être bouleversée par l'espoir de deux
millions!'[7] From this point on, the word *esteem* is recurrent in
Stendhal's analyses of Octave's meditations on Armance. He is not
in love with the girl; but it is intolerable to him that one who has
earned his *esteem* should unjustly deny him hers. To clear himself
in her eyes, he requires merely a few words in private, which is
precisely what she will allow him no opportunity for. His colourless life is thus temporarily orientated towards the reconquest of
her *esteem*, and, being forced to concentrate his attention on his
cousin, unwittingly he falls in love with her. 'Il estimait Armance
beaucoup et pour ainsi dire uniquement; il se voyait méprisé par
elle, et il l'estimait précisément à cause de ce mépris. N'était-il pas
tout simple de vouloir regagner son estime? Il n'y avait là nul
désir suspect de plaire à cette jeune fille.' When at last the chance
is given him to justify himself, he ends his little speech to Armance
by recalling the remark about him she had made to Méry and
adding: 'Ce mot a disposé de ma vie; depuis ce moment je n'ai
pensé qu'à regagner votre estime.' (It is at this point that, not
surprisingly, her nerves get the better of Armance and she has to
withdraw; though not before she has pronounced the formula of
absolution: 'Vous avez toute mon estime.')[8]

There is something very Jane-Austenish in this kind of bloodless moral tussle—we may be reminded, in this instance, of Darcy's
efforts to regain the esteem of Elizabeth Bennet after she has made
it plain, by the manner in which she rejects his first proposal, how
thoroughly he has incurred her contempt. What is peculiar to
Stendhal—or at any rate far removed from Jane Austen—is that

[6] *Le Mariage de Figaro*, i. iv; *De l'amour*, i. 54; *Correspondance*, i. 184.
[7] *Armance*, p. 50.   [8] Ibid. 69, 81, 82.

in this passage his hero, and elsewhere in *Armance* his heroine, appear to reckon that the most shaming of indignities is to be suspected of an undue concern about money. Certain virtues are taken for granted: Octave would never dream that anyone should doubt his courage, any more than Armance that anyone should impugn her chastity; but slanderous tongues could credibly hint that he was become purse-proud and she a mercenary schemer. When a fault is widely current, people prefer to believe that none of their neighbours is exempt. In the society of which he wrote, the rarest of virtues was disinterestedness; hence the touchiness of both his main characters if anything occurs to cast doubt on their utter indifference to wealth, or suspicion on their refusal to join in the universal struggle for riches. Octave tells Armance he can live on five francs a day and can earn twice the sum any time as an industrial chemist; and we have seen with what strange equanimity Armance receives the news that she has inherited a fortune.

Is this a mark of their caste? They are both of noble birth, and in considering cupidity to be the stigma of base souls they are, in a sense, reverting to ancestral type. The feudal barons who were Octave's forbears, the boyars who were Armance's, if they found themselves impoverished, were wont to win new estates at the point of the sword. Hoarding, husbanding, investing were practices proper to the burgher, the kulak; to people of that sort it was allowable to 'talk money' since money meant so much to them. A nobleman who did the same transgressed the aristocratic code; hence Octave's horrified disgust at his uncle's ill-concealed excitement when the news of the indemnity reaches him,[9] this uncle who, ranking as a Commander in the Order of the Knights of Malta, yet demeans himself to speculate in the funds and sees no harm in so doing.

But Julien Sorel, Lucien Leuwen, Mina Vanghen (in *Le Rose et le Vert*), Lamiel finally, all share the same conviction that whoever bows down before what one of Balzac's characters, in a famous tirade, called 'la toute-puissante pièce de cent sous', whoever adjusts his human respect for his neighbour to an estimate of his neighbour's income, is quite simply beneath contempt. And Julien Sorel, Lucien Leuwen, Mina, and Lamiel are all of them members

---

[9] 'Cette âme vulgaire qui, avant ou après la naissance, ne voyait au monde que l'argent...' is how Stendhal, and not Octave, describes M. de Soubirane (*Armance*, p. 42).

of the third or fourth estates, and consequently cannot be said to derive from their aristocratic nurture and traditions the conviction that money-making is low and money-makers contemptible. The point is that all these, and Octave and Armance too, were in this respect self-projections of Stendhal who, though never spendthrift and never—or only for one short period in his life—really well off, frequently confessed to a distaste amounting to loathing of the class of people whose principal preoccupation is what they and what the Joneses earn. 'Une horreur presque hydrophobique', he calls it in the *Souvenirs d'égotisme*, adding: 'La conversation d'un gros marchand de province grossier m'hébétait et me rendait malheureux pour tout le reste de la journée.'[1] It was, he explained, a phobia contracted in childhood, and we can turn to the *Vie de Henri Brulard* for further details. He writes there, for instance, that he had never been able to think of money without disgust. 'En avoir ne me fait aucun plaisir, en manquer est un vilain malheur'. Rather than wrangle, how often has he allowed himself to be cheated by Italian shopkeepers! As for the moneyed class, 'J'ai toujours et comme par instinct... profondément méprisé les bourgeois.' — 'La conversation du vrai bourgeois sur *les hommes et la vie*... me jette dans un *spleen* profond quand je suis forcé par quelque convenance de l'entendre un peu longtemps.'[2] The *Mémoires d'un touriste* record a tremendous attack of this 'spleen' when, on the road from Dol to Saint-Malo, the writer found himself obliged to share the coach with a crew of 'bourgeois riches ou plutôt enrichis' to whom he listened impatiently as gravely they discoursed on their own persons, their wives, their children, their . . . pocket-handkerchiefs, all, if one was to believe them, vastly superior to the persons, wives, children, and pocket-handkerchiefs of everyone else. The Tourist tried to turn the talk on to politics. 'Ils se sont mis à louer bêtement la liberté et de façon à en dégoûter, la faisant consister surtout dans le pouvoir d'empêcher leurs voisins de faire ce qui leur déplaît.' He would have liked to horsewhip the lot of them; and ruefully reflected that, had he been travelling instead with five reactionaries, at least he would have heard some refined conversation, while their political views could hardly have been more preposterous and ungenerous. The fit of misanthropy which this encounter brought on was such that, on arriving at Saint-Malo, he was rude to his hostess; took an omnibus in high dudgeon

---

[1] *Souvenirs d'égotisme*, p. 93.   [2] *Vie de Henri Brulard*, i. 92, 27, 271.

to view the birthplaces of Chateaubriand and Lamennais; and lost
his way out of sheer disinclination to address himself to a fellow
creature.[3]

Between the Tourist and Stendhal there is virtual identity;
between Stendhal and Octave (and Armance who, intellectually, is
Octave's mirror) a near identity, particularly in respect of such fits
of misanthropy brought on by a sense of superiority to the common
herd. In analysing this feature of Stendhal's first hero, we shall be
analysing one that they all share; though in none is it so marked,
so radical, as in Octave. Octave is a nineteenth-century Alceste
disgusted, not at men's insincerity, but at their vulgarity. Lacking
his creator's mercurial and gregarious disposition, he is a more
consistent and thoroughgoing misanthropist; what Beyle felt only
in moments of ill humour and could usually dispel by retreating
into a reverie, the Vicomte de Malivert feels almost incessantly and
can relieve only by explosions of murderous rage directed sometimes against others, sometimes on himself.

It will be remembered that the comment Armance made to
Méry, which so stung Octave, combined two criticisms: that the
young man had had his head turned by the expectation of two
millions; and that, after all, he was just the same as everyone else.
Of the two imputations Stendhal does not say which Octave
resented more; certainly the second is as ill-founded as the first.
An aspect of Octave's character that Stendhal stresses quite as
forcibly as any other is his *singularity*; something encountered
again, incidentally, in Julien, though Julien's singularity has a
rather different origin. Symptomatic of Octave's singularity is his
indifference to the honours that ordinary men compete for. In the
very first paragraph of his novel Stendhal informs us that his hero
had hoped to serve for a short while in a regiment, after which he
would have resigned his commission and held himself in readiness
to join the army again should war break out, caring little whether
he fought it as a lieutenant or with the rank of colonel. 'C'est un
exemple' Stendhal adds, 'des singularités qui le rendaient odieux
aux hommes vulgaires.' Odious, perhaps, but conspicuous too;
when he goes into the world, his lack of ambition and contempt for
those who cherish ambitions set him apart: 'Il n'y avait pas
jusqu'au dédaigneux silence que lui inspirait tout à coup la présence

---

[3] *Mémoires d'un touriste*, ii. 182–8.

des gens qu'il croyait incapables de comprendre les façons de
sentir élevées, qui ne passât pour une singularité piquante.'⁴
Those who are closest to him and see most of him are more
sensitive than the rest to this strangeness in Octave. Mme de
Malivert, in particular, senses in him 'quelque chose de sur-
humain; il vit comme un être à part, séparé des autres hommes';
and even M. de Soubirane, obtuse and frivolous old man though
he is, ventures, when talking about him to Mme de Malivert, to
remark on the 'something strange' in his nephew.⁵ The young man
himself is as conscious as any of this quality, to the point where one
wonders if he is not deliberately cultivating it. 'J'ai par malheur
un caractère singulier, je ne me suis pas créé ainsi; tout ce que j'ai
pu faire, c'est de me connaître. Excepté dans les moments où je
jouis du bonheur d'être seul avec toi [he is speaking to his mother],
mon unique plaisir consiste à vivre isolé, et sans personne au
monde qui ait le droit de m'adresser la parole.'⁶ It is hardly possible to say whether his bearishness causes his 'strangeness', or the
reverse; but it seems that Octave genuinely suffers from the role
of outsider that nature has forced upon him. 'Je vois les plus
pauvres, les plus bornés, les plus malheureux, en apparence, des
jeunes gens de mon âge, avoir un ou deux amis d'enfance qui
partagent leurs joies et leurs chagrins. Le soir, je les vois s'aller
promener ensemble, et ils se disent tout ce qui les intéresse; moi
seul, je me trouve isolé sur la terre. Je n'ai et je n'aurai jamais
personne à qui je puisse librement confier ce que je pense.'⁷ In all
this one would not be wrong in detecting a strain of Byronic affectation—on Stendhal's part quite as much as on Octave's. For
Armance is a period piece on top of all else, discreetly flavoured
with a romanticism which tends rather to the melancholic than
to the lugubrious and enhances today the faintly archaic charm
of the work.⁸

The commentators of *Armance* will remind us, of course, that
Octave feels himself an outsider because his sexual inadequacy
cuts him off from other men and robs him of assurance in his deal-
ings with women. This is clear enough: an invert can at least resort

⁴ *Armance,* pp. 6, 77.   ⁵ Ibid. 18, 47.   ⁶ Ibid. 14.   ⁷ Ibid. 39–40.
⁸ The book, says Levin, 'languishes under the spell of romanticism. Both the
elusive Armance de Zohiloff and the melancholy Octave de Malivert suffer from
fainting-fits; their trysting place is the tomb of Abelard; and their love is confirmed by a letter written in blood' (*The Gates of Horn,* p. 113). Cf. also Blin,
'Étude sur *Armance*' (in the Fontana edition of the novel), p. liii.

to the confraternity of inverts, but the impotent is truly alone. Eunuchs have always had a reputation for malevolence, and it is hardly necessary to suppose that Stendhal needed to read Pinel's *Traité médico-philosophique sur l'aliénation mentale et la manie* before it could occur to him that impotence would incline his hero to misanthropy. But quite apart from the pathological aspect, Stendhal had only to enlarge and extend certain tendencies of his own nature in order to arrive at the 'being apart' that was Octave. Given a personality richly enough endowed and, above all, sufficiently explored, analysed, and understood, a writer will draw from himself all the fictional succedanea he will require; which all the same are never, and never can be, as complex and as charged with explosive potentialities as himself.

When Octave tells Armance how all his efforts to make friends result only in increasing the antipathy with which he is universally regarded, he is voicing a complaint which Beyle himself had more than once made in respect of his own character. The young men with whom Octave goes riding in the Bois de Boulogne have hardly got to know him, he declares, before some unlucky remark of his estranges them. 'Quand enfin au bout d'un an, et bien malgré moi, ils me comprennent tout à fait, ils s'enveloppent dans la réserve la plus sévère et aimeraient mieux, je crois, que leurs actions et leurs pensées intimes fussent connues du diable que de moi.'[9] The passage echoes, with more dignity, an observation found in Stendhal's personal writings. He too used to rue, but half humorously, the dislike he aroused wherever he went: 'Les hommes les plus doux, quand ils ont subi ma connaissance pendant six mois, donneraient six francs pour me voir tomber dans un trou plein de boue au moment où je me prépare à entrer dans un salon. Cependant, je ne hais personne…'[1]

Octave's singularity forces him in on himself and turns him into 'un être tout mystère'—a phrase Stendhal uses in a brief paragraph in chapter xi. He continues: 'Jamais d'étourderie chez lui, si ce n'est quelquefois dans ses conversations avec Armance… On ne pouvait lui reprocher de la fausseté; il eût dédaigné de mentir, mais jamais il n'allait directement à son but.' On a couple of occasions

---

[9] *Armance*, pp. 155–6.
[1] Letter to Sophie Duvaucel, 7 Mar. 1830 (*Correspondance*, vi. 294). Stendhal used approximately the same illustration in a letter to Mme Jules Gaulthier, 14 Mar. 1836 (ibid. x. 17).

we see this ingrained love of mystery at work within him. One evening, leaving the theatre, he enters a restaurant and 'fidèle au mystère qui marquait toutes ses actions', orders a bowl of soup and a candle to be brought to him in a private room. Having locked himself in, he reads two newspapers which he had bought previously, carefully burns them, and calls for his bill. Stendhal adds no explanation. Conceivably in the theocratic police state towards which France was evolving under Charles X, precautions of this sort were not inadvisable for a young man of Octave's class who wished to read the opposition press. Stendhal is more explicit in his comments on Octave's behaviour towards Armance's aunt, Mme de Bonnivet, a slightly crackbrained religious enthusiast who hopes to 'convert' him. Octave is careful not to dash her hopes; the young man 'qui se croyait si exempt de fausseté, ne sut pas se défendre d'un mouvement de plaisir à la vue d'une fausseté que le public allait se figurer sur son compte'.[2] Something of this gratuitous delight in misleading others may be observed again in Roizand, the hero of *Une Position sociale*.[3] Once more, Stendhal needed only to copy, and exaggerate, certain habits of his own. The autobiographical fragment called *Souvenirs d'égotisme* covers the years immediately preceding the writing of *Armance*: the picture Stendhal draws of himself at this period is of a man with an inner life altogether other than might have been thought if one had judged him on his reputation. He passed as a libertine and a cynic, a 'monster of immorality'; he was, in fact, a gentle dreamer, his thoughts for ever dwelling, innocently, rapturously, or miserably, on the obdurate Mathilde Dembowski, left behind in Milan. To some extent, as he admits, he deliberately duped his friends for fear they should divine his secret preoccupation.

The perpetual fear of being 'found out' was largely responsible, no doubt, for Stendhal's intriguing habit of making personal notes in a private polyglottal shorthand. One such instance we quoted at the beginning of this study; there are hundreds of others over which the specialists have pored, sometimes to very good purpose. This was another personal idiosyncrasy with which he felt he could appropriately enrich the character of Octave. At the end of the

---

[2] *Armance*, pp. 47–48, 66.
[3] Of whom Stendhal wrote 'son orgueil aurait été au désespoir de laisser deviner ses sentiments' (*Mélanges de littérature*, i. 85). Roizand, similarly, deceives Mme de Vaussay by pretending an interest in theological speculation which he does not feel.

second chapter of *Armance* the events of the day, now known to the
reader, are summarized by the hero in a series of staccato notes,
meaningless to anyone so indiscreet as to open the notebook; but,
for further security, transliterated into the Greek alphabet, while
the notebook, once this cabbalistic rite has been performed, is
tucked away in a secret drawer.[4]

All these mysterious exercises, meaningful only to himself,
betray in Octave (and, through him, in the author of *Armance*) a
degree of introversion that verges on abnormality. There are, certainly, times when Narcissus yearns to see some other reflection
than his own. 'Sans être souverain, j'ai soif de l'*incognito*... J'éprouve
un besoin impérieux de voir agir un autre vicomte de Malivert'—
and he discloses to Armance a long cherished plan to assume the
identity of a former valet of his and enter the service of some young
English duke doing the Grand Tour.[5] Stendhal, in the *Souvenirs
d'égotisme* once more (pp. 48–49), wrote of the delight he used to
take 'à me promener fièrement dans une ville étrangère (Lancaster,
Torre del Greco, etc.), où je suis arrivé depuis une heure et où je
suis sûr de n'être connu de personne... Me croira-t-on?' he asks;
'je porterais un masque avec plaisir, je changerais de nom avec
délices... mon souverain plaisir serait de me changer en un long
Allemand blond et de me promener ainsi dans Paris.' The fantastic
miscellany of pseudonyms that Stendhal invented to disguise the
authorship of his books and the provenance of his letters (129 of
them, if Léautaud's count is correct) shows how genuine and com-
pulsive was this 'love of wearing masks'.

Not quite eccentric enough to put into execution his scheme of
donning a valet's livery, Octave obtains some relief from the
oppressive sense of his inescapable coincidence with himself, by
participating in those bawdy-house orgies which were a feature of
Restoration 'high life' and which Balzac occasionally takes pleasure

---

[4] The note is carefully dated. Octave has a passion for recording the dates of
the slightest events in his life which again he shared with his creator. On the eve
of his intended departure for Greece (prevented, in the event, by his duel), his
mind is brought back to Armance when he reads a legend he had engraved on
one of his pistols: 'Armance essaye de faire feu avec cette arme, le 3 septembre
182*.' Stendhal continues: 'Tous les objets qui l'environnaient portaient les
marques du souvenir d'Armance. L'abrégé de ce nom chéri, suivi de quelque
date intéressante, était écrit partout' (*Armance*, p. 193). One is irresistibly
reminded of the 'inscriptions chiffrées' on the study walls of the hero of Fromen-
tin's *Dominique*, also known to be an autobiographical importation into the novel.

[5] *Armance*, pp. 153–5.

in describing (*La Peau de chagrin, Illusions perdues*, &c.). 'Le besoin d'agir et le désir d'observer des choses nouvelles l'avaient poussé à voir la mauvaise compagnie, souvent moins ennuyeuse que la bonne... le mauvais ton permet de parler de soi, à tort et à travers, et l'on est moins isolé... On peut se croire vingt amis intimes, dont on ne sait pas le nom.' Here again, there is reason to suppose that Stendhal added a touch of self-portraiture to the composite figure of his hero.[6]

For all this, Octave is not a copy of Stendhal; it would be truer to call him a self-caricature, or to regard *Armance*, in so far as *Armance* is a simple frame for the hero, as an essay in self-criticism. Sainte-Beuve once declared of Lamartine that he was ignorant of everything but his own soul; if this dictum, applied to Stendhal, seems strained, at least it can be ventured that he knew nothing quite so thoroughly as himself. He is one of a distinguished though heterogeneous band of major French writers which, even if one leaves aside the poets, includes Montaigne, Rousseau, and Proust: such men as constructed their best work out of nothing more substantial than their own endless self-questioning, self-analysis, self-communing. 'Il faut se posséder pour bien parler, il faut peut-être *posséder son âme...,*' Stendhal noted in his diary in 1805, 'pour bien écrire.'[7] Raphael could not have painted the *Madonna alla seggiola*, nor Racine have known what words to put in the mouths of Oreste and Phèdre, unless painter and poet had had sensibilities rich enough, and been swayed by passions strong enough, to draw from their own souls the ingredients and the very stuff of their artistic masterpieces.[8] For himself, Stendhal became convinced at an early stage that, as he put it, 'je ne puis être bon, si je suis jamais bon, que dans ce que je tirerai tout à fait de mon cœur'.[9]

This does not mean that one is justified in endorsing extreme

---

[6] *Armance*, pp. 112–13. 'Si je rencontre une jeune femme française et que, par malheur, elle soit bien élevée, je me rappelle sur-le-champ la maison paternelle et l'éducation de mes sœurs, je prévois tous ses mouvements et jusqu'aux plus fugitives nuances de ses pensées. C'est ce qui fait que j'aime beaucoup la mauvaise compagnie, où il y a plus d'*imprévu*' (*Pages d'Italie*, p. 120).

[7] *Journal*, ii. 14.

[8] We summarize and paraphrase here two passages found respectively in the *Vies de Haydn, de Mozart et de Métastase* (p. 133) and the *Histoire de la peinture en Italie* (ii. 51). Whether Stendhal's interpretation of the process of invention and creation in Raphael and Racine was correct or not is a point scarcely worth examining here.

[9] *Journal*, v. 245 (1 July 1814).

views regarding the subjectivity of Stendhal's fiction. One is not called on to agree with Fineshriber who says that Stendhal's books are not novels at all but 'virtually letters to himself . . . a psychological portrait of the author . . . an uninterrupted autobiography'; or with Lalo when he maintains that, if one accepts Stendhal's metaphor for a novelist as a man bearing a mirror, then one must distinguish between Stendhal and his successors, for 'whereas Balzac, Flaubert, Zola, for example, carry this mirror along the by-paths, directing it towards the wayfarers and the landscapes, Stendhal reflects and admires in it only himself'.[1] If we limit ourselves to *Armance*, it would be patently false to assert that, for all his carefully cultivated self-awareness, Beyle can be identified with the irritable, hypersensitive, moody self-tormentor that he created in Octave. Intellectual curiosity was what chiefly impelled Stendhal to examine his own reflection in the mirror; Octave is moved to do so chiefly by dislike of everything he sees as soon as he turns his back on it. In the second chapter of the novel Stendhal records a significant piece of day-dreaming on the part of his hero: it relates to a vast room, to which he alone would have the key, and on the walls of which would be fixed three enormous mirrors, seven feet high. Nothing remotely resembling such a fantasy can be found anywhere in the diaries or private papers of Stendhal. The Egotist was not Narcissus.

Each of Stendhal's heroes exists half within him, half outside him. In Octave, what is independent is, broadly, whatever is stipulated by his class origins. A realization of class difference and, what was more important, of class conflict, was one of Stendhal's principal bequests to the French novel. Nothing like it had been dreamed of by his eighteenth-century predecessors: Diderot's Jacques permits himself to be impertinent to his master, but never shows himself envious of his master's social position; Figaro's portentous sneer: 'Vous vous êtes donné la peine de naître', was uttered in a play. The French Revolution, which substituted 'classes' for 'estates', rumbles behind every one of Stendhal's novels, not excluding *La Chartreuse de Parme*.

Himself a somewhat depressed member of the fast-rising professional middle class, Stendhal views his hero—and his heroine too— as pathetic survivals from a gracious but irretrievably superseded

---

[1] Fineshriber, *Stendhal the romantic rationalist*, pp. 30, 38; Lalo, *L'Art et la vie*, i. 46.

past. They win his respect—and ours—only because they are completely lucid about their situation. In his fourteenth chapter, which consists almost entirely of a conversation between the two young tories, this situation is exposed with verve and brilliance. It starts with a complaint (one which Mathilde de La Mole will repeat in *Le Rouge et le Noir*) about the tedious shallowness of conversation in the drawing-rooms of the reactionaries, where the fear of being improper, not to say seditious, obliges every guest to stick to 'safe' topics. 'Toujours la chasse, la beauté de la campagne, la musique de Rossini, les arts! et encore ils mentent en s'y intéressant. Ces gens ont la sottise d'avoir peur, ils se croient dans une ville assiégée et s'interdisent de parler des nouvelles du siège. La pauvre espèce! Et que je suis contrarié d'en être!' Armance suggests he might try calling on the besiegers—but no: Octave quails at the idea of visiting, say, a banker's house, where the talk might be more lively, but where some infringement of the code of politeness he is used to is certain to upset him. 'Que me fait l'esprit d'un homme? ce sont ses manières qui peuvent me donner de la tristesse.' Armance does her best to get him to surmount this squeamishness. 'Comment connaître les hommes si vous ne voyez qu'une classe? Et la classe la moins énergique parce qu'elle est la plus éloignée des besoins réels!' But Octave feels himself hopelessly identified with his own class, however anachronistic it may be in an industrial society. 'Depuis que la machine à vapeur est la reine du monde, un titre est une absurdité, mais enfin je suis affublé de cette absurdité. Elle m'écrasera si je ne la soutiens.' Were he to have himself announced as plain mister when entering the banker's drawing-room, he would feel like Rousseau's dog, named Duke, whom his master called Turk if a duke happened to be visiting him. 'Au fond, vous et moi,' he tells Armance, 'nous ne voulons certainement pas vivre avec ces gens-là; mais sur beaucoup de questions nous pensons comme eux... Nous sommes comme les prêtres des idoles du paganisme, au moment où la religion chrétienne allait l'emporter. Nous persécutons encore aujourd'hui, nous avons encore la police et le budget pour nous, mais demain peut-être, nous serons persécutés par l'opinion.' To which Armance retorts: 'Je vois quelque chose de plus faux dans notre position, à vous et à moi. Nous ne sommes de ce parti que pour en partager les malheurs.' Octave ignores this wry sally and proceeds to elaborate a typically tortuous plan for obtaining an introduction to liberal

circles without being regarded as a deserter by the conservatives.
He wants to meet General Foy (the Gladstone or the Lloyd George
of the day). 'N'est-ce pas une chose humiliante, reprit Octave, que
tous nos soutiens, et enfin jusqu'aux écrivains *monarchiques* chargés
de prôner tous les matins dans le journal les avantages de la
naissance et de la religion, nous soient fournis par cette classe qui
a tous les avantages, excepté la naissance?' This had always been
the case, even under Louis XIV; but Octave is too dejected to make
the observation.

The passage is an excellent example of the peculiar double irony
of Stendhal, which makes him so intriguing and—to some—so
exasperating a writer. He is certainly criticizing here the upper
class of his day, comprising those depleted remnants of the pre-
revolutionary aristocracy who returned or re-emerged with
Louis XVIII, and pretended nothing had happened between
1789 and 1815 to alter their position or make obsolete their privileges. But he is also criticizing their critic, Octave. He does this
indirectly by placing at the head of his chapter an epigraph (in
Italian) the tenor of which is that the young are apt either to overlook or to overstress the blemishes they observe in the society in
which they move; and directly by inserting footnotes at the bottom
of two pages in which he, as author, denounces Octave's errors and
illusions. These footnotes are perhaps mere precautionary dis-
claimers; in which case the irony is triple. But it is hard to avoid
the impression that Stendhal's attitude towards his solemn hero is
secretly derisive. He maintained—in a memorandum dated 5 June
1828, evidently intended as notes for a preface:

> Quoique non impuissants, les jeunes privilégiés comme le chevalier
> de Rohan sont ou jeunets ou *aussi* malheureux que l'impuissant Octave.
> Voilà leur ridicule.
> Impossible en 1828 qu'un *jeune homme* se dise: 'Hé bien, j'en prends
> mon parti, ces avantages sont injustes, mais puisqu'ils viennent me
> chercher, j'en profiterai.'
> Plus impossible encore qu'après un tel propos il ait un moment
> heureux.
> Ce n'est pas en un siècle moral et où l'on se juge sans cesse que l'on
> verra naître un caractère capable de braver de bonne foi le remords...[2]

The moral of *Armance*, if we are to believe the author, is: if you
hatch out with wings, don't make your life a burden to yourself

---

[2] *Mélanges intimes et Marginalia*, ii. 81–82.

because you are not like the farmyard poultry. It is possible to have too tender a social conscience; the unscrupulous young man (the Chevalier de Bonnivet, in *Armance*) may be odious, but the over-scrupulous young man is slightly comic.

The corollary of Octave's over-scrupulousness is that he has a strong and exquisitely developed sense of what he owes to others, and dreads nothing so much as that he might embark on a course of action which could wrong them or cause them to think less of him. Duty and self-esteem are key-words, repeated almost *ad nauseam*; it was with this in mind that Stendhal flattered himself *Armance* was comparable to *La Princesse de Clèves*. His sense of duty is Octave's sole resource, and provides him with his only motive for activity of any sort; without it he would lapse into the lethargy of an Oblomov. Even his studies in chemistry were under-taken, or so we are told, in obedience to the call of duty. It is in the name of duty that he suppresses the irritation that his uncle's society causes him, and his mother knows him well enough to guess that a mistaken interpretation of his duty leads him to fre-quent Mme d'Aumale, a notorious flirt. His very features and deportment betray his enslavement to the idea of duty, to the point of making him look positively English at times, says Stendhal.

As the only son of a family of ancient lineage, Octave has one imperative duty laid on him—to continue the line. And this duty he cannot, of course, discharge. This explains up to a point why he is so anxious to invent other duties, of a kind he can fulfil. But beyond this, the moral fervour which such a preoccupation seems to prove has evoked grateful comment from a number of Sten-dhal's critics, particularly among those sprung from Protestant societies; and we are not infrequently invited to admire this dis-tinctive sense of duty by which Octave and certain later figures, Julien and Lucien, are said to achieve a sort of secular sainthood.

The fundamental characteristic of Beyle's principal personages, who, measured by the current standards of morality, have no conscience and no morals, is, that they have evolved a moral standard for themselves. That is what every human being ought to be capable of doing, but what only the most highly developed attain to: and it is this capacity of theirs which gives Beyle's characters their remarkable superiority over other characters whom we have met with in books and real life. They keep an ideal, which they have created for themselves, constantly before their eyes, and have no peace until they have won self-respect.

Thus the nineteenth-century Danish literary historian, Georg Brandes.[3] A similar view is expressed, but in terms even more rhapsodical, by two contemporary American commentators. The first views the efforts of Stendhal's heroes to adhere to a line of conduct which will satisfy their sense of duty, as matching the strict self-mastery of Christian ascetics who strive to attain purity of soul;[4] while the second evokes, to explain Stendhal's supposed idealism, 'the artificial heroic spirit of ancient Rome' according to which 'Antony will do nothing unworthy of Antony; Caesar must live up to a public idea of Caesar which he has himself created. Perhaps it was this notion,' continues Adams, 'that a man owes a duty to his own definition of himself, which furnished to Stendhal the seed for his concept of Beylism...'[5]

Beylism is a term which, ever since Léon Blum made it the centre of his neat but untrustworthy little book on Stendhal, has acquired an extraordinary extension, so that it is currently used to cover any and every facet of what appears to be Stendhal's philosophy of life. Stendhal himself used it sparingly, and only at one particular period of his life, between 1811 and 1813, when his worldly affairs were prospering and before he had experienced any grave emotional disappointments. The word, far from connoting any such strenuous spiritual gymnastics as Adams suggests, implies, if we go back to the actual texts in which Stendhal uses it, no more than a hedonistic doctrine of which the first rule is: Do not kick against the pricks. His friend Louis Crozet has fallen hopelessly in love: 'il en est triste et attristant. C'est ce que je lui dis sans cesse à lui-même pour le rendre un peu beyliste; mais il regimbe.' If his mistress is deaf to entreaty, the *beyliste* will turn elsewhere. Given that happiness is the principal object of life, it is irrational to make oneself unhappy seeking it where it cannot easily be found. Alfieri's career provides a further example. 'Il eût eu plus d'esprit, plus de talent et plus de bonheur en ne voulant pas lutter de caractère et d'orgueil avec des institutions inébranlables'; and Stendhal, ever on the watch for suitable subjects for the stage, thinks he has found in Alfieri's character, seen from that angle, 'le sujet d'une comédie destinée à ramener ces bilieux pleins de vertu au beylisme. Elle

---

[3] *Main Currents in Nineteenth-Century Literature*, vol. v, p. 230.
[4] Everett Knight, 'Stendhal et André Gide', *French Review*, vol. xxiv (1951), pp. 468–9.
[5] R. M. Adams, *Stendhal: Notes on a Novelist*, p. 184.

ridiculiserait le Misanthrope de Molière...'⁶ From Alceste to Octave
is a short step, as we have seen already. Stendhal uses the term again on a couple of occasions in letters to Félix Faure. On 24 August 1812, after a poignant account of his moral distress during the Russian campaign, he says how deeply he longs to return to Italy, and how sorely he is tempted to solicit a minor post in Rome; but the check to his career which this step would represent makes him hesitate. In this, he acknowledges, he is 'sinning against *beylisme*' which, we must deduce, teaches that one should never set one's social position, one's career, one's income, higher than one's chances of private happiness. In the second letter to Faure, written later in the same year, the 'principles of *beylisme*' are invoked in connexion once more with their mutual friend Crozet, and again with regard to Rousseau whose *Confessions* Stendhal has been re-reading. Of Rousseau he writes:

C'est uniquement faute de deux ou trois principes de *beylisme* qu'il a été si malheureux. Cette manie de voir des devoirs et des vertus partout a mis de la pédanterie dans son style et du malheur dans sa vie. Il se lie avec un homme pendant trois semaines: crac, les *devoirs* de l'amitié, etc. Cet homme ne songe plus à lui après deux ans; il cherche à cela une explication noire. Le *beylisme* lui eût dit: 'Deux corps se rapprochent; il naît de la chaleur et une fermentation, mais tout état de cette nature est passager. C'est une fleur dont il faut jouir avec volupté, etc.' Saisis-tu mon idée? Les plus belles choses de Rousseau sentent l'empyreume pour moi, et n'ont point cette grâce *corrégienne* que la moindre ombre de pédanterie détruit.⁷

An over-developed sense of what is due to others, and of what is due to oneself from others, is a sort of moral pedantry. It is contrary to *beylisme*. And who evinces it more consistently, more impenitently, than Octave de Malivert?

Beylisme, in its primitive sense and in the only sense in which Stendhal ever used the word, has much to do with the hunt for

---

⁶ *Journal*, iv. 76–78.
⁷ *Correspondance*, iv. 65–69. 'Sentent l'empyreume', perhaps: 'smell of charred vegetables' (*empyreuma*, 'the burnt smell imparted by fire to organic substances', *O.E.D.*). As for the 'grâce corrégienne', a precise interpretation is difficult, but there are two texts which throw some light on Stendhal's meaning: the definition he gives of Correggio's art in the *Histoire de la peinture en Italie* ('peindre comme dans le lointain même les figures du premier plan'); and the observation made by a minor character in *La Chartreuse de Parme* (Canon Borda) about Fabrice, whose attractiveness is, he says, due above all to 'un certain regard chargé de douce volupté... une physionomie à la Corrège'.

happiness, *la chasse au bonheur*. But happiness is to be sought, not by charging after it like the buffalo, but with the butterfly's vagabond approach. One might finally define the doctrine as a kind of desultory *egoism* (happiness has reference after all only to the ego) from which, however, *egotism* (the constant referring of everything to oneself) is banished.

The hero of *Armance*, this 'bilieux plein de vertu' with his 'manie de voir des devoirs partout', is the supreme offender against *beylisme* properly understood; and, unless one supposes Stendhal's outlook to have undergone total revision between 1812 and 1826 (it had admittedly been modified and a little darkened), Octave is not a hero proposed for our admiration, but a figure who is meant to command, at best, our indulgent sympathy. His obsessive fear of losing his self-esteem, his sense of aloneness, and his introversion, all show him to be the complete egotist; while his apprehension of the overriding duty he owes to mother, father, uncle, cousin, and all others in his circle, proves him to be without the least trace of saving egoism. Hence it is not surprising that happiness, always, according to Stendhal, a rare and sporadic state, passes him over altogether. The novelist describes him on one occasion as 'cette âme, affaissée et désorganisée en quelque sorte par l'absence si longue de tout bonheur'.[8] But it can be seen too that, to the extent that he is prepared to scale down his expectations of others and allow himself to be a little less morally fastidious, he becomes a happier and a saner man, and Stendhal correspondingly warms to him. During one of the few brief periods when Armance's ministrations take effect, his misanthropy is observed to weaken,

le monde lui semblait moins haïssable et surtout moins occupé de lui nuire. Il se disait qu'excepté dans la classe des femmes dévotes ou laides, chacun songeait beaucoup plus à soi, et beaucoup moins à nuire au voisin qu'il n'avait cru l'apercevoir autrefois.

Il reconnut qu'une légèreté de tous les moments rend tout esprit de suite impossible; il s'aperçut enfin que ce monde qu'il avait eu le fol orgueil de croire arrangé d'une manière hostile *pour lui*, n'était tout simplement que mal arrangé. Mais, disait-il à Armance, tel qu'il est, il est à prendre ou à laisser. Il faut ou tout finir rapidement et sans délai par quelques gouttes d'acide prussique ou prendre la vie gaiement. En parlant ainsi, Octave cherchait à se convaincre bien plus qu'il n'exprimait une conviction...[9]

8 *Armance*, p. 32.   9 Ibid. 107–8.

In the end, of course, Octave does finish everything with a few drops of self-administered poison. It is not only a fitting end to the novel, Octave being so devitalized by the 'absence si longue de tout bonheur' that he has no more chance of life, ultimately, than a plant deprived of sunlight; it is also symbolically fitting, since Octave, feeding on himself, ends in total self-consumption. His will to live is under attack from the start, and long before the occurrence of the misfortunes and vexations which the novel relates, we are to understand that he has been yearning for release, is more than half in love with easeful death, that his mind is fixed on some transcendental state. The idea of suicide presents itself several times (his duel with M. de Crêveroche would have been a form of suicide, if it had had a different outcome, even though he had not provoked his opponent); and when he finally forms the resolution to marry Armance and leave her a widow within a month, he regains a certain serenity: 'l'idée de la mort venait le consoler et rendre le calme à son cœur.' He accomplishes stoically the duties laid on a bridegroom. 'Rien ne lui était pénible; c'est que rien ne lui inspirait plus d'intérêt. Il était mort au monde.'[1] He dies as Narcissus in the legend, still unable to wrest his eyes from his own reflection, and leaving Armance, like another Echo, to pine and perish in her turn.

From the beginning, there has been greater disagreement about the value of *Armance* than about the value of Stendhal's other completed novels. 'All my friends find it detestable,' the author wrote to Sutton Sharpe, the barrister who had acted as his guide in England; 'and I find them coarse.'[2] Romain Colomb, his cousin and executor, who wrote one of the first biographical sketches of Stendhal after his death, could find little good to say about the work, but confirmed that Beyle felt for it the same sort of predilection as parents often do for 'a child with rickets, or one of subnormal intelligence or naturally perverse'.[3] There were moments no doubt when Beyle found his cousin 'coarse'. In our own day, there have been serious critics of Stendhal who have refused to take the work seriously. Bardèche called *Armance* 'a disappointment, a deviation in Stendhal's intellectual development . . . a failure as a novel'. On the other hand Thibaudet, whose opinion is usually

---

[1] Ibid. 306–7, 310.   [2] *Correspondance*, vi. 239.
[3] Colomb, *Notice sur la vie et les ouvrages de M. Beyle*, 2ᵉ édition (1854), p. lxxxviii.

worth considering, called it 'a novel of accomplished mastery in execution and style, the finest, most subtle, most rich in implications perhaps that he ever wrote', while Gide, though he admitted that the novel was 'disconcerting', rated it 'the most delicate and best written of all Stendhal's books'.[4]

No one pretends that *Armance* is a great novel, while those who would maintain that it is a good novel are few. But those who dismiss it as a bad novel are being either hasty or insensitive. Its qualities are not easy to define: they are not of the kind to linger on the palate long after the book has been closed; or else they are qualities the common reader does not look for in a novel, and perhaps ignores when he meets them. It is arguable that Stendhal was too interested in the states of mind of his characters, and too little interested in the events that precipitated their changes of mood; and he may be reproached with indulging too readily in the pleasure of describing states of mind and changes of mood. Too often the narrator steps back, leaving the 'analyst of the human heart' to tell us what Octave, what Armance, thought or felt. Most readers run their eyes indifferently over such pages—and who shall say they are wrong? For the few, however, these are the passages that count, and they are irreplaceable.

The epigraph Stendhal chose for the twentieth chapter of *Armance* was an exchange between Othello and Iago: 'A fine woman! a fair woman! a sweet woman!—Nay, you must forget that.—O, the world has not a sweeter creature.' Octave has broken brutally and, he thinks, irreparably, with Armance. After such unpardonable harshness on his part, any reconciliation seems out of the question, and he makes the necessary arrangements for his departure for Greece, where he hopes to fall fighting the Turk. 'Essayerons-nous de rappeler,' asks Stendhal, 'les différents genres de douleur qui marquaient chaque instant de sa vie? Le lecteur ne se lassera-t-il pas de ces tristes détails?' If we were to answer these rhetorical questions we should say that it will depend once more who the reader is. Far from tiring of them, the few who share his vision and sensibility will find these 'details', with which the rest of Stendhal's chapter is filled, not only deeply moving but almost intolerably so. For he is writing still—as he always would, for the rest of his life—out of the memory (more keen, because nearer, in

---

[4] Bardèche, *Stendhal romancier*, pp. 138, 147; Thibaudet, *Stendhal*, p. 92; Gide, *Incidences*, pp. 176, 187.

1826) of the loss of Mathilde Dembowski. In calling the resulting emotional crisis *grief* ('douleur'), Stendhal was following closely—though perhaps without knowing it—Burke's definition: 'If the object of pleasure be totally lost, a passion arises in the mind which is called grief.' What *Armance* gives us at this point is not moralistic definitions but classic illustrations. No one, probably, who has ever experienced Burke's 'pleasure totally lost' can fail to recognize in Stendhal's illustrations, these 'melancholy details' as he calls them too modestly, something corresponding to his own memories of a time of loss. Octave has the illusion of voices murmuring in his ear, 'et cette sensation étrange et imprévue l'empêchait d'oublier un instant son malheur'. He cannot see an A or a Z in an advertisement or a shop-sign 'sans être violemment entraîné à penser à cette Armance de Zohiloff qu'il s'était juré d'oublier... Il essaya de se causer une douleur physique assez violente toutes les fois que son esprit lui rappelait Armance. De toutes les ressources qu'il imagina, celle-ci fut la moins inefficace.' He cannot bear company and sends his valet out of the house to make some purchases; five minutes later 'souffrir dans la solitude était devenu le pire des tourments', and a chance visitor, whom at another time he would have sent packing as soon as he decently could, is kept talking for a full hour.

Not only the tragic emotions are so illustrated in *Armance*; Stendhal refines his style to an exquisite simplicity in order to embrace all the shifting pastel shades of tenderness in the relations between his lovers. 'Comme, se voyant sans cesse, ils pouvaient se parler rarement sans être entendus, ils avaient toujours dans leurs courts moments de liberté tant de choses à s'apprendre, tant de faits à se communiquer rapidement, que toute vaine délicatesse était bannie de leurs discours.' Their association, too innocent to be called love, too intimate to be called friendship, is a kind of conspiracy of candour. 'La conversation était sérieuse, grave, mais d'un intérêt touchant. Les sentiments osaient se montrer sans aucun voile. A la vérité, on ne parlait que de sujets peu capables de compromettre, mais le charme céleste de la candeur n'en était pas moins vivement senti...'[5] Love may be, in this novel, no more than love's speech, but with what pure eloquence this speech is phrased! And when, in his twenty-third chapter, Stendhal permits Octave at last, on what he thinks is his death-bed, to make the avowal of

[5] *Armance*, pp. 106, 100.

his passion, the language in which the scene is reported, direct, devoid of grandiloquence and all facile pathos, redeems whatever tiresome feinting there may have been in the lovers' earlier sentimental encounters.

Il y avait une heure qu'Octave goûtait pour la première fois de sa vie le bonheur de parler de son amour à l'être qu'il aimait.

Un seul mot venait de changer du tout au tout la position d'Octave et d'Armance; et comme depuis longtemps, penser l'un à l'autre occupait tous les instants de leur existence, un étonnement rempli de charmes leur faisait oublier le voisinage de la mort; ils ne pouvaient se dire un mot sans découvrir de nouvelles raisons de s'aimer.

This is the most intimate of music: not yet the symphonic splendours of *Le Rouge et le Noir*, nor the ethereal harmonies of *La Chartreuse de Parme*. *Armance* is a *nocturne*; and though it must be granted that Beethoven and Bach are the greater composers, there are moments when it is permissible to prefer Chopin.

IV ⬝ THE DREAMER

I N concentrating attention on the hero in Stendhal's novels, we
are bound to neglect many other facets of his work which are,
strictly, not at all negligible. Any specific critical approach to a
great writer has the disadvantage that it excludes, or at the least
occludes, every other approach. This is the price that has to be
paid for incisiveness; the alternative is to risk saying nothing in
the vain attempt to say everything. No one who ventures to speak
or write about Stendhal can fail to be painfully aware at almost
every turn of how much he is forced to disregard, of the many
reservations and attenuations that have to be suppressed; until he
is constrained to find what reassurance he can in Baudelaire's consoling maxim: 'Pour être juste, c'est-à-dire pour avoir sa raison
d'être, la critique doit être partiale, passionnée, politique, c'est-à-
dire faite à un point de vue exclusif, mais au point de vue qui
ouvre le plus d'horizons.'[1]

Fortunately, in treating of *Le Rouge et le Noir*, the drawback of
the particular exclusiveness we are adopting is less apparent.
Stendhal himself originally intended to entitle the book *Julien*,
and customarily refers to it by this name alone in his letters and
private memoranda. From the moment when, in the fourth chapter,
he introduces us to his hero, perched on a cross-beam under the
roof of his father's saw-mill, he never allows us to lose sight of
him. Even when Julien is not actually present, he furnishes the
text of conversation between whatever characters occupy the stage
for the time being: Mme de Rênal and her husband, M. de La
Mole and Pirard, Mathilde de La Mole and her father. There are
passages in *Lucien Leuwen*, and longer ones in *La Chartreuse de
Parme*, in which Lucien and Fabrice and their concerns are temporarily in eclipse: we are invited to interest ourselves in François
Leuwen's parliamentary career, in Mosca's endless fencing to
maintain his position at the Court of Parma. Such episodes have
no parallel in *Le Rouge et le Noir*. The book is filled with remarkable

---

[1] *Salon de 1846 (A quoi bon la critique?).*

characters, some lovable, some detestable, some laughable, some
simply astonishing; but none of them, not even Mathilde, risks
overshadowing Julien, whereas it is not absolutely certain that in
the preceding novel we are meant to take more notice of Octave
than of Armance. *Le Rouge et le Noir* may or may not be Stendhal's most perfect achievement; but it is certain he never created
a character more complex, more haunting, more controversial than
Julien.[2]

Next to nothing is known about how the novel came to be
undertaken; it has not even been settled beyond reasonable doubt
when Stendhal started to write it and for how long previously he
had been brooding over his subject. Did Julien first confront his
maker in the shape of some nameless working lad, an ostler, perhaps, or a boatman, briefly encountered by Beyle on one of his
many journeys, with a look of intelligence on his face ill befitting
a rustic, and a flash of indignation in his eye? Or did he begin as
an embryonic idea to which the imagination gradually added the
cellular tissue of humanity? If this is what happened, the idea is
not far to seek, and we have already quoted it in one formula:
Armance asking her lover: 'Comment connaître les hommes si
vous ne voyez qu'une classe? Et la classe la moins énergique parce
qu'elle est la plus éloignée des besoins réels!'[3] What Armance is
expressing here is a favourite theory of Stendhal's: the higher an
individual stands in the social hierarchy, the less he is required to
exert himself, and the less, consequently, he needs to display that
primitive virtue: *energy*. In the *Promenades dans Rome*, the travel-
book which Stendhal intercalated between *Armance* and *Le Rouge
et le Noir*, we may read passage after passage treating of energy
and its decline in the cultivated classes. Energy is 'la qualité qui
manque le plus au dix-neuvième siècle. De nos jours on a trouvé
le secret d'être fort brave sans énergie ni caractère. Personne ne
sait vouloir; notre éducation nous désapprend cette grande science.'
Education, good manners, in a word, *civilization*, dilute the energy
of a nation; the process starts, naturally, in the upper levels of
society which are the most refined. 'La civilisation étiole les âmes.
Ce qui frappe surtout, lorsqu'on revient de Rome à Paris, c'est
l'extrême politesse et les yeux *éteints* de toutes les personnes qu'on

---

[2] 'Si *la Chartreuse de Parme* est le plus beau livre de Stendhal, Julien Sorel
est pourtant son chef-d'œuvre' (A. Suarès, *Portraits*, p. 186).
[3] Cf. above, p. 85.

rencontre.' — 'Paris est-il sur la route de la civilisation véritable?
Vienne, Londres, Milan, Rome, en perfectionnant leurs façons de
vivre, arriveront-elles à la même délicatesse, à la même élégance,
à la même absence d'énergie?'[4] Vienna, London, evidently on the
way to becoming 'unreal cities' long before *The Waste Land*.
The topic arises naturally in the *Promenades dans Rome*, a book
in which much is made of the contrast between the backward and
ill-policed populations of southern Italy and the relatively advanced
society of northern France. But the same ideas are met with in
almost all Stendhal's writings in the eighteen-twenties: in his art-
criticism, for instance, where one would hardly expect to find them.
'Rien n'est fait pour étioler la manière de sentir comme un séjour
un peu prolongé à Paris. Tant de gens respectables dans les salons
ont intérêt à flétrir toute énergie du nom de grossièreté.' And, more
pointedly: 'L'opinion à Paris *abhorre l'énergie*. Elle n'a pardonné à
Napoléon qu'en le voyant prisonnier sur le rocher de Sainte-
Hélène.'[5] Napoleon is inescapable in this context. The French
Revolution, in Stendhal's reading of history, marked the end of a
period during which the highly refined manners of the upper classes
had steadily sapped their vitality. In 1792 the rude, unpolished
representatives of lower ranks in society came to the head of
affairs: Danton, Saint-Just, Collot d'Herbois. The revolutionary
wars provided further openings for the energetic plebeian: Hoche,
the ex-stable-boy, and Jean-Victor Moreau became generals. 'A ce
moment, le plus grand des annales de la France, la politesse fut
proscrite par des lois. Tout ce qui avait de la politesse devint juste-
ment suspect à un peuple enveloppé de traîtres et de trahisons...'[6]
The Cato, the stern republican Roman, who co-existed in
Stendhal with the dilettante-dandy, must be noted as simply one
of the more rebarbative elements in this unmanageable personality.
There is undeniable justice in Lytton Strachey's criticism: 'It was
the energy of self-assertiveness that pleased Beyle; that of self-
restraint did not interest him.'[7] Passages such as those quoted
suggest that Stendhal's ideal should logically have been the enemy

---

[4] *Promenades dans Rome*, i. 309; ii. 179–80; iii. 200.
[5] *Mélanges d'art*, pp. 121, 187. The first of these remarks occurs in an article
published in the *Journal de Paris* in 1824; the second in an essay, 'Des beaux-
arts et du caractère français', which appeared in the *Revue trimestrielle* in 1828.
[6] *Napoléon*, i. 198–200. Stendhal wrote his uncompleted *Vie de Napoléon*
at Milan, 1817–18.
[7] *Books and Characters*, p. 274.

of civility; perhaps, after all, Molière's Alceste. His heroic age is not always the Revolution; sometimes he seems to want to shift it back to the early seventeenth century, the time of the wars of the Fronde,[8] which suggests that there is no absolute incompatibility between Mathilde de La Mole's form of nostalgia and Julien's: both look back, at any rate, to a time of turmoil and civil strife. Sometimes Stendhal even pretends to hanker after the Dark Ages and is capable of advancing that 'le *principe énergique* était plus fort que parmi nous dans la société du dixième siècle'.[9] But one may question his seriousness here, and also when, deploring the poor musical taste of his day, he declared: 'Si le ciel nous donne un peu de guerre civile, nous redeviendrons les Français énergiques du siècle de Henri IV et de d'Aubigné; nous prendrons les mœurs passionnées des romans de Walter Scott. Au milieu du fléau de la guerre, la légèreté française se renfermera dans de justes bornes, *l'imagination* renaîtra, et bientôt sera suivie par la musique.'[1] Was a musical revival worth a civil war? Not a question which, in his more Neronic moments, Stendhal was disposed to consider.

In suggesting that the rudimental Julien-idea is to be sought in this theory of a correlation between the refinements of civilization on the one hand, and a withering of the will on the other, we have in mind Stendhal's own interpretation of *Le Rouge et le Noir* as an attack on the stranglehold of the proprieties which in his view inhibited the French ruling class, in the period of which he was writing, from offering any effective resistance to the forces that were to sweep them away. In a letter to Sophie Duvaucel written on 20 January 1831 he inquired whether she had received her copy, and in case she had, he adjured her not to read 'ce plaidoyer contre la politesse qui *use la force de vouloir*'.[2] Julien, it seems, was conceived as the Goth at the gates: the struggle for existence had sharpened his wits and his appetite and, once at the capital, he found nothing between himself and domination but a clique of bloodless, over-bred patricians. This subject, the doom of an aristocratic, conven-tion-ridden, unenterprising class, undermined and overthrown by the new men emerging from lower social strata, might have been

---

[8] 'Alors, on trouvait chez le paysan, chez le noble, chez le bourgeois, une énergie que l'on ne connut plus en France après les soixante-douze ans du règne de Louis XIV. En 1640 le caractère français osait encore désirer des choses énergiques' (*Le Chevalier de Saint-Ismier: Romans et nouvelles*, ii. 81).

[9] *Mémoires d'un touriste*, i. 129.

[1] *Vie de Rossini*, i. 285.   [2] *Correspondance*, vii. 56.

peculiarly topical in 1830, but it had haunted Stendhal's mind for a full quarter of a century. His play *Les Deux Hommes* has already been mentioned in connexion with the origins of *Armance*; in tracing the personal sources of *Le Rouge et le Noir* we are brought back to the same piece, and specifically to a speech put in the mouth of the 'raisonneur' in the play, Valbelle. The essential seed, later to flower in the scathing sketches of the De La Mole circle, is buried here in the chaotic mass of papers which represent Stendhal's effort to fit *Les Deux Hommes* for the stage.

Cela se fait-il, cela ne se fait-il pas, voilà la grande question que se font tous les jeunes gens; dans la conversation ils ne cherchent nullement à s'instruire mais uniquement à briller, et sont plus contents d'avoir fait un mauvais calembour que d'avoir appris une vérité utile. Aussi, qu'il ne vienne une révolution, que quelque grand intérêt force à s'occuper sérieusement d'une vérité à trouver, ou d'une grande entreprise à exécuter, vous voyez tous nos élégants disparaître et tous les grands hommes, gloire de la nation et envie de la postérité, sortir de la classe bourgeoise où le besoin ramène à la vérité.[3]

Valbelle's little sermon would have been written in 1803 or 1804. The example of Diderot's *comédie bourgeoise* must be held responsible for the pomposity of the tone and perhaps also for the attribution of virtue to 'la classe bourgeoise'. As time went on, Stendhal looked progressively farther and farther down the ladder of society to identify the class 'où le besoin ramène à la vérité', the class which was to re-energize the nation. Energy was the monopoly, now of the 'petite bourgeoisie', now of the peasant-farmer ('petits propriétaires à 20 louis de rente'), or the shopkeeper. In 1826 he even professed to find it exclusively among convicts.[4] Balzac, in creating Vautrin, was to exploit this particular vein. Stendhal himself, though at the end of his career he planned to introduce an intelligent and unscrupulous criminal as the hero of *Lamiel*,[5] settled in the main for the relatively law-abiding and honest class of artisans to represent the social reservoir of 'energy'. A *cause célèbre* in the Pyrenean town of Bagnères-de-Bigorre gave him a pretext for an inappropriately extended development in the

[3] *Théâtre*, ii. 238–9.
[4] *Rome, Naples et Florence*, i. 180–1.
[5] Possibly in imitation of an early thriller by Balzac which had been republished in 1837 under the title *Argow-lè-Pirate*. The suggestion is made by A. Ruff, *L'Esprit du mal et l'esthétique baudelairienne* (1955), p. 137.

Promenades dans Rome which is commonly—and justly—regarded as foreshadowing one of the themes of *Le Rouge et le Noir*, that of the lower-class boy whose 'energies', finding no outlet in a hierarchical society, vent themselves in violent and ultimately criminal activity. It was probably in April 1829[6] that Stendhal became acquainted with the history of Adrien Laffargue through reading about it in the *Gazette des Tribunaux*, a newspaper which specialized in accounts of the more sensational court-cases and which he used to recommend enthusiastically to intending English travellers in France.[7] Laffargue, a clever, rather moody cabinet-maker, fell out with his mistress, a certain Thérèse Castadère. The tiff became a bitter quarrel which ended in bloodshed: Laffargue got hold of a pistol, fired two shots at Thérèse (of which only the second hit her) and, to make sure she was dead, finished up by cutting her throat. He was apprehended immediately and offered no resistance. Thanks largely to Thérèse's humble station in life and her tarnished reputation, Laffargue, though found guilty by the assize court at Pau, was sentenced to a mere five years' imprisonment.

Possibly to satisfy his publisher, who had found the last volume of the *Promenades dans Rome* a little short of matter, Stendhal introduced into it a fairly full account of Laffargue's evidence and that of the witnesses, and summarized the more dramatic passages of the trial. The moral that he drew in conclusion is what interests us:

Tandis que les hautes classes de la société parisienne semblent perdre la faculté de sentir avec force et constance, les passions déploient une énergie effrayante dans la petite bourgeoisie, parmi ces jeunes gens qui, comme M. Laffargue, ont reçu une bonne éducation, mais que l'absence de fortune oblige au travail et met en lutte avec les vrais besoins.

Soustraits, par la nécessité de travailler aux mille petites obligations imposées par la bonne compagnie, à ses manières de voir et de sentir qui étiolent la vie, ils conservent la force de vouloir, parce qu'ils sentent avec force. Probablement tous les grands hommes sortiront désormais

---

⁶ According to C. Liprandi who has made the definitive study of the question in his exhaustive monograph, *Au cœur du 'Rouge': l'affaire Laffargue et 'le Rouge et le Noir'* (1961).

⁷ 'An Englishman who proposes visiting France, and who understands our language, cannot better prepare himself for his journey than by reading a year's file of the *Gazette des Tribunaux*' (*New Monthly Magazine*, vol. xvi (May 1826), p. 510); 'an excellent paper, which I recommend to all the English who wish to make themselves acquainted with the state of things in France' (ibid. vol. xvii (Oct. 1826), p. 303).

de la classe à laquelle appartient M. Laffargue. Napoléon réunit autrefois les mêmes circonstances: bonne éducation, imagination ardente et pauvreté extrême.[8]

The same elements were to be present in Julien too: a good education, an ardent imagination, and extreme poverty;[9] and Julien belongs strictly to the same class as Laffargue, that of the skilled manual workers: we see him on one occasion exercising his handicraft, when he fits up book-shelves for Chélan, the parish priest at Verrières (book I, chapter xxii).

An earlier criminal case, also reported in the *Gazette des Tribunaux*, that of Antoine Berthet, provided Stendhal with the broad outline of his plot. Berthet was a village boy of humble birth (his father a blacksmith) who was found a position as tutor in the manor-house of his native Brangues. He had some sort of intrigue with the squire's lady, Mme Michoud de la Tour, and was sent away to the seminary at Belley. Expelled from this establishment, he returned to Brangues, only to find another young man installed as tutor and, he suspected, enjoying Mme Michoud's favours in his place. He wrote her a number of threatening letters which appear to have had the curious result that the Michouds exerted themselves to secure him a place in another seminary, this time at Grenoble. He was kept here only a month, and was then offered another situation as tutor by a certain Comte de Cordon. He had not been long in this household when he started an apparently fairly innocent romance with Mlle de Cordon, the discovery of which led to his dismissal. He returned to Brangues, desperate at these continual checks, and the series of letters to Mme Michoud was resumed. This time Berthet was threatening her not with exposure but with

---

[8] *Promenades dans Rome*, iii. 200–1. Cf. ibid. ii. 248: 'L'an passé, les tribunaux nous ont appris plusieurs assassinats commis par amour; les accusés appartenaient tous à cette classe ouvrière qui, grâce à sa pauvreté, n'a pas le temps de songer à l'opinion du voisin et aux convenances. M. Laffargue, ouvrier ébéniste, auquel la cour d'assises de Pau vient de sauver la vie, a plus d'âme à lui seul que tous nos poètes pris ensemble, et plus d'esprit que la plupart de ces messieurs.' That Stendhal denominates Laffargue's social status now as 'working-class', now as 'lower middle-class', indicates merely that the modern distinction between the terms was unknown to him.

[9] On two separate occasions in *Le Rouge et le Noir*, Stendhal gives it to Julien to use the very phrase he had applied in the *Promenades* to Laffargue: 'cette classe d'hommes de cœur qui, après une bonne éducation, n'a pas assez d'argent pour entrer dans une carrière' (i. 165); and: 'cette classe de jeunes gens qui, nés dans une classe inférieure et en quelque sorte opprimés par la pauvreté, ont le bonheur de se procurer une bonne éducation' (ii. 448).

death; a threat he eventually attempted to carry out, firing a shot at her during mass in the parish church of Brangues, and then turning the pistol on himself. He succeeded however only in wounding his victim and in breaking his own jaw. He was committed for trial, found guilty, and executed. The disparity between the treatment he received at the hands of the law and that which was meted out to Laffargue must have been due to the difference in social status between the two women involved and, more particularly, to the fact that Berthet, by shedding blood in a place of worship, had rendered himself guilty, in the eyes of the Church at least, of sacrilege.

In the transposition he made of it, the Berthet affair was sufficiently recognizable for the Michoud de la Tour family to bear Stendhal a perennial grudge thereafter.[1] Nevertheless, he cannot be accused of copying more than a few incidents in the life of the unfortunate young man who was guillotined in 1828. Julien's behaviour and, in general, his character bear no resemblance to Berthet's. The only evidence on which we may judge what sort of a person Berthet was is the press-report of the trial which Stendhal himself read (not necessarily at the time of its publication, at the end of December 1827).[2] He emerges as an obviously unbalanced, weak-minded though clever boy, with no inordinate ambitions: he never seems to have aspired to anything higher than a position as country incumbent. At the end of a long training in theology (unlike Julien, he had been a seminarist for four years *before* he became tutor; this course was interrupted by ill-health) his superiors decided he was unfitted to have a cure of souls; a verdict he accepted unwillingly. 'It is a great pity I have failed the career I destined myself for; I should have made a good priest' he remarked in one of his letters to Mme Michoud. Words which, by no stretch of the imagination, can one conceive Julien ever being so naïve as to employ.

---

[1] A curious piece of information given in a communication from a great-grand-niece of the original Mme Michoud. See J. Rodes, 'Stendhal et la famille Michoud de la Tour', *Le Divan*, no. 167 (1931), pp. 129–30.

[2] In addition, a fascinating document has recently come to light: the account (written in 1886 by a collateral descendant of Louis Michoud) of Berthet's behaviour while a tutor, according to the tradition preserved orally in the family. The most suggestive point that emerges is that Berthet held political opinions judged to be subversive. See V. Del Litto, 'En marge du *Rouge et Noir*. L'affaire Berthet racontée par une petite-nièce de Louis Michoud de la Tour', *Stendhal Club*, no. 14 (1962), pp. 148–63.

Berthet was without Julien's imagination, without Julien's vaulting ambition. He is sent to Belley, returns to Brangues; to Belley a second time, and again returns to Brangues; to Grenoble, to Virieu, to Morestel, and each time returns tamely to Brangues. Julien's one idea is to 'make his fortune', which means leaving Verrières and, preferably, going to Paris. Berthet resented having no future but that of a 'dominie at a wage of 200 francs', but his resentment was directed not against the social order but against the Michouds, who had proved incapable of finding him a satisfactory position. Julien takes little notice what salary is being paid him, and is outraged only that he needs to earn his living while the privileged members of society, to whom he feels himself superior, have no money cares and idle away their time. Berthet's crime was prompted by sheer despair at finding himself dismissed from every post to which he was appointed, mingled with some jealousy of his thirty-six-year-old mistress who had taken another lover and whom his letters failed to frighten. Whatever the motives of Julien's crime, they were certainly not Berthet's. At his trial, Berthet defends himself volubly, puts on a show of penitence, accuses Mme Michoud of having corrupted his innocence, then, after his condemnation, when he has lodged his appeal, retracts these accusations. Julien preserves a proud silence, and speaks only when it appears he is on the verge of acquittal; what he says then is calculated to ensure that the jury should not return a verdict in his favour; he refuses to appeal, in spite of every pressure that is brought on him to do so. Julien, finally, was out to kill, and never entertained the idea of suicide: Berthet represents himself as torn, up to the very moment of action, between the idea of taking his own life and that of forcing his guilty mistress to 'appear beside him at the bar of Divine Justice', as he puts it.

Neither Berthet nor Laffargue were obvious types of the angry social misfit, the 'plebeian in revolt' that Stendhal wished to picture in Julien. They were skeletal figures—wire structures—of no value until imagination had deposited its crystals on them. They were, to use another of Stendhal's metaphors, *pilotis*, piling to support the visible superstructure. What caused Julien to be called into being was an intellectual need on the part of his creator. Octave had afforded him an opportunity to cast an eye in imagination over the social scene from one of the topmost rungs of the ladder; in Julien he wanted to see it as it appeared from one of the lowest.

Neither position was one he himself occupied, or ever had or ever would. The areas in which Julien's spirit and Stendhal's overlap are not what could be called the socio-political ones. Stendhal gave Julien many of his own qualities: a sense of 'difference' from the common herd, of 'singularity'; an invincible distrust of intellectual authority; an excessive sensitivity to real or supposed offences; and, above all, a profound disrespect for established religion which was, for instance, completely opposed to Berthet's way of thinking. But Julien's class-consciousness, his hostility to his social superiors, constitutes an irreducible originality. Stendhal does not merely fail to share it; he fails to sympathize with it and, in so far as it was possible for him as novelist to do so, condemns it. For Julien, in allowing himself to be consumed with resentment and 'impotent hatred' of those in a higher station, sins against *beylisme*. No less than Octave's, but for different reasons, Julien's life-story is an object lesson on the danger of flouting those 'principles of *beylisme*' which Stendhal had developed in his letters to Félix Faure.

His hatred of 'the rich' creates, from the very start, misunderstandings between himself and Mme de Rênal, when the situation is such that no development appears more likely than that the two should drift into some such idyllic attachment as linked Jean-Jacques Rousseau and Mme de Warens at Les Charmettes.[3] The first meeting between the two, when Julien presents himself as the new tutor (chapter vi), is bathed in a creamy glow of tender promise. These two delightful creatures, Julien with his great dark eyes and curly black hair, standing at the garden gate in his shirt sleeves with his jacket on his arm; Mme de Rênal with a shawl thrown round her bare arms and a soft perfume clinging to her summer dress; the warmth of the day, their isolation, the sensual charm each radiates and each responds to; Julien's rapture and astonishment at hearing himself politely spoken to by so beautifully dressed a lady; Mme de Rênal's joy and relief at finding a timid, almost girlish stripling when she expected a shabby, grim-faced, ill-washed ecclesiastic: everything in this scene, at once so poetic and so unsentimentally observed, hints at a future of unclouded happiness—everything but the last, portentous incident. The idea crosses

[3] If Rousseau's account is to be trusted (*Confessions*, book III). In age and social status there is little difference between Julien and Jean-Jacques, and between Louise de Rênal and Louise de Warens, whose names are even somewhat reminiscent the one of the other. See J.-B. Barrère's invaluable study, 'Stendhal et le chinois', *Revue des sciences humaines*, fasc. 92 (1958), pp. 437–61.

Julien's mind that he should kiss her hand; he nerves himself to make this incongruous gesture, not as a homage to beauty but because he considers it 'une action qui peut m'être utile, et diminuer le mépris que cette belle dame a probablement pour un pauvre ouvrier à peine arraché à la scie'. This *mépris* is postulated: neither by word, deed, or look does Mme de Rênal manifest *disdain*, for indeed, as we know, her heart is quite guiltless of it. But Julien detects it everywhere. After he has been some months in their employ, Mme de Rênal tries to make him a present of money to buy some linen, having noticed, simply, that he is short of shirts. Immediately he flares up. Does she think he is a domestic? 'Je suis petit, madame, mais je ne suis pas bas.' Independence of spirit is admirable; rudeness is not. His outburst upsets and silences Mme de Rênal at the time; but on reflection she is impressed by it, and tries to soothe his ruffled pride by even greater kindness. Julien remains as bristly as ever: 'Voilà, se disait-il, comme sont ces gens riches, ils humilient, et croient ensuite pouvoir tout réparer par quelques singeries.'[4] Whatever she does, Julien will never see the woman in her, but only the representative of her class which is at enmity with his. She, on the other hand, is only too sensible of the handsome boy in Julien. To fortify her weakening virtue, she switches to treating him more coldly; Julien thereupon deduces that he is being 'put in his place'.—'Il se souvint du rang qu'il occupait dans la société, et surtout aux yeux d'une noble et riche héritière', and he rounds on himself in fury for expecting anything but slights from these insolent aristocrats. Why cannot he school himself to be as indifferent to their rebuffs as to the favours they bestow? He cannot forget that Mme de Rênal first saw him in his working clothes; the idea even crosses his mind to pay court for preference to her friend, Mme Derville; 'ce n'est pas qu'elle fût plus agréable, mais toujours elle l'avait vu précepteur honoré pour sa science, et non pas ouvrier charpentier, avec une veste de ratine pliée sous le bras, comme il était apparu à madame de Rênal';[5] Stendhal adds, in the next paragraph, that this vision, as it happened, remained Mme de Rênal's most cherished memory.

When she becomes his mistress his conquest is a class triumph. Though he no longer fears to be regarded as 'un amant subalterne, à cause de sa naissance obscure', the satisfaction he feels is, in part at least, compounded of 'la joie de posséder, lui pauvre être

---

[4] *Le Rouge et le Noir*, i. 67–69.   [5] Ibid. 122, 139.

malheureux et si méprisé, une femme aussi noble et aussi belle'. Not that he trusts her, even after she has yielded. 'Il se dit: Elle est bonne et douce, son goût pour moi est vif, mais elle a été élevée dans le camp ennemi.'[6] Stendhal has no need to stress what Julien misses, and what he mars, by closing his eyes to the obvious and persisting in thinking of his mistress as a class enemy. By showing in the same detail the thoughts and emotions of Mme de Rênal— never was a woman more devoid of snobbery, or of the least ink- ling of class-distinctions, than she—he can leave it to his reader to draw his own conclusions; at the most, a rapid aside (as when Stendhal qualifies as 'foolish' Julien's idea that he was regarded as 'un amant subalterne', a backstairs lover) is enough to make the point.

No woman, probably, who ever read *Le Rouge et le Noir*, could forgive Julien for turning Mme de Rênal's love for him into a private symbol of the overthrow of her social class by his. He is not, of course, quite so insensible as this analysis suggests; and eventually, after the great crisis precipitated by the illness of her youngest son, he does receive the ultimate revelation of passionate love. Mme de Rênal, who is completely devoted to her three boys and is, by train- ing and temperament, deeply religious, regards the child's fever as a warning from on high: she must break with Julien if Stanislas is to live. Her inability, even so, to give up her lover, is over- whelming and surprising proof to Julien of the genuineness of her passion which he had always half doubted. Stanislas recovers but his mother does not regain her former indifference to the moral implications of her adultery. She tells Julien she is certain of eternal damnation—had God meant to save her he would have taken her son. Hell, with all its terrors, lies beyond the grave but even so she cannot repent, and like a heroine in a play by Corneille she declares that she would commit her transgression again if it were still to be committed. When—hypocritically, for he is simply scared at the thought of what this distraught woman might do—he suggests that to appease God they should live chastely in one another's society, she answers, holding his head at arm's length between her hands: 'Et moi, t'aimerai-je comme un frère? Est-il en mon pouvoir de t'aimer comme un frère?' Julien yields at last.

La méfiance et l'orgueil souffrant de Julien, qui avait surtout besoin d'un amour à sacrifices, ne tinrent pas devant la vue d'un sacrifice si

[6] *Le Rouge et le Noir*, i. 160, 164.

grand, si indubitable et fait à chaque instant. Il adorait madame de Rênal. Elle a beau être noble, et moi le fils d'un ouvrier, elle m'aime... Je ne suis pas auprès d'elle un valet de chambre chargé des fonctions d'amant. Cette crainte éloignée, Julien tomba dans toutes les folies de l'amour, dans ses incertitudes mortelles.[7]

Julien's second mistress is even higher placed socially than his first; his suspicions of her motives are as a consequence even deeper, and, it must be confessed, justly so, up to a point. Between him and Mathilde there is no such breathtaking first meeting as occurred outside the french windows in the garden at Verrières. He finds himself sitting opposite her at table when he first dines with the De La Mole family. He observes with indifference her blonde hair, fine figure, and flashing eyes, and prefers her brother, a bluff and brainless cavalry officer. In succeeding days he avoids speaking to her, and is furious when he has to take her orders. Privately, he catalogues the defects of her person and character: her tallness, her pallor, her 'colourless' hair, her immodestly low-cut dresses, everything about her, in fact, that makes her different from Mme de Rênal whose submissiveness he mentally contrasts with Mathilde's imperiousness, whose warmth and gentleness he opposes to the coldly sarcastic witticisms this spoilt Parisian doll permits herself. He snubs her, ignores her pointedly when he can do so with impunity, or tries to outrage her by voicing opinions calculated to upset her aristocratic prejudices.

This conduct has the totally unintended effect of causing Mathilde first to distinguish him from the undistinguished press of her well-born suitors, then to seek his company, admire the penetration of his views, confide in him some of her own. Julien softens: 'il oubliait son triste rôle de plébéien révolté.'[8] This is not the first time that Stendhal uses the formula, nor will it be the last.[9] On this occasion the phrasing is important: Stendhal is implying that Julien is not naturally the discontented commoner: he is *acting a part*, and a 'dismal' one at that. But perhaps Mathilde too is acting a part in some conspiracy to shame him; hand in glove with her brother, no doubt, whose indifference to his sister's

[7] Ibid. 202, 204.   [8] Ibid. ii. 139.
[9] 'Israël Bertuccio n'a-t-il pas plus de caractère que tous ces nobles Vénitiens? se disait notre plébéien révolté...' (*Le Rouge et le Noir*, ii. 126; the reference is to Casimir Delavigne's tragedy *Marino Faliero*, first performed in 1829). 'Nous trouverions dans son âme du plébéien révolté' (ibid. 376: letter from Mathilde to her father).

association with their father's base-born secretary is highly suspect:
'ne devrait-il pas s'indigner de ce que sa sœur distingue un *domestique* de leur maison?'[1] A household servant—Julien had over-
heard a doddering duke so denote him, and could neither forgive
nor forget the impertinence.

Mathilde's flattering attentions alter his opinion of her in more
than one respect; there is now fascination in her great blue eyes;
but it is, nevertheless, not with the gratitude of an ardent lover
that he reads the first love-letter she sends him. Stendhal, who
sometimes uses language gracelessly, but never carelessly, speaks
four times in a single page (chapter xiii of the second part) of the
joy this letter gives him. Joy is the egotist's substitute for happiness.
There is joy in the thought that he, a 'poor peasant', should be
honoured with a 'declaration of love from a great lady', that young
Sorel in his suit of black should be preferred to the Marquis de
Croisenois (her fiancé) who has moustaches, a pretty wit, and a
handsome uniform . . . and one of whose ancestors followed Saint-
Louis to the Crusades. A twinge of compunction makes him hesitate a moment. He has many moral obligations to Mathilde's
father, who has treated him with unwavering courtesy and kindness.
'Cet éclair de vertu disparut bien vite. Que je suis bon, se dit-il;
moi, plébéien, avoir pitié d'une famille de ce rang! Moi, que le duc
de Chaulnes appelle un domestique!' His indignation feeds on the
wildest fancies, all based on the supposition that Mathilde is
leagued with her friends and family to do him injury. Croisenois,
maybe, has been alerted to send a lackey to wrest Mathilde's letter
from him, the calculation being that Julien will shoot the lackey,
which will be the pretext to have him thrown into jail.

Et j'aurais quelque pitié de ces gens-là, s'écria-t-il en se levant impé-
tueusement! En ont-ils pour les gens du tiers état quand ils les tien-
nent! Ce mot fut le dernier soupir de sa reconnaissance pour M. de La
Mole qui, malgré lui, le tourmentait jusque-là... Il faut en convenir,
le regard de Julien était atroce, sa physionomie hideuse; elle respirait le
crime sans alliage. C'était l'homme malheureux en guerre avec toute
la société.

Or so at least Stendhal would have us believe. In reality, if we strip
away the mask of the romantic outlaw which it has pleased him to
fix on Julien at this critical moment, beneath there glares out at us

---

[1] *Le Rouge et le Noir*, ii. 144.

the frightened face of a boy tormented by hallucinations of his own making. Croisenois has no inkling of what is going on; if he had, he would hardly know what to do about it. Mathilde, far from despising Julien for his lowly origins, despises Croisenois, her brother Norbert, and all the other elegant young nonentities of her circle for not resembling Julien in his independence of spirit, his intrepid intellect, his scorn of conventional attitudes. Julien is living a dream. His very words show him fatally out of touch with his time: 'Do they show any mercy to men of the third estate ...'— the *third estate*, has he forgotten, stormed the Bastille and abolished *lettres de cachet* before he was born. There is no *third estate*. The governments of the Restoration imprisoned Béranger for his seditious songs, Courier for his seditious pamphlets: but these men were imprisoned for sedition, not for the seduction of patrician girls. Julien thinks and acts as though it were only yesterday that the Duc de Rohan told his lackeys to beat up Voltaire.

Julien is a man in a dream at Verrières and here in Paris; it would be more fashionable to say that Stendhal shows him, everywhere except in the last ten chapters of the novel, living an inauthentic life, defining himself in advance of being. He does not in fact *feel* himself as the 'poor peasant from the Jura mountains', the 'carpenter's son', the 'plebeian in revolt'; this is how it suits his self-pity, but also his ambition, to see himself; this is the tragic part for which he has cast himself. He acts, in his time, many other parts: he plays Napoleon, Danton, Richelieu, even a real stage character, Tartuffe. No other man ever sees him either as poor peasant, or as a reincarnation of these figures of the past. M. de Rênal sees him as a competent but uppish private tutor, who confers an expensive *cachet* on the Mayor of Verrières. Pirard sees him as a brilliant pupil, probably unfitted, however, for the priesthood. For M. de La Mole he is that rare acquisition, an intelligent and completely trustworthy personal secretary. For Altamira he is another rarity, a serious-minded Frenchman, while for Korasoff he is the perfection of imperturbable dandyism. Men have little difficulty in defining him, though they all define him differently and none as he defines himself. Women have a clearer intuition of Julien's ceaseless struggle to make himself other than he is, and are alternately fascinated and terrorized.[2]

---

[2] 'Votre Julien est bien violent, il m'effraie', says Mme Derville to her friend (*Le Rouge et le Noir*, i. 100). Awe and fear enter into Mme de Rênal's sentiments:

Among the models Julien proposes to himself and tries to live
up to, Napoleon has a privileged position. The others serve as
occasional guides. Danton stands for all the fierce, *energetic*,
remorseless idealists whom the eruption of 1793 threw up. Stendhal qualified him (in his *Mémoires sur Napoléon*) as 'cette âme
hautaine' and as 'l'homme dont aucune des révolutions qui, depuis,
ont été essayées en Europe, n'a montré l'égal'.[3] There are two occasions in *Le Rouge et le Noir* when Julien's thoughts are drawn to
Danton. At the Duc de Retz's ball (book II, chapter ix) he spends
his time in conversation with the aristocratic Italian refugee Altamira; among other matters, they discuss the question (more novel
then than it is today) whether, in political life, ends sanctify means.
Was Danton justified in shedding blood to establish the Revolution?
Julien does not hesitate: 'si, au lieu d'être un atome, j'avais quelque
pouvoir, je ferais pendre trois hommes pour sauver la vie à quatre.'
Are there any commandments a great man may not break? 'Ce
grand Danton a volé. Mirabeau aussi s'est vendu. Napoléon avait
volé des millions en Italie, sans quoi il eût été arrêté tout court
par la pauvreté, comme Pichegru...' Certain heroes of Dostoevsky
reason along similar lines. Actually, Julien is no more a social
revolutionary than Raskolnikov. When he does acquire 'a scrap of
power' he uses it capriciously or self-interestedly. The lucrative
directorship of the workhouse at Verrières, which Valenod has to
relinquish when he succeeds M. de Rênal as mayor, Julien causes
to be given to his own father; he thinks it amusing to have another
vacant office at Verrières filled by a known fool (Cholin); subsequently he discovers, without any great remorse, that his quirkish
ruling disappointed the expectations of a far worthier candidate,
Gros, the impoverished teacher of mathematics whom he had
known as the only honest man in Verrières.

Properly, Julien's career resembles Danton's in no other respect
than that it ends on the scaffold. After the excited talk with

'Son génie allait jusqu'à l'effrayer; elle croyait apercevoir plus nettement
chaque jour le grand homme futur dans ce jeune abbé. Elle le voyait pape, *elle
le voyait premier ministre comme Richelieu*' (ibid. 170; my italics). Mathilde, at
the end of her first private conversation with Julien, 'eut peur, ne put soutenir
son regard, et recula deux pas' (ibid. ii. 131); this fear contributes to the
emotions which make her hesitate before committing herself irrevocably: 'La
profondeur, *l'inconnu* du caractère de Julien eussent effrayé, même en nouant
avec lui une relation ordinaire' (ibid. 183).

[3] *Napoléon*, ii. 85. The *Mémoires*, unlike the *Vie de Napoléon*, were written
subsequently to *Le Rouge et le Noir* (in 1836–7).

Altamira, his thoughts do not revert to his great predecessor until
he finds himself in the condemned cell. Here he remembers being
told how Danton, on the eve of his execution, made a jest about the
verb 'to be guillotined', which ought to be shown in the grammars
as defective, since it cannot be used in the first person of the past
tense. He also recalls that Danton is supposed to have broken down
and wept at the foot of the scaffold; but at least Danton had the
excuse of having achieved great things in his life. 'Moi seul, je sais
ce que j'aurais pu faire... Pour les autres, je ne suis tout au plus
qu'un PEUT-ÊTRE.'[4]

One of Julien's dreams is of rising to power through the Church.
'Que de cardinaux nés plus bas que moi et qui ont gouverné!'[5]
This dream is as unreal as his others, since he is not a citizen of the
Papal States. In France, in spite of the power briefly wielded in
the eighteen-twenties by the Church party (the 'congrégation'),
there was little chance that the nineteenth century would see a
re-emergence of the great cardinal-ministers of the seventeenth.
In Julien's room in the Hôtel de La Mole there is a bust of Richelieu,
which seems to frown at him severely when he wonders whether
he is being rash in responding to Mathilde's advances. This is perhaps a case of imaginative contamination. Richelieu was remembered as the statesman who brought to heel the factious nobles
of France. Mathilde—who lives in the past as much as Julien
does, and more openly—has chosen as her 'models' the turbulent
feudal magnates whom Richelieu tamed. But if on this occasion
he imitates Richelieu for audacity, he copies Tartuffe for caution,
'son maître Tartuffe, dont il savait le rôle par cœur', says Stendhal.
On two later occasions Stendhal shows Julien acting under the
inspiration of Molière's arch-crook.[6]

Julien Sorel is one of those literary creations whose folly or perversity must be blamed on an abuse of literacy. Don Quixote and
Emma Bovary are of the same kind: reading has turned their brains
or corrupted their morals. In this Julien stands in contrast to

---

[4] *Le Rouge et le Noir*, ii. 452–3, 456.   [5] Ibid. 174.
[6] Deliberating how to answer the Marquis's reproaches when his liaison with
Mathilde is discovered, 'la réponse fut fournie par le rôle de Tartuffe. — *Je ne
suis pas un ange...*' (cf. Act III, scene ii: 'Ah! pour être dévot, je ne suis pas
moins homme'). The following day he thinks of enlisting Pirard's help, but he
knows that the priest will be too indignant to give him a hearing. 'Le génie de
Tartuffe vint au secours de Julien: Eh bien, j'irai me confesser à lui' (*Le Rouge
et le Noir*, ii. 364, 367).

Octave and Lucien, who are mathematicians, and to Fabrice, who is an ignoramus. Julien is a great lover of literature, addicted indifferently to Horace and Voltaire; one day perhaps some *stendhalien* will draw up a list of all the authors and books he can be shown to have studied. His reading during his boyhood is necessarily confined to the 'thirty or forty volumes' which an old army surgeon, his only childhood friend, bequeathed him on his death-bed. Among them are Rousseau's *Confessions* ('le seul livre à l'aide duquel son imagination se figurait le monde'), a copy of Napoleon's dispatches, and Las Cases's record of the Emperor's conversations at St. Helena, the famous *Memorial* published in 1822–3. 'Il se serait fait tuer pour ces trois ouvrages.'[7] It was the *Memorial* that his father knocked into the stream when he caught him reading at work.

There is an element of the fortuitous in Julien's choice of Napoleon as lodestar, since it hung on the chance that it should have been a veteran of Napoleon's armies who befriended him in his lonely boyhood and lent him books. It has been advanced more than once that, in making Julien a victim of the Napoleonic myth, Stendhal was using him to express a political attitude which, in 1830, it would have been unwise for the author to avow openly.[8] That he was a secret adherent of Bonaparte after Waterloo is a legend which seems to have been propagated by Beyle himself, and is another instance of the delight he took in mystifying or shocking his friends. In his notorious *H.B.*, a brochure published seven years after Stendhal's death, Prosper Mérimée wrote: 'It was difficult to know what he thought of Napoleon. His almost invariable practice was to argue against whatever opinion was being advanced. Sometimes he spoke of him as a *parvenu* dazzled by false glitter, continually breaking the rules of logic. At other times he adopted a tone of admiration verging on idolatry. He was by turns as critical as Courier and as servile as Las Cases.'[9] His private papers, inaccessible to Mérimée, show Stendhal to have held consistently a perfectly coherent view: that Napoleon was a benefactor of the nation until he betrayed the Revolution—until, in other words, he signed the concordat, had himself crowned emperor,

---

[7] *Le Rouge et le Noir*, i. 34.
[8] Cf. M. David, *Stendhal*, p. 36; H. Jacoubet, *Variétés d'histoire littéraire*, p. 245; &c.
[9] *Portraits historiques et littéraires* (ed. P. Jourda), p. 157.

and attempted to reconstitute court society. In addition, Stendhal was impressed by the tragic dignity of the lonely figure on St. Helena. So diluted an admiration is very different from Julien's passionate devotion to the memory of the Emperor. In fact, it was perhaps with the idea of suggesting how remote his own point of view was from Julien's, that Stendhal included, at the beginning of the second part of *Le Rouge et le Noir*, an apparently otiose dialogue in the chapter entitled 'Les Plaisirs de la Campagne'. Julien is on his way to Paris to take up his duties under M. de La Mole. In the stage-coach he listens to a conversation between two travellers, one of whom (Saint-Giraud) is not merely Stendhal's mouthpiece but quite clearly Stendhal himself in almost every particular. 'J'aime la musique, la peinture,' he declares; 'un bon livre est un événement pour moi; je vais avoir quarante-quatre ans.' Stendhal was forty-seven in the year that *Le Rouge et le Noir* was published. It is not impossible that when he wrote these pages he was giving Saint-Giraud his own age, or in other words that they antedate considerably the composition of the novel.[1] Saint-Giraud's jeremiad is very much in the key of certain laments Stendhal is known to have uttered in his forty-fourth year—in an article written for the *New Monthly Magazine*, 18 September 1826, and in two separate passages in the 1826 edition of *Rome, Naples et Florence*.[2] The gist is that a man who wants a quiet life, free from political embroilment, must give up the notion that anything of the sort can be found in the country. Your neighbours will not allow you to be a neutral: you have the choice of promising your vote to the tories and enduring the innumerable vexations the whigs will be sure to put on you, or vice versa. In the end you will be driven to sell up and return to the capital, 'chercher la solitude et la paix champêtre au seul lieu où elles existent en France, dans un quatrième étage, donnant sur les Champs-Élysées'. And in the final analysis, who is responsible for this state of affairs? continues Saint-Giraud heatedly. 'Ton empereur, que le diable emporte' (his friend Falcoz, whom he is addressing, is a Bonapartist). 'Qui me chasse de ma terre?... Les prêtres, que Napoléon a rappelés par son concordat... Y aurait-il aujourd'hui des gentilshommes insolents, si

---

[1] The discrepancy in ages is noted by Aragon (*Lumière de Stendhal*, pp. 52–53) who, however, omits to draw the conclusion that seems inescapable.

[2] See C. Liprandi, 'Sur un épisode du *Rouge et Noir*: Les Plaisirs de la Campagne', *Revue des sciences humaines*, fasc. 68 (1952), pp. 295–313.

ton Bonaparte n'eût fait des barons et des comtes?...' The whole
of this passage is strongly reminiscent of the satiric dialogues for
which Paul-Louis Courier was famous at the time. The two
speakers, Saint-Giraud and Falcoz, take no further action in the
novel and in fact never appear elsewhere than in this chapter;[3]
which gives additional force to the theory that the passage was an
unpremeditated intercalation, having been extracted by Stendhal
at a late stage from his unpublished papers. Its importance in the
novel, once more, is that it underlines the divergence between the
author's feelings about Napoleon and the hero's. Julien is a silent
listener, intervening shyly only once, and then snubbed by Saint-
Giraud. The criticism of his idol that he is forced to hear makes no
impression on him. His first action on arriving in Paris is to take a
cab in spite of the lateness of the hour, and drive out to view
Joséphine's house at Malmaison.

'Toute vraie passion', comments Stendhal here, 'ne songe qu'à
elle.' Julien's devotion to Napoleon bears all the marks of a private
cult: is it not, in fact, his substitute for religion? To divulge the
mystery to the profane would be blasphemy: on one occasion,
before the story proper opens, he had been so indiscreet as to
betray in words his admiration for Napoleon, and to punish himself had worn his arm in a sling for two months. Thereafter he hides
away to read the sacred books that retrace for him Napoleon's life
and exploits, and never lets the hallowed name cross his lips. He
has his relic: a portrait of the Emperor in a little black cardboard
box, with inscriptions on the back which testify to his devotion.
There is a tragi-comic incident (chapter ix of the first part) concerned with this box. Julien has hidden it in his mattress; he learns
by chance that the Mayor of Verrières (in accordance with the still
simple country ways of that time) is having the straw in all the mat-
tresses renewed by two servants under his personal supervision.
Julien begs—almost orders—Mme de Rênal to retrieve the portrait before her husband arrives at his bed; this she goes to do,
'pâle comme si elle fût allée à la mort', for she, of course, thinks the
portrait is of Julien's sweetheart.

A secret cult; a solitary one too. Bonapartism became a live
issue again in the late forties, after Stendhal's death; in the late
twenties, with Napoleon's only son a boy in his teens living under

[3] Though Stendhal was careful to mention them by name in the first part of
Le Rouge et le Noir (i. 219, 265).

surveillance at Schönbrunn, it was a cause which had no predictable future. 'The delusion which led us', wrote Stendhal in 1825, 'to regard Buonaparte as the perfect model of a hero, as eminently useful to France, is now vanished, or holds its empire only over the minds of shopmen and country lieutenants on half-pay. What was in 1818 the nearly unanimous sentiment of all the strong and generous spirits of France is now fallen into a mere common place, condemned in good society.'[4] After the death of the old veteran who had communicated the faith to him, Julien never again encounters a fellow believer. It would be incredible that none existed, but, like him, they are silent. Only once, at Besançon, he overhears talk between two stonemasons working on the other side of the seminary wall, which shows the memory of 'the Other One' to be still alive among the common people. They regret his disappearance for roughly the same reasons as Julien: 'un maçon y devenait officier, y devenait général, on a vu ça.'[5] His Bonapartism is one of the few real links connecting Julien with the proletariat from which he springs and which he claims to represent.

The example of Napoleon is a poison that works by over-stimulation: at once forcing his growth and blighting him inwardly. It is what turns him into the monster of single-minded egotism that he is, but it is also what makes him, ultimately, a tragic figure. The explanation of Julien's failure to achieve in the world that happiness groped after by each of Stendhal's heroes, is implicit in the words he uses in a candid moment to Mme de Rênal, though subsequently he retracts them nervously. 'Ah! s'écria-t-il, que Napoléon était bien l'homme envoyé de Dieu pour les jeunes Français! Qui le remplacera?... Quoi qu'on fasse, ajouta-t-il avec un profond soupir, ce souvenir fatal nous empêchera à jamais d'être heureux!'[6] The point is not so much that, for a post-Napoleonic generation, the road to fortune is coloured black, not red (being the winding path of intrigue, hypocrisy, petty infamies, instead of the earlier royal road of virile, full-blooded valour); rather, it is that the incredible fulfilment of Napoleon's own ambitious dream has so dazzled the imaginative adolescent that he cannot conceive of happiness

[4] *London Magazine*, new series, vol. ii, pp. 570–1.
[5] *Le Rouge et le Noir*, i. 352. Cf. *Rome, Naples et Florence*, i. 63: 'J'ai passé deux heures au milieu des ouvriers à écouter leurs propos. A chaque instant Napoléon est mêlé à saint Charles. Tous deux sont adorés.' This was at Milan however, not Besançon. San Carlo is the patron saint of the Milanese.
[6] *Le Rouge et le Noir*, i. 163–4.

except in terms of the realization of some equally fabulous ambition. The proper gloss on Julien's melancholy outburst is a couple of sentences in Stendhal's *Promenades dans Rome*, the book which, as has been noted, immediately preceded *Le Rouge et le Noir*. 'Parce qu'un lieutenant d'artillerie est devenu empereur, et a jeté dans les sommités sociales deux ou trois cents Français nés pour vivre avec mille écus de rente, une ambition folle et nécessairement malheureuse a saisi tous les Français... En présence des plus grands biens, un bandeau fatal couvre nos yeux, nous refusons de les connaître comme tels, et oublions d'en jouir.'[7] The blindness or malady which Stendhal diagnosed here and which he illustrated in his novel as it affected a chosen representative of the Restoration period, was, as he saw it, a disorder widespread among his contemporaries even after 1830: Napoleon's shadow was a long one. When in 1837 Stendhal was writing up his tour of France, he was still acutely aware of the unlucky legacy of misguided ambition which Napoleon's career had bequeathed to the younger generation; but he was also, very possibly, thinking of *Le Rouge et le Noir* when he wrote, in the *Mémoires d'un touriste*, of

cette malheureuse soif de jouissance et de fortune prompte, qui est la folie de tous les jeunes Français. De quelque côté qu'ils regardent ils voient un lieutenant d'artillerie qui devient empereur, un postillon qui devient roi de Naples, un ouvrier chapelier qui devient maréchal, le précepteur du seigneur de leur village qui devient pair de France et millionnaire... Toute cette malheureuse jeunesse française est donc trompée par la gloire de Napoléon et tourmentée par des désirs absurdes. Au lieu d'*inventer* sa destinée, elle voudrait la *copier*; elle voudrait voir recommencer, en 1837, le siècle qui commença en 1792 avec Carnot et Dumouriez.[8]

Murat, whom Napoleon created King of Naples in 1808, was an innkeeper's son. The hatter who became field-marshal is probably Jourdan, who had a drapery business at the time of the Revolution. The 'tutor of the lord of the manor' sounds very like Julien Sorel, who might well have entered the peerage and become a millionaire if the guillotine had not abridged his career.

The vital criticism that Stendhal makes of his hero, implicitly in *Le Rouge et le Noir* and obliquely in this passage of a later work, is that he is living not his own life, but a modified *copy* of another's.

[7] *Promenades dans Rome*, ii. 182–3.
[8] *Mémoires d'un touriste*, iii. 288–90.

He misses happiness, or all but misses it, through trying to live up to an alien ideal. Stendhal's language is existentialist in anticipation: Julien does not *invent* himself, he conforms to a borrowed model. He and Mathilde (who has a different model, placed in a more remote past, the queen of Navarre who was the mistress of one of her ancestors) are two of a piece: hence, initially, their secret sympathy, but, since each pursues incompatible dreams, hence too the secret rivalry which poisons their relations. Julien cannot be both Napoleon and Boniface de La Mole, nor Mathilde both Joséphine de Beauharnais and Marguerite de Navarre. Mme de Rênal, on the other hand, is always authentically herself; and hence is perpetually discovering herself, in love, in jealousy, in forgiveness, and finding true happiness or true horror in what she discovers. She is innocent, and she sins; she is the faithful wife, and deceives her husband, and repents, and returns to the fold, and transgresses again. 'Aucun projet ne paraissait dans toute cette conduite. Elle se croyait damnée sans rémission, et cherchait à se cacher la vue de l'enfer en accablant Julien des plus vives caresses.'[9] She is not erratic, but she is no conformist, and she never acts a part. One cannot conceive, for example, that she should ever think of herself as a second Francesca da Rimini. She *invents* her destiny, outwardly humble but infinitely richer in spiritual content than that of the haughty aristocratic girl who temporarily supplants her.

To accuse Julien of folly for allowing his ambitious dream to come between himself and happiness is all very well; but it must not be overlooked that without this dream he would not have compelled Stendhal's interest or ours. Born in the eighteenth century, he might have furnished a duplicate of the amiable 'paysan parvenu' Marivaux depicted in Jacob. Born when he was, on the morrow of the battle of Austerlitz, it is inevitable that he should resolve to 's'exposer à mille morts plutôt que de ne pas faire fortune'.[1] His ambition is responsible for his exacerbated pride, his distrust of every man and every woman, his secretiveness and love of solitude, his prickly imperviousness to affection and his self-pity, his machiavellian dissimulation and patient cultivation of the difficult art of hypocrisy: everything in fact about him that made an earlier generation of critics regard *Le Rouge et le Noir* as a novel with a villain-hero.[2] But it is hard to hate this dreamer. His ambition is rooted in a chimerical fantasy, and for this he must be forgiven, where the coldly practical schemer would not be forgiven. Julien stands with Don Quixote, among the elect, on the other side of the bar from Maupassant's Bel-Ami with whom some mistakenly confuse him.

He is a man of infinite plans who owes his success to the fact that nearly all the plans he makes luckily miscarry. He plots in minute detail the seduction of Mme de Rênal, to the point of committing the grand design to paper. It avails him nothing: he owes his conquest to his youthful charm, to the impression he has already, quite unintentionally, made on her, to the compassion he arouses when, overcome by nervous exhaustion, he bursts into tears at her bedside; a piece of weakness that was certainly unpremeditated when he formed the resolution to enter her room on a given night. At his theological college he thinks naïvely to win respect and favour by excelling at his studies; the result is the opposite of what he anticipated: he falls under suspicion of spiritual pride, for the Church requires other qualities than intellectual prowess in her parish priests. Chazel, a fellow seminarist who deliberately sows howlers in his Latin unseens, promises far better in the eyes of his superiors. At Paris, he never proposed to make Mathilde de La Mole fall in love with him; in fact, he kept her at arm's length; which is just why she fell in love with him. When later she turns against him, he commits one tactical error after another in vain attempts to win her back. He reconquers her only when he abandons the struggle to succeed by his own devices, places himself in the hands of a friend (Prince Korasoff), and humbly puts into operation a fool-proof plan devised by a friend of this friend, an acknowledged expert in the art of bringing recalcitrant beauties to heel.

Never was a young man so assured that he was shaping his own destiny, and so hugely mistaken. His errors arise invariably from what Stendhal calls his 'imagination', his 'wild imaginings', his

Vogüé who called him 'une âme méchante', Caro who said he was 'le plus infâme petit roué qu'il y ait au monde' (*Stendhal et le beylisme*, p. 93). Julien still succeeds occasionally in arousing virtuous indignation among schoolgirls who are required to read the book, and among certain others: thus, quite recently, in a curious essay entitled 'Julien Sorel ou le complexe de David', Jean Damien asserted: 'On cherchera en vain une noble pensée, un beau geste, une belle action à inscrire à son crédit sur le livre de notre morale' (*Stendhal Club*, no. 4 (1959), p. 310).

'imagination always darting to extremes'. This is what is responsible for his miscalculations at the seminary. 'Égaré par toute la
présomption d'un homme à imagination, il prenait ses intentions
pour des faits, et se croyait un hypocrite consommé.'[3] Imagination
raises him at times to an unwarranted pitch of optimism, but it
may also plunge him into equally unfounded despair, as when,
thinking Mathilde's reaction against him to be due to his unworthi-
ness, he lapses into a paroxysm of self-loathing. Stendhal calls this
'imagination renversée' and adds, in explanation: 'il entreprenait
de juger la vie avec son imagination. Cette erreur est d'un homme
supérieur.'[4]

It had been Stendhal's error too, often enough. In showing his
hero incapable of seeing situations steadily and dealing with them
firmly he was drawing on the memory of the many mortifications
his own over-lively imagination had brought on him. He too had
elaborated pointless schemes for the reduction of one woman's
virtue and been completely taken by surprise when another girl
blurted out that she was in love with him.[5] The contradiction
between Stendhal's unbridled imagination (he used to compare
himself to a skittish horse[6]) and his pretentions to rational
behaviour did not escape the more percipient of his friends. 'All
his life,' wrote Mérimée, 'he was dominated by his imagination,
and in everything he did, acted impulsively and enthusiastically.
Nevertheless, he prided himself on behaving always in conformity
with the dictates of reason. . . .'[7] François Bigillion, one of his boyhood companions of whom we may read in the Vie de Henri Brulard, warned him that he would be better guided by his level-headed
friends than by his own unsteady temperament. 'For the sake of
your own happiness, never act in accordance with your inclinations.
Your imagination blinds you to reason.' Henri Gagnon, his grandfather, whose letters are peppered with good advice, likewise put
him on his guard against this dangerous faculty. 'The sword wears
out the scabbard, my boy; your ardent imagination makes you
more unhappy than the circumstances in which you are placed
would warrant.'[8] The two letters containing these remonstrances

[3] Le Rouge et le Noir, i. 311.   [4] Ibid. ii. 234.
[5] Alexandrine Daru in 1811, Giulia di Rinieri in 1830.
[6] 'Un cheval ombrageux', one that takes fright at shadows. Stendhal used the
metaphor in letters to Pauline (1812) and Mme Curial (1824). Correspondance,
iv. 20, and vi. 81.   [7] Mérimée, op. cit., p. 155.
[8] Lettres à Stendhal . . . recueillies . . . par V. Del Litto, i. 185; ii. 48.

were both written to Beyle when he was at Marseilles, having
settled there temporarily in pursuance of a peculiarly chimerical
vision: that of making his fortune in an export-and-import business
at a time when the Continental System was wreaking havoc with
overseas trade.

Some eight years after *Le Rouge et le Noir* was published, Stendhal had the idea of writing a companion novel, the hero of which
would be a young man anxious, like Julien, to make his way in
the world, but differing from Julien in not being impeded by the
visionary streak. He was to be a realist in the basest sense of the
word. 'L'âme passionnée, le jeune Jean-Jacques, s'attache aux prédictions de son imagination, Robert ne fait cas que de ce qu'il voit.'
Robert was to be devoid of imagination; hence the curious title,
A-Imagination, which Stendhal gave to the few pages he dictated
of this work. His intentions, as stated in a preliminary note, con-
firm what has been advanced in respect of *Le Rouge et le Noir*.

L'auteur voulait, il y a dix ans, faire un jeune homme tendre et honnête, il l'a fait ambitieux mais encore rempli d'imagination et d'illusion
dans Julien Sorel. Il prétend faire Robert absolument sans imagination
autre que celle qui sert à inventer des tours pour parvenir à la fortune;
mais il ne s'amuse pas à se figurer la fortune et ses plaisirs. L'expérience
lui a déjà appris que ces imaginations-là ne se réalisent point; *alors
comme alors*, dit-il, c'est sa maxime favorite.

Stendhal sums up his conception of this anti-hero in a single
phrase: 'Sa lorgnette n'est jamais ternie par le souffle de l'imagination.'[9]

The consequence is that Robert is a bigger rascal than any
invented by the masters of the picaresque. He is ready to perform
whatever shabby service may be required of him provided he is
well paid. He cuts out a viscount who is in love with a wealthy
widow, and when challenged to a duel, proposes that the disappointed suitor should buy him off instead: 'Donnez-moi cent mille
francs et je fais qu'elle prenne de la haine pour moi.'[1] The subject
was probably too unpleasant to be long pursued: the fragment
that found its way on to paper consists mainly in scenarios.

The case of Robert is interesting because it suggests a correlation in Stendhal's judgement between moral depravity and the lack
of imagination. Hence it is possible to maintain that Julien's

imagination is the morally purifying element in him. The 'superiority' it confers on him is the superiority of the man whose mind, fixed as it is on some sublime and unattainable goal, is incapable of stooping to certain forms of meanness. For a poor peasant boy who knows well he will have to struggle for his bare livelihood, he is shown as extraordinarily unconcerned about questions of money: a minor implausibility essential if Stendhal was to adhere to the image he wanted to give of a hero raised above baseness by the power of the imagination. It is his father who argues for hours with M. de Rênal about his starting salary. He is given a rise which he neither wants nor expects; from something he said, his employer deduced he was tempted to take a better position elsewhere; in fact, when later Valenod offers him a salary of eight hundred francs, two hundred more than Rênal pays him, it never occurs to him to accept. When he leaves the mayor's household he prefers to borrow a small sum from his friend Fouqué rather than accept a gratuity from Mme de Rênal's husband. This is one respect in which Julien's sense of values is anything but distorted. In the De La Mole drawing-room, one evening, he sees the wealthy Baron de Thaler (in whom Stendhal is supposed to have portrayed one of the Rothschilds) mercilessly ragged by the same young dandies who would not dare to speak an uncivil word to the modest secretary living on his quarterly salary. 'Une telle vue guérit de l'envie', he reflects.[2] But Julien is the last man to need curing of that kind of envy. It is not merely that he is disinterested; he is what the world calls unworldly. He is, in short, a poet, in the sense that Stendhal judged himself to be one when he first arrived in Paris: 'Je n'étais point *ficelle*, fin, méfiant, sachant me tirer avec un excès d'adresse et de méfiance d'un marché de douze sous, comme la plupart de mes camarades... J'étais dans les rues de Paris un rêveur passionné, regardant au ciel et toujours sur le point d'être écrasé par un cabriolet.'[3]

One of his teachers at the seminary takes Julien with him to assist in decorating the cathedral for the Corpus Christi celebrations. After the procession has left, priest and pupil remain to protect the rich hangings against thieves. The bells begin to toll in the almost empty cathedral. Julien is transported by the sound: 'Son imagination n'était plus sur la terre.' The incident (chapter

---

[2] *Le Rouge et le Noir*, ii. 67.
[3] *Vie de Henri Brulard*, ii. 191. Cf. above, p. 49.

xxviii of the first part) allows Stendhal to lead on to the following passage:

> Les sons si graves de cette cloche n'auraient dû réveiller chez Julien que l'idée du travail de vingt hommes payés à cinquante centimes, et aidés peut-être par quinze ou vingt fidèles. Il eût dû penser à l'usure des cordes, à celle de la charpente, au danger de la cloche elle-même qui tombe tous les deux siècles, et réfléchir au moyen de diminuer le salaire des sonneurs, ou de les payer par quelque indulgence ou autre grâce tirée des trésors de l'Église, et qui n'aplatit pas sa bourse.
> Au lieu de ces sages réflexions, l'âme de Julien, exaltée par ces sons si mâles et si pleins, errait dans les espaces imaginaires. Jamais il ne fera ni un bon prêtre, ni un grand administrateur. Les âmes qui s'émeuvent ainsi sont bonnes tout au plus à produire un artiste...

Le Rouge et le Noir contains just enough such passages to indicate the silhouette of the authentic Julien, which social pressures and the drive to 'succeed' mask for most of the time. When Mme de Rênal and the children move from Verrières to their summer residence at Vergy, a different Julien, forgetful of the past and neglectful of the future, emerges briefly. 'Après tant de contrainte et de politique habile, seul, loin des regards des hommes, et, par instinct, ne craignant point madame de Rênal, il se livrait au plaisir d'exister, si vif à cet âge, et au milieu des plus belles montagnes du monde.' When Mme Derville arrives on a visit, he treats her confidently as a friend who must share his love of nature, and takes her to the spot from which the best view can be had. Then there is a certain evening which Julien spends as usual in the open, seated between his mistress and Mme Derville under an enormous lime-tree, for coolness' sake.

> Julien ne pensait plus à sa noire ambition, ni à ses projets si difficiles à exécuter. Pour la première fois de sa vie, il était entraîné par le pouvoir de la beauté. Perdu dans une rêverie vague et douce, si étrangère à son caractère, pressant doucement cette main qui lui plaisait comme parfaitement jolie, il écoutait à demi le mouvement des feuilles du tilleul agitées par ce léger vent de la nuit, et les chiens du moulin du Doubs qui aboyaient dans le lointain.[4]

But, adds Stendhal in the next sentence, 'cette émotion était un plaisir et non une passion'. When he retires a little later to his room, it is to take up his book and pore once again over Napoleon's

---

[4] *Le Rouge et le Noir*, i. 89, 116.

reminiscences. 'A vingt ans, l'idée du monde et de l'effet à y pro-
duire l'emporte sur tout.'

The concluding chapters of *Le Rouge et le Noir*, on which we
have not touched at all so far, show how in the end this 'passion'
expires, leaving room for the reflowering, in memory and reality,
of this 'pleasure':

> Toutes les passions s'éloignent avec l'âge,
> L'une emportant son masque et l'autre son couteau.

Julien, locked away, within a few weeks of execution, can let fall
the vizard and let drop the knife.

No incident in the novel has incurred so much criticism and
aroused so much speculation as Julien's attempt on Mme de
Rênal's life which, although unsuccessful, ruins a career of unlimited promise and delivers him to the executioner. The situation
which Stendhal has reached in chapter xxxv of the second part of
Le Rouge et le Noir can be summarized in a few lines. Mathilde,
discovering that she is with child by Julien, tells her father that
they must marry. The Marquis de La Mole, another 'homme à
imagination', had dreamed of seeing his daughter marry into a
ducal family. His fury is boundless but he is obliged to yield to the
realities of the situation; to make the match socially a little more
acceptable, he has a minor title conferred on Julien, procures him a
commission in the hussars, and settles an income on him. He delays
giving his final consent only in order to complete his inquiries into
Julien's character. These inquiries result in a letter from Mme de
Rênal in which Julien is described as an ambitious young man who
profits by his sexual attractions in order to enslave and dishonour
whatever woman has most credit in the household in which he is
serving.

M. de La Mole warns Mathilde he will never consent to her
marriage with a man of this type. Julien, having been shown Mme
de Rênal's letter, tells Mathilde her father's decision is perfectly
understandable. Without another word he takes horse for Verrières, where he arrives on a Sunday morning. He purchases a pair
of pistols and tells the gunsmith to load them for him; enters the
church as mass is being celebrated; and sees Mme de Rênal a
few pews away. He hesitates for so long as she is clearly visible.
But when she lowers her head Julien fires once at the kneeling
figure bathed in the red light which streams through the crimson

awnings hung over the windows of the church. With the first shot he misses; he fires again and she falls.

Émile Faguet, at the beginning of this century, was apparently the first commentator to complain that this train of incidents was in total contradiction with the psychology of the various characters involved in them.[5] M. de La Mole ought to have reflected that little weight could be given to the denunciation of a jealous cast-off mistress. Mathilde, instead of sending Julien an agitated and despairing summons, ought to have waited for her father to come round to a more rational way of thinking. Julien, finally, ought to have seen that nothing was to be gained by assassinating his accuser. Whatever he may say or think, the Marquis is in no position to forbid or defer indefinitely his daughter's marriage to Julien.

Faguet suggests two reasons why Stendhal should have set plausibility at defiance here. In the first place, the fashion of the day required a melodramatic finish to a novel. There may be something in this, even though Stendhal had contented himself with an ending in a minor key for *Armance*. The successful novels—*Les Chouans, Notre-Dame de Paris, Indiana*—published in France about the same time as *Le Rouge et le Noir* were nothing if not sensational; and Stendhal was not indifferent to the claims of the contemporary romantic sensibility.[6] His concessions to this taste, however, though real, are seldom so conspicuous, and they must be looked for in rather subtler touches. To take but one instance, a careful reading of *Le Rouge et le Noir* allows one to detect traces of a kind of fate symbolism (admittedly more German than French in inspiration[7]) which might be held to represent a passing obeisance to romanticism. Has it ever been observed how, on three crucial occasions, the hero finds himself *in a church hung with red draperies* of one sort or another? When he enters the church at Verrières with intent to murder, 'toutes les fenêtres hautes de l'édifice étaient voilées avec des rideaux cramoisis'. The detail echoes an earlier incident which took place in the cathedral at Besançon, the

---

[5] *Politiques et moralistes*, iii. 51–54.

[6] Catalogues of the 'romantic' elements in *Le Rouge et le Noir* have been attempted by P. Bourget, *Nouvelles pages de critique et de doctrine*, i. 37; P. Jourda, 'Un centenaire romantique', *Revue des cours et conférences*, vol. xxxii (1931), pp. 308–14; J.-B. Barrère, loc. cit. 453–4; &c.

[7] Stendhal probably never read Kleist, but he did know, as we have seen, *Die Wahlverwandtschaften*.

gothic pillars of which, in celebration of the Corpus Christi holi-
day, were encased in 'une sorte d'habit de damas rouge' rising to
thirty feet; it was here, behind one of these red pillars, that Julien
saw Mme de Rênal unexpectedly for the first time since he left
Verrières. The shock of seeing him caused her to swoon away.
Both these occasions are no doubt meant to recall the experience
Julien had when he was on his way, for the first time, to the
Rênals' house. On a whim, he entered the church—later to be
the scene of his criminal attempt—and found it 'sombre et solitaire.
A l'occasion d'une fête, toutes les croisées de l'édifice avaient été
couvertes d'étoffe cramoisie. Il en résultait, aux rayons du soleil, un
effet de lumière éblouissant, du caractère le plus imposant et le
plus religieux.' Julien picks up a scrap of newspaper in the Rênal
family pew. On one side are printed the words: 'Détails de l'exécu-
tion et des derniers moments de Louis Jeanrel, exécuté à Besançon,
le...', and on the other the beginning of a sentence: 'Le premier
pas...' Julien, on leaving the church, imagines he sees blood spilt
on the floor. A closer inspection shows the illusion to have been
created by drops of holy water which shine red in the red light
which streams through the red curtains.[8] So discreet a use of
omens and portents does not suffice to make *Le Rouge et le Noir* a
schicksalsroman,[9] and perhaps, after all, bearing in mind Stendhal's
literary preferences, it might be safer to trace such features to
Shakespeare rather than to contemporary romantic literature. His
admiration of *Macbeth* would have been strong enough to tempt
him to this distant imitation.

Faguet's other suggestion is that Julien would not have been, as
Stendhal wanted him to be, a second Laffargue, a man of 'energy',
if he had not sooner or later tried to kill someone. Stendhal's conception of energy was a little more subtle than this: strength of
character does not necessarily display itself in homicide. Nevertheless, the opinion that Stendhal's invention here was not altogether
free received powerful reinforcement when the story of the
seminarist of Brangues came to light. At the time Faguet was
writing, Stendhal's incontrovertible use of this *cause célèbre* had
not yet been fully established. Some of the most authoritative of

[8] *Le Rouge et le Noir*, ii. 392; i. 339, 42–43.
[9] For a more extended discussion of the point, see S. de Sacy, 'Le Miroir sur
la grande route', *Mercure de France*, vol. cccvi (1949), pp. 64–80, and E. B. O.
Borgerhoff, 'The Anagram in *Le Rouge et le Noir*', *Modern Language Notes*,
vol. lxviii (1953), pp. 383–6.

his modern critics suppose that Stendhal's hand was in a sense forced by the necessity to dovetail Julien's career into the historical framework provided by Berthet's, even though Julien did not have Berthet's motives for murder or the character that might have led him to commit it.[1] Other apologists suppose Julien to have lapsed, at this point in the story, into a psychopathic condition, and are prepared to back up this theory with a wealth of clinical detail.[2]

In reality, it is unnecessary to suppose either that Stendhal was being clumsy or that Julien had taken leave of his senses. The incident, artistically desirable in that it provides a 'strong' climax, is also well-founded psychologically and, if the phrase may be used, poetically true.

Well-founded psychologically, because Julien's violent reaction is perfectly explainable as that of a man of spirit who has been, to use an expressive contemporary word, 'smeared'. The question is not whether Mme de Rênal's accusation is true or false; the question is not even whether Mme de Rênal believes what she has written (it emerges later that she composed the letter at the prompting of her confessor). The point, as Julien sees it, is that, in everyone's eyes but his own, the picture that has been drawn of him corresponds a shade too closely to reality. It is undeniably true that, in the two households in which he served, he 'dishonoured the woman who had most credit'. His motives were not ignoble, or not as ignoble as the letter suggests; but who will believe him, when the motives attributed to him are so plausible? The essence of a 'smear' is that it presents a portion of the truth and adds a degrading lie which nothing in what is known of the truth contradicts. Whatever protestations he may now make, and however M. de La Mole may profess to accept these protestations, Julien could never be sure that, in his heart, the Marquis will not continue to believe that he had been forced to yield his daughter to a scheming adventurer. Like Octave in this, Julien cannot endure not to be esteemed by those he respects. M. de La Mole himself, baffled by the enigmas

---

[1] L. Blum, op. cit. 86–88; J. Prévost, Les Épicuriens français, p. 95, and La Création chez Stendhal, p. 269; M. Bardèche, Stendhal romancier, p. 186; F. O'Connor, The Mirror in the Roadway, pp. 53–54; &c.

[2] H. Martineau, L'Œuvre de Stendhal, pp. 405–10; C. Liprandi, Au cœur du 'Rouge', p. 241. The chief point in favour of this explanation is that Stendhal himself speaks of 'l'état d'irritation physique et de demi-folie où il était plongé depuis son départ de Paris pour Verrières' (Le Rouge et le Noir, ii. 402).

in Julien's character, is convinced of at least one thing: 'il est impatient du mépris... [il] ne peut supporter le mépris à aucun prix.'[3]
With absolute logic, Julien chooses the only course which can
efface this suspicion, because it is the very last course of action that
would be expected of an ambitious schemer: committing murder in
broad daylight and insisting, when interrogated, that the crime
was premeditated. It is not an act of despair, for Julien has no
reason to despair: he can still marry the Marquis's daughter and
progress to the summits of society on which after all there is room
for men with far more on their conscience than the seduction, for
mercenary reasons, of their employer's daughter. It is not an act of
despair, it is not even an act of vengeance, as he pretends to Mathilde.
It is an act of self-justification. It cuts short his life, ruins his hopes,
but ensures at least that no man will think him a wily scoundrel.[4]

The poetic truth of the episode lies in the opportunity it provided
Stendhal to reveal in the end the authentic Julien, who had occasionally emerged in the early chapters, but who subsequently, in
the 'little world' of the seminary and in the 'great world' of Paris,
had drowned more and more deeply in a murk of artificiality. At
Besançon he was still an apprentice in the art of suppressing his
own personality. 'Après plusieurs mois d'application de tous les
instants, Julien avait encore l'air de *penser*. Sa façon de remuer les
yeux et de porter la bouche n'annonçait pas la foi implicite et
prête à tout croire et à tout soutenir, même par le martyre.'[5] But
the more he committed himself to his ambition, the easier he found
it to act the parts required of him: the part of the perfect secretary,
the part of the intrepid horseman, the part of the confidential
agent. M. de La Mole asks him to post himself at the door of the
Opéra, at half past eleven every evening, to observe the deportment of young men of fashion, and imitate them. He forms a close
friendship with a charming exquisite, the Chevalier de Beauvoisis,
and learns so well the art of foppishness that in London, in the
native land of dandyism, he eclipses all rivals. Later, he acts for

---

[3] *Le Rouge et le Noir*, ii. 379.
[4] This interpretation was touched on, but not satisfactorily explored, by
Mlle H. Bibas ('Le double dénouement et la morale du *Rouge*', *Revue d'histoire
littéraire de la France*, vol. xlix (1949), pp. 21–36) and, before her, by J. Decour
in his suggestive essay entitled simply 'Stendhal'; published clandestinely during
the war, these pages were reprinted after the Liberation in *La Nef*, no. 3 (1944),
pp. 8–16.
[5] *Le Rouge et le Noir*, i. 321.

weeks on end the part of devoted admirer of a pious prude in order to humiliate Mathilde and tame this notorious shrew. Stendhal, it is true, professes to admire the 'courage' with which Julien feigns indifference to his mistress and admiration for Mme de Fervaques;[6] but is this not another instance of the 'double irony', noted earlier, of the commentator who hides his deepest meaning under a screen of deceptive transparency?

All through the second part of this novel, Julien is becoming *civilized*; at the end of it, he is on the point of reaping civilization's rewards. 'My adventure is over,' he exclaims the evening he learns that he now ranks as a lieutenant of hussars; 'mon roman est fini, et à moi seul tout le mérite.'[7] He sacrifices all these rewards by a single act of *energy*, making the most uncivilized, most ungentlemanly gesture of shooting down the woman who had impugned his honour, for all the world like a Corsican cut-throat.

He is recompensed by a serenity which he had never known before, save in brief snatches in the garden at Vergy and in the mountains above Verrières. His prison-cell is at the top of a tower, with a 'superb view', and here, writes Stendhal (chapter xxxvi), 'son âme était calme... La vie n'était point ennuyeuse pour lui, il considérait toutes choses sous un nouvel aspect. Il n'avait plus d'ambition. Il pensait rarement à mademoiselle de La Mole';— instead, his mind reverts with persistence to Mme de Rênal, 'surtout pendant le silence des nuits, troublé seulement, dans ce donjon élevé, par le chant de l'orfraie'. The cry of the osprey—an unusually evocative touch which is premonitory of the zone of poetry into which Stendhal is now moving.

Chose étonnante! se disait-il, je croyais que par sa lettre à M. de La Mole elle avait détruit à jamais mon bonheur à venir, et, moins de quinze jours après la date de cette lettre, je ne songe plus à tout ce qui m'occupait alors... Deux ou trois mille livres de rente pour vivre tranquille dans un pays de montagnes comme Vergy... J'étais heureux alors... Je ne connaissais pas mon bonheur!

Julien, by the proximity of death, is suddenly aged, as though a man's age depended not on the number of years lived but on the time left for him to live.

The happiness of the dreamer takes charge, with this difference, that formerly his dreams were of the future, and of clashes with

---

[6] *Le Rouge et le Noir*, ii. 340, 342, 344.   [7] Ibid. 383.

men, triumphs over women, the battle of the sexes, and the war of the classes. Now he has done with *the others*. He shuts his ears to news of the outside world; cuts as short as he decently can his conferences with defending counsel; is impatient with his faithful friend Fouqué, who is pathetically plotting his escape from prison, and even more impatient with Mathilde. 'A vrai dire il était fatigué d'héroïsme.' He implores them not to trouble him:

— Laissez-moi ma vie idéale. Vos petites tracasseries, vos détails de la vie réelle, plus ou moins froissants pour moi, me tireraient du ciel... Que m'importent *les autres*? Mes relations avec *les autres* vont être tranchées brusquement. De grâce, ne me parlez plus de ces gens-là...

Au fait, se disait-il à lui-même, il paraît que mon destin est de mourir en rêvant...

Il est singulier pourtant que je n'aie connu l'art de jouir de la vie que depuis que j'en vois le terme si près de moi.[8]

He barely conceals from Mathilde the fact that his first love fills his thoughts. Before the trial he had been flooded by memories of incidents thought forgotten; Verrières and Vergy had completely displaced Paris in his thoughts, and he was truly happy only when, left in complete solitude, he was free to relive that more distant past. In the court room only the presence of Mme Derville has power to draw him out of his glacial indifference to the proceedings: he imagines she is there as Mme de Rênal's emissary. The following day, in the condemned cell, he is woken by Mathilde, frantic with grief and with the sense of failure. He is silent when she seeks, by entreaty, argument, and invective, to dissuade him from refusing to appeal against his sentence. He is not listening to her. Instead, his imagination shows him, in a vision of hallucinatory intensity, Mme de Rênal's bedroom in the house at Verrières, the local newspaper, with the story of his execution emblazed on its front page, as it lies on the orange counterpane, Mme de Rênal's hand crumpling its pages convulsively, the tears coursing down her face. . . .

The undeserved and crowning happiness is when Mme de Rênal, braving scandal and her husband's interdict, visits him in prison. Stendhal implies, in the few brief scenes in which he shows them together, something which a younger novelist than he could never have suggested, at any rate with such conviction: that the

[8] Ibid. 427, 435.

transcendent enchantment of love comes with the sharing of the past in recollection.

The other incidents in this culminating drama—Mathilde's intriguing, her furious and helpless jealousy, the attempted bribery of justice, Julien's appearance in court and deliberate taunting of the jurymen to ensure they should not acquit him—all these seem vaguely unreal, for we see everything with minds clouded by the powerful emanation of Julien's enraptured dream-state. Even his bitter animadversions against society, his anguished speculations on the after-life, seem less important than the granting of this unforeseen happiness. They do, however, succeed in making his death seem real, the finality absolute, even though, when he reaches the moment of death, Stendhal avails himself of his supreme resource: silence.

Jamais cette tête n'avait été aussi poétique qu'au moment où elle allait tomber. Les plus doux moments qu'il avait trouvés jadis dans les bois de Vergy revenaient en foule à sa pensée et avec une extrême énergie.

Tout se passa simplement, convenablement, et de sa part sans aucune affectation.[9]

The writer who was to narrate so scrupulously the gruesome tortures inflicted by her judges on Beatrice Cenci, says no more than this touching the execution of Julien Sorel.

He had not been allowed to refuse the consolations of religion, but had made it clear to the priest that he repented of nothing in his life. 'J'ai été ambitieux, je ne veux point me blâmer; alors, j'ai agi suivant les convenances du temps.'[1] The words are addressed, on a deeper level, by Stendhal to the reader. If Julien was for most of his life misguided it is the ethos of his age that should be blamed. Napoleon is a symbol, a pretext, no more. The historical moment called for the kind of single-minded, resolute *arrivisme* that Julien did his best to display. One way or another, betrayal was inescapable: Julien's choice lay between betraying his soul through hardness and betraying his spirit through softness. Had he remained at Verrières, had he accepted the profitable partnership which Fouqué offered him in his timber business, he would perhaps have been happy, but he would not have been a hero; it is required of Aeneas that he leave Carthage and her queen, even though this Aeneas goes to found no new city. It would be naïve to write down *Le*

⁹ *Le Rouge et le Noir*, ii. 492.   ¹ Ibid. 490.

Rouge et le Noir as a sermon on the folly of human ambitions; for things could not have been otherwise. But it is obviously far more than a piece of social satire; though it might not be altogether misplaced to speak of it as a piece of sublimated social history. Stendhal had perhaps something of the sort in mind when he gave his novel the sub-title *Chronique du XIXe siècle*.

But any formula seems intolerably constricted. 'Every time you discuss Stendhal, you are left with the impression that you have said nothing at all, that he has eluded you, and that everything remains to be said. In the end you have to resign yourself and restore him to his unpredictable and miraculous utterance.'[2] *Le Rouge et le Noir* acts, in its own way, as Stendhal does in his larger fashion: the book, and the man, defy criticism, if criticism is the art of throwing a net of convincing approximations over the protean masterpiece or artist. It is not criticism merely to marvel. But in that case criticism is here powerless, for in the last resort there is nothing we can do but marvel at the sheer intellectual brilliance with which Stendhal has connected his several explosive themes in an ordered system, presented the complex totality lucidly and exhaustively, and irradiated the whole with that strange stark poetry which is peculiarly his own.

[2] J. P. Richard, *Littérature et sensation*, p. 116.

V ⁎ THE UNHEROIC HERO

I N the autumn of 1830, even before *Le Rouge et le Noir* was on display in the Paris bookshops, Henri Beyle found himself once more a paid servant of the government: the government not of imperial France now, but of a constitutional monarch who preferred an umbrella to a sabre and was rumoured to indulge in an occasional flutter on the stock market: 'le plus fripon des Kings', Stendhal called him privately. The new consul at Civitavecchia found his duties not onerous but excessively tedious; the hot little seaport was the dullest hole. True, Rome was not far away and he had a number of good friends in Rome. But too many pleasure trips to the capital brought sharply worded reprimands from the authorities in Paris. Complaints of the grey monotony of his existence recur with desolating regularity in Stendhal's private correspondence during these years; they were veiled complaints because letters might be read in transit and an incautious phrase, deciphered by an enemy, might rob him of the post which, however hated, did at least give him the wherewithal to eat and a modicum of consideration among his fellows. So he exhaled his dissatisfaction in the third person and in a more illegible scrawl even than was his habit. 'L'ennui étouffe ce pauvre garçon; il était cent fois plus heureux no. 71 [Stendhal's Paris address had been, before he left for Italy, 71 rue de Richelieu]; il lui aurait fallu cinquante louis de rente de plus et non pas dix mille francs à manger bêtement, par exemple en voitures qu'il faut avoir ici de certains jours. Enfin il meurt d'ennui...' He had some leave due in 1833 but, for fear of what might happen in his absence (his deputy at Civitavecchia was a sly and envious Levantine), hesitated about spending it in Paris, 'quoique j'aie soif d'une conversation qui soit autre chose qu'une cérémonie. Il ne m'est plus donné d'entendre un mot qui me surprenne...'[1] The talk that habitually goes on around him sends him to sleep, and he wakes up to utter a string of incongruities, to the great scandal of the company he is in.

[1] *Correspondance*, viii. 57, 69.

He went on leave, however, in spite of his misgivings; but on his return to the Papal States it needed only a few months of the old routine to bring on his discontent once more.

Je commence à être bien las du métier… Que sert de pouvoir jouer le deuxième rôle à Abeille [*Abeille*, in Stendhal's private code, stood for Civitavecchia], si le bavardage important, l'air *important*, la façon grave de parler des occupations du matin et de la correspondance du dernier courrier, sont mon *horreur*? Rien ne me semble bête, au monde, comme la gravité… Mourrai-je étouffé par les bêtes? Il y a grande apparence. Je suis aimé, considéré, j'ai eu le meilleur morceau d'un poisson de quatorze livres, le meilleur de son genre [this was at a dinner given in his honour the previous day]… mais je crève d'ennui.

He had stayed up till one in the morning reading Dante, but even Dante affords no solace—the poem is too familiar to charm him any more.[2]

During this brief snatch of home leave in 1833 Stendhal had been asked by an old friend, Mme Jules Gaulthier, to look through a novel she had written. It is to be hoped the perusal of the manuscript succeeded for a few days in distracting the corpulent consul from his chronic spleen. The lady had asked for criticism, and Stendhal criticized, firmly but not unkindly. Most of his strictures bore on style. Mme Gaulthier was advised to delete at least fifty superlatives from each chapter; to write 'fetch me my horse' instead of 'draw hither with my steed'; and to clear her head of pretentious phraseology by reading Marivaux's *Vie de Marianne* and Mérimée's *Chronique de Charles IX*. The two letters that contain Stendhal's comments[3] permit certain deductions to be made about the contents of Mme Gaulthier's novel (it was never published, and the paper it was written on went no doubt to kindle fires in winters now long fled). The title she had chosen was *Le Lieutenant*; Stendhal suggested, as being more explicit: *Leuwen or the Student sent down from the École Polytechnique*. It is reasonable to suppose, then, that her hero Leuwen, having had his studies abruptly terminated at this famous school which Stendhal had been intended to enter in 1799, took a commission in the regular army. Next, Stendhal speaks of 'l'amitié ou la liaison d'Olivier pour Edmond', and adds (one of the few compliments he paid Mme Gaulthier): 'Le caractère d'Edmond, ou l'*académicien futur*, est

---

[2] Ibid. 346–8.
[3] 4 May and 8 November 1834: *Correspondance*, viii. 270–2, and ix. 31–33.

ce qu'il y a de plus neuf dans *Le Lieutenant*.' Finally, Mme Gaulthier's hero, this ex-polytechnician regimental officer Olivier Leuwen, was to fall in love. This detail emerges from a passing admonishment: 'Ne jamais dire: "La passion brûlante d'Olivier pour Hélène." Le pauvre romancier doit tâcher de faire croire à la *passion brûlante*, mais ne jamais la nommer: cela est contre la pudeur.'

It is known that Stendhal began writing his novel *Lucien Leuwen* only a few days after sending the first of these letters to Mme Gaulthier. All the features of Mme Gaulthier's story which may be deduced from his comments are reproduced in the first part of *Lucien Leuwen*: Lucien disobeys an order confining students of the Polytechnique to their quarters during a period of popular unrest in Paris and is in consequence expelled; he is made second lieutenant in the 27th Lancers; he has a close friend Ernest Dévelroy whose ambition is to be elected to the Academy of Sciences; and of course he falls in love. Given all this, the conclusion is almost inescapable: Stendhal, notoriously ungifted for the invention of plot, appropriated Mme Gaulthier's story, having by the severity of his criticisms taken the preliminary precaution of deterring her from publishing on her own account. Admittedly the points of contact that can be established are few, and touch on relatively minor matters, all to do with the initial situation. Perhaps the most important factor in Lucien's destiny is that he is the only son of a millionaire, and we have no means of knowing whether this idea came to him from Mme Gaulthier or not. Judging from the number of different alternative plans that Stendhal drew up for later developments in the plot, one would be disposed to agree with Martineau that *Le Lieutenant* can have been at most a 'springboard' for his imagination.[4]

The process by which Stendhal arrived at the starting-point of *Lucien Leuwen* seems thus as satisfactorily established as one could hope. But there is one other circumstance which raises an awkward doubt about the interpretation of these events.

Eight years previously Stendhal had published the second of his two pamphlets *Racine et Shakspeare*: the work was a light-hearted discussion, part theoretical, part polemical, about the type of play most suitable for putting on the stage in 1826. At one point Stendhal introduces a simile of unusual elaboration to paint the state of

---

[4] *L'Œuvre de Stendhal*, p. 454.

mind of people of taste and sensibility, who have never seen any
tragedy acted which did not conform strictly to the conventions of
seventeenth-century drama, and whose eyes are suddenly opened to
the needlessness of these conventions. When this revelation is
vouchsafed them,

beaucoup de gens sincères avec eux-mêmes, et qui croyaient leur âme
fermée à la poésie, respirent; pour la trop aimer, ils croyaient ne pas
l'aimer. C'est ainsi qu'un jeune homme à qui le ciel a donné quelque
délicatesse d'âme, si le hasard le fait sous-lieutenant et le jette à sa garnison, dans la société de certaines femmes, croit de bonne foi, en voyant
les succès de ses camarades et le genre de leurs plaisirs, être insensible
à l'amour. Un jour enfin le hasard le présente à une femme simple,
naturelle, honnête, digne d'être aimée, et il sent qu'il a un cœur.[5]

This passage hardly needs modification to become a synopsis
of Lucien's adventures in the first volume of the novel. 'Délicatesse d'âme' he has in good measure. Influence secures him an
army commission and in the third chapter Lucien is shown riding
with his brother officers to the garrison town of Nancy where he is
to be stationed. We have already seen how he believed himself to
be proof against love;[6] Mme de Chasteller is precisely the 'femme
simple, naturelle, honnête' who will force him to confess himself
mistaken.

Students of Stendhal have long been aware of the existence of
this evident forecast of *Lucien Leuwen*, unaccountably turning up
in a treatise on romanticism published years before he read Mme
Jules Gaulthier's still-born novel *Le Lieutenant*. The two facts
have been registered; no attempt has been made to link them. Any
such attempt must, of course, be conjectural in the extreme—
which is no reason why it should not be made.

It was on 24 February 1810 that Stendhal was introduced to the
two La Bergerie sisters, the younger of whom bore the epicene
name Jules. He found them both 'less Raphaelesque' than he had
been led to suppose by his old school friend Louis Crozet, who had
been passionately in love with the elder, Blanche. But even at this
date, Stendhal admitted to a preference for Jules—'mais son mérite
est encore un peut-être à mes yeux'[7] (she was twenty and on the

[5] *Racine et Shakspeare*, pp. 111–12.
[6] See above, p. 43.
[7] *Journal*, iii. 273. See also H. Martineau, *Petit dictionnaire stendhalien*,
pp. 238–9.

verge of marriage). The meeting had no immediate sequel and it was not until around 1826 that Stendhal began a regular exchange of letters with Jules, now the wife of a tax official. It is more than likely that his correspondent was at this time reading whatever he published, and read, therefore, this second part of *Racine et Shakspeare* which came out precisely in 1826. And it is at any rate within the bounds of possibility that the sketch of the young second lieutenant who believes himself to be cold-hearted and undergoes a conversion, was marked by Mme Gaulthier, pondered on, and eventually expanded into the story of Olivier Leuwen and Hélène.[8] If this is admitted, then it must be granted that in appropriating *Le Lieutenant* in so cavalier a fashion, Stendhal was doing no more than reaping what he had sowed, and *Lucien Leuwen* would be that exception among his works, a story invented for all intents and purposes by himself.

It was never published during his lifetime. So long as the Orleanist régime, on which he depended for his salary, endured, he could not have brought it out without the most savage emasculation of the political satire which is particularly violent in the second part.[9] Perhaps the knowledge that it could probably appear only after his death discouraged Stendhal from persevering with the labour of revision. He dictated from his own corrected manuscript the first seventeen chapters and part of the eighteenth; this fair copy, which breaks off in the middle of the episode of the Countess de Commercy's ball, was published with the title *Le Chasseur vert* by Stendhal's executor, Romain Colomb, in a volume of

---

[8] The curious surname Leuwen may too have been originally taken by Mme Gaulthier from Stendhal. There is, in *Le Rouge et le Noir*, an episodic figure of the name of Liéven, 'ancien lieutenant du 96ᵉ', who agrees to act as Julien's second in his duel with M. de Beauvoisis. The same name, Liéven, was given to the hero of Stendhal's short story *Le Philtre*, 'jeune lieutenant du 96ᵉ régiment en garnison à Bordeaux'; Mme Gaulthier could have read *Le Philtre* in the *Revue des Deux Mondes* in 1830. In the manuscript of Stendhal's novel, Leuwen is occasionally spelt Lieven.

[9] 'Tant que pour vivre je serai obligé de servir le Budget je ne pourrai print it, car ce que le Budget déteste le plus, c'est qu'on fasse semblant d'avoir des idées.' The statement is made in a will which Stendhal dated from Rome, 17 Feb. 1835 (*Mélanges intimes et Marginalia*, i. 29–32); by the 'Budget' he means, of course, the Treasury. He bequeathed the manuscript to his sister Pauline, but not without some trepidation lest, having lapsed into piety, she consign it to the flames. *Tempora mutantur*. He recommended it should be entrusted to some professional writer for revision of the style, but not to Balzac at any price; Mérimée would be the man for the job, were it not that Mérimée 'scarcely deigns to write his own works . . .'.

Nouvelles inédites issued in 1855. Later editors have added to this fragment their decipherment of the remainder of the manuscript, all in Stendhal's crabbed hand, full of deletions, alternative readings, marginal comments, and little crosses against the words he intended to change. No doubt the day will come when the piety of *stendhaliens* will require the facsimile publication of these five volumes, preserved at Grenoble: they constitute a unique source of information not only about the creative process in Stendhal, but even about such fascinating trivia as his idiosyncratic pronunciation of certain words, preserved in the mis-spellings of the amanuensis.[1]

The original design allowed for three parts: the first set in Nancy, the second in Paris, the third in Rome. The book as we have it ends with Lucien's departure for Italy to take up his post as secretary in the French embassy at Rome. Here the intention was that Lucien should start an intrigue with the ambassador's wife, incur her enmity, and lose his post through her machinations. Reduced to poverty, he would finally meet Mme de Chasteller again and marry her.[2] On 28 April 1835, after he had been working on the novel for rather less than a year,[3] Stendhal decided to suppress the third part. (This was not indolence: he recognized the unwisdom of introducing a bevy of new characters two-thirds of the way through the novel.) *Lucien Leuwen* ends, therefore, a little in the air for most tastes. Stendhal certainly intended to engineer the reunion of the lovers at the end, after Lucien has learned that his suspicions of Mme de Chasteller's virtue were outrageously unjust. But he never settled how this consummation was to be achieved. Mme de Chasteller's last appearance is in chapter xli; the novel stops at chapter lxviii. In the interval she continues, though absent, to occupy Lucien's thoughts, and Stendhal traces delicately the process by which the harsh indignation of the betrayed lover is replaced by softer moods of understanding, forgiveness, and idealization until finally Mme de Chasteller becomes the object of a sentimental cult, to the point that when Lucien takes another

---

[1] See A. Rousseaux, *Le Monde classique*, pp. 145 et seq.

[2] This is the gist of the various plans reprinted in *Mélanges intimes et Marginalia*, ii. 210, 214–15, 244–5.

[3] It was on the night of 8/9 May 1834, between 11.30 p.m. and 1.30 a.m., that Stendhal gave up the idea of correcting his friend's novel and decided 'de ne pas send it to Mme Jules, mais d'en make un opus'. The excuse he gave himself is as tortuous as the jargon in which he recorded this momentous decision: 'Avec cette lady, cela tomberait rapidement dans le *non lu* des cabinets littéraires pour femmes de chambre' (*Mélanges intimes et Marginalia*, ii. 214).

mistress Stendhal compares him, with characteristic irreverence, to St. Peter denying the Christ. It may be ventured that this transmutation of an unhappy love-affair into a poignant and ennobling memory is more touching, and even more true to life, than would have been the conventional happy ending that Stendhal contemplated, with all misapprehensions banished and a humdrum marriage indemnifying the lovers for their past tribulations.

Such an ending would, besides, have been wildly uncharacteristic of Stendhal. It is, nevertheless, significant of his intentions in this novel that Lucien, alone among his heroes, is suffered to survive. Octave commits suicide, Julien is beheaded, Fabrice, in his charterhouse, outlives Clélia by less than a year. Mina de Vanghel and Hélène di Campireali both stab themselves, and Lamiel, had that novel been finished, would have perished in a great fire which she herself had lit. Only Lucien does not die. Certain critics find it hard to forgive him this. They accuse him of acquiescing in infamy—the supposed infamy of Mme de Chasteller, the real infamy of the government of Louis-Philippe which he consents to serve.

Infamy and shame, this is what Lucien feels, in a world in which he cannot succeed in isolating himself, in which he cannot live a life divorced from politics, a life of the imagination, sincere and human, as he would wish. This is not granted him. Neither is it granted to Julien or to Fabrice, but they are strong enough to accept imprisonment and death, or rather, to choose prison, the cloister, and death; this is their way of handing back their ticket of admission, as Ivan Karamazov will express it later, the only way that Stendhal the pessimist thought a man could keep his humanity and his freedom. It is beyond Lucien to die. He breaks down and weeps; bitter tears, salt tears, and will not be comforted.[4]

Lucien, it must be confessed, is not well liked by Stendhal's critics. In his study *The Unheroic Hero* Raymond Giraud chooses three fictional characters to illustrate his subject: Balzac's César Birotteau, Flaubert's Frédéric Moreau, and Lucien Leuwen. Giraud acknowledges that Lucien is worthy to be called 'hero' in that he is a man of sensibility and a man of honour; he is 'unheroic' by the force of circumstances, since his good qualities can find no employment in the situation in which he finds himself. Mario

---

[4] L. Maranini, *Visione e personaggio secondo Flaubert ed altri studi francesi*, p. 143. In her last sentence, the critic is referring to Lucien's fit of crying after the mud-throwing episode at Blois (chapter xlix).

Bonfantini accords Lucien 'il carattere assai poco eroico'; even before he is launched on his career Lucien 'has already betrayed, not his caste, but his ideals; and not out of an understandable and human desire to rise, like Julien . . . but out of pure baseness, out of pusillanimity when faced with the difficulties which it should have been his business to overcome and with the solicitations of an over-affectionate family'.[5] Finally, the whole argument of Gilbert Durand's essay, 'Lucien Leuwen ou l'héroïsme à l'envers',[6] is that Lucien is *par excellence* the unheroic hero, the hero who is the reverse of heroic, and that for that very reason Stendhal realized his novel was a failure and left it unfinished. Durand understands the word 'heroic' in the sense in which it is applied to the protagonists of all the myths, legends, and epics of folklore and early literature.

The central question which it is proposed to examine in this chapter is whether this deprecatory view of Lucien, which a fair body of informed criticism has adopted, is the proper one.

The obvious starting-point is a comparison with the central figure of the preceding novel. Lucien Leuwen and Julien Sorel have one thing in common: they are of an age. Calculation from the dates and allusions to contemporary events in the novels shows that they must both have been born around 1808. In other words, they belong to a generation for whom Napoleon was a captive and exiled Titan, not the invincible general or all-powerful emperor. This is what marks them off from Fabrice who was just old enough to have served in Napoleon's last battle.

Lucien's attitude to Napoleon is, however, as unlike Julien's as it could be. It is arguable that the difference has something to do with the fact that Lucien's studies have been in the field of applied mathematics, while Julien received his training in theology. Julien is more at home with cults. Temperamentally, too, Lucien is less of a dreamer than Julien, and far too hard-headed to indulge in any kind of mythopoeia: it never occurs to him to take Napoleon as a model. He is not unresponsive to the stirring epic that closed when he was still a small boy. 'Les récits de la vie du jeune général Bonaparte, vainqueur au pont d'Arcole, me transportent; c'est pour moi Homère, le Tasse, et cent fois mieux encore.'[7] But his

---

[5] M. Bonfantini, *Stendhal e il realismo*, pp. 176–7.
[6] *Stendhal Club*, no. 3 (1959), pp. 201–25.
[7] *Lucien Leuwen*, i. 114.

good sense also shows him that were a new Napoleon to arise, to restore the military prestige of France, the first casualty would be civil liberties; and the journalist who questioned the veracity of a dispatch from the front would be shot as a traitor. A little wire-pulling on his father's part, and Lucien is commissioned in the Lancers: he enters, at a nod, the career that Julien was forced to renounce early on with a heavy heart. But Lucien joins the army merely to give himself some occupation. He is young enough to indulge momentarily in day-dreams about the romance of war; he sees himself wounded and being tended by a Swabian village lass. But he knows this to be an idle fancy (for Fabrice, it will be reality, except that the girl, Aniken, is Flemish not Swabian). And in a trice he wakes up to reality and predicts for himself a future which is, point by point, realized in the first part of the novel: 'Je deviendrai un pilier du café militaire dans la triste garnison d'une petite ville mal pavée; j'aurai, pour mes plaisirs du soir, des parties de billard et des bouteilles de bière, et quelquefois le matin, la guerre aux tronçons de choux, contre de sales ouvriers mourant de faim.'[8] Vigny's *Servitude et grandeur militaires*, a book strictly contemporary with *Lucien Leuwen*, is full of variations, unrelieved, however, by Stendhal's wry humour, on this theme of the plight of the peace-time soldier whose only function is to suppress the occasional proletarian riot.

Lucien is, then, born too late, but no more than Julien. If Julien is, all considered, less dissatisfied, it is because he has a purpose in life: to get to the top. Lucien is already at the top; he has everything, intelligence, good looks, money, an indulgent father who will open for him whatever doors he wants opened. Hence, of course, his frustrated dissatisfaction, his uncertainty. What has he done to deserve these privileges?

La Chartreuse de Parme presents a hero no less privileged—well born, handsome, a young charmer whom no man can dislike and no woman resist, who has the most powerful of patrons to smooth the path of his rather languid ambition. Yet Fabrice is undisturbed by the moral problem that torments Lucien: of all Stendhal's heroes, he is the very image of the happy man.

One reason we have touched on already: Fabrice was not born too late—at sixteen he heard the cannon of Waterloo and for the rest of his life, for better or for worse, he will be the man who bore

[8] *Lucien Leuwen*, i. 21.

arms under Napoleon. The importance of this, however, is more symbolic than psychological. Fundamentally, the great advantage that Fabrice possesses over Lucien is that he is not burdened with Lucien's conscience. His conscience performs the same function for Lucien as his ambition for Julien: it makes him interesting to the reader, which, as we have seen, is what Stendhal principally demanded of the hero of a novel; but it also makes him unhappy, not with Julien's divine discontent, but with a bitter and fretful unhappiness.

Lucien Leuwen is, as Jean Prévost observed, a book 'steeped in moral concerns';[9] the same critic remarks how certain minor characters, Ernest Dévelroy, Coffe, perform the function of an 'external conscience' for the hero. The 'conscience' that Dévelroy embodies, however, is social rather than moral. This ambitious young prig, who tries to further his own career by shameless toadyism, reads Lucien lectures on his indolence, his indifference to what people of consequence think of him, his refusal to indulge in the play-acting that society requires of a young man who has still to make his mark. Dévelroy calls his cousin 'un enfant, et, qui pis est, un enfant content'. He reproaches him with his dependence on his father, and affects high indignation when Lucien expresses disgust at the 'vileness' of a certain time-serving, boorish, sponging lieutenant-colonel. 'N'as-tu pas de vergogne, à ton âge, de n'être pas en état de gagner la valeur d'un cigare?... Vil ou non, il t'est mille fois supérieur; il a agi et tu n'as rien fait... M. Filloteau [the colonel in question] fait peut-être vivre son père, vieux paysan; et toi, ton père te fait vivre.'[1]

Through Dévelroy speaks the querulous voice of the quint-essential middle-class ethos. Fortunately we hear little more of him after he has done Lucien the disservice, in these first chapters, of pushing him into the army where no one is under the illusion he is living on his pay: his first action after joining his regiment is to purchase the most expensive horse in Nancy, his second, to rent the lodgings occupied by the colonel of the battalion they are relieving. His father's cheques keep him going as before. Why on earth, asks the editor of the local left-wing paper with whom Lucien strikes up a friendship, why on earth did you join the army? Lucien's answer is evidence of his lucidity, if not of his strength of character:

[9] *La Création chez Stendhal*, p. 295.   [1] *Lucien Leuwen*, i. 15, 25.

Pour me mettre en état de gagner quatre-vingt-dix-neuf francs par mois et ma propre estime, j'ai quitté une ville où je passais mon temps fort agréablement.

— Qui vous y forçait?

— Je me suis jeté de ma pleine volonté dans cet enfer.

— Eh bien! sortez-en et fuyez.

— Paris est maintenant gâté pour moi; je n'y serais plus, en y retournant, ce que j'étais avant d'avoir revêtu ce fatal habit vert: un jeune homme qui peut-être un jour sera quelque chose. On verrait en moi un homme incapable d'être rien, même sous-lieutenant.

— Que vous importe l'opinion des autres, si, au fond, vous vous amusez?

— Hélas! j'ai une vanité que vous, mon sage ami, ne pouvez comprendre; ma position serait intolérable; je ne pourrais répondre à certaines plaisanteries...[2]

Never again will Lucien be the giddy youth who had gaily answered his cousin's admonishments by proclaiming his indifference to the judgements of society. Having once undertaken to prove to himself that he could serve his country as well as the next man, Lucien is caught: his *vanity* will not allow him to back down.

The fruit of vanity is joylessness, and his first few weeks of army life are intensely miserable. Lucien takes himself very seriously, will never laugh at himself or suffer another to laugh at his expense. One of the few talents he prides himself on is his ability to manage a horse; when, on his first arrival at Nancy, he is thrown in front of his troop, the mortification he feels is altogether disproportionate to the gravity of his misadventure. 'Notre héros', observes Stendhal at this point, 'subissait les conséquences de cette éducation de Paris, qui ne sait que développer la vanité, triste partage des fils de gens riches.' The following day, Lucien is inducted into his regiment with the usual solemn mummery. He comports himself with the most icy self-possession, but his anxiety lest a false move provoke a single smile reduces the whole ceremony to a difficult but empty piece of drill. Though patriotic enough, he is too self-conscious to respond to the symbolic significance of this initiation into the honourable profession of arms; and so, when the parade is over, he feels mortally depressed. 'N'eût-il pas mieux valu', asks Stendhal, 'être fou de bonheur, comme l'eût été, dans la position de Lucien, un jeune homme de province, dont l'éducation n'eût pas coûté cent mille francs?'[3] As Julien would have been.

[2] *Lucien Leuwen*, i. 129.   [3] Ibid. 80, 98.

Vanity forbids him to take any part in the pleasures normal to his age. Fear lest this vanity should be ruffled by their banter makes him treat his fellow officers with frigid politeness, and they respond in kind. Lucien, left to himself, is bored to tears. It is hereabouts that Stendhal compares him to 'un jeune protestant. L'abandon était rare chez lui;... une vanité puérile, une crainte extrême et continue de manquer aux mille petites règles établies par notre civilisation, occupait la place de tous les goûts impétueux qui, sous Charles IX, agitaient le cœur d'un jeune Français.'[4] Lucien's vanity is *puérile*. As Dévelroy had said and as Stendhal insists, time after time, he is still a child.

Le lecteur est supplié de ne pas le prendre tout à fait pour un sot: ce cœur était bien jeune encore. — Lucien était jeune, c'est-à-dire injuste. Fort de ses loyales intentions, il croyait tout voir, et n'avait pas encore vu le quart des choses de la vie. — Le lecteur bénévole est prié de considérer que notre héros est fort jeune, fort neuf et dénué de toute expérience... C'était à cette époque une âme naïve et s'ignorant elle-même;... il ne savait pas ce qu'il serait un jour.[5]

Stendhal had made the same vague prophecy of future development with regard to Julien, but at the end, not at the beginning, of *Le Rouge et le Noir*. 'Il était encore bien jeune; mais, suivant moi, ce fut une belle plante. Au lieu de marcher du tendre au rusé, comme la plupart des hommes, l'âge lui eût donné la bonté facile à s'attendrir, il se fût guéri d'une méfiance folle... Mais à quoi bon ces vaines prédictions?'[6] For Julien is to die at twenty-three. Lucien, however, has a future and this fact accounts for the care with which the novelist defines his point of departure and tracks his progress, a progress which, morally at least, follows the contours of the author's own. With *Lucien Leuwen* Stendhal came nearest to writing a fictional autobiography, and it is not irrelevant to note that when he abandoned the novel, in November 1835, it was to set to work immediately on his autobiography proper, the *Vie de Henri Brulard*, which was initially conceived as a voyage of self-discovery. 'Je me suis dit: je devrais écrire ma vie, je saurai peut-être enfin, quand cela sera fini dans deux ou trois ans, ce que j'ai été, gai ou triste, homme d'esprit ou sot, homme de courage ou peureux, et enfin au total heureux ou malheureux.'[7] Lucien is nagged by the same demon of self-questioning. 'Mais, en vérité, je ne sais pas ce

---

[4] Ibid. 120.
[5] Ibid. 124, 188, 215–16.
[6] *Le Rouge et le Noir*, ii. 410–11.
[7] *Vie de Henri Brulard*, i. 6.

que je suis, et je donnerais beaucoup à qui pourrait me le dire.'
On his return from his mission to Caen (in the second part of the
novel) he is not in the least concerned how his immediate chief,
the Minister for the Interior, will regard his failure to secure the
election of the government's nominee, but immensely concerned
to know what his handling of the business has taught him about
himself. 'Quelle opinion dois-je avoir de moi-même?' he asks his
parents, after telling them the whole story. 'Ai-je quelque valeur,
voilà ce que je vous demande.'[8] Lucien steers no fixed course, but
is for ever taking his bearings; in this quite unlike his predecessor
Julien, but very like his creator Henri Beyle.

There are episodes, particularly in the first part of *Lucien
Leuwen*, which clearly transpose certain events in Beyle's life. The
circumstances in which Lucien's popularity declines among the
gentlefolk at Nancy recall how Beyle found himself ostracized at
Milan, in 1820-1, when the absurd story got about that he was an
agent of the French government; the Abbé Rey (whom Lucien
had tartly snubbed for refusing church burial to a freethinking
cobbler) spreads the rumour that Lucien has been dispatched to
Nancy by the authorities to report on the political opinions of the
local notabilities. Similarly the scheme concocted by Sanréal, Roller,
and their friends to rid the town of Lucien by forcing him to fight
a succession of duels, may be a reminiscence of a similar threat
to Stendhal's life made in 1816 by a number of Bonapartists at
Grenoble, who regarded him as a deserter because he had stayed
abroad during the 'Hundred Days'.[9]

Numerous are the observations on Lucien's character which
repeat Stendhal's reflections on his own. M. Leuwen is constantly warning his son against taking an exaggerated view of the
importance of men and affairs: 'Tu fais des héros, en bien ou en
mal, de tous tes interlocuteurs. *Tu tends tes filets trop haut*, comme
dit Thucydide des Béotiens.'[1] The same expression was, apparently,
used of Beyle by his friend Fiore.[2] More than any other of

---

[8] *Lucien Leuwen*, ii. 76; iii. 210.

[9] A biographical detail revealed by F. Vermale, 'Stendhal six mois après
l'affaire Didier', *Petite Revue des bibliophiles dauphinois*, vol. iv, no. 6 (1940-2),
pp. 395-406.

[1] *Lucien Leuwen*, i. 110. Coffe makes an identical remark after taking Lucien
to task for talking over the heads of a group of electors at Caen: 'Vous avez eu
cent fois trop d'esprit pour ces animaux-là. *Vous tendez vos filets trop haut*' (ibid.
iii. 89-90).

[2] 'Encore aujourd'hui, l'excellent Fiore (condamné à mort à Naples en 1800)

Stendhal's heroes, Lucien shares his creator's highly indeterminate and, in the last resort, negative political outlook. Lucien arrives at Nancy with a vague reputation for republicanism: he owes this to the circumstances in which he was expelled from the École Polytechnique. Overtures are made to him anonymously by a group of seditious warrant-officers; but regretfully, Lucien decides he cannot support them. There are too few of their persuasion; they would do better to emigrate to the land of the free. He, Lucien, would not accompany them. 'Je m'ennuierais en Amérique, au milieu d'hommes parfaitement justes et raisonnables, si l'on veut, mais grossiers, mais ne songeant qu'aux *dollars*... Ce pays modèle me semble le triomphe de la médiocrité sotte et égoïste...'[3] At that period, when every country of any importance in the Old World was ruled by an absolute or constitutional monarch, the United States was the cynosure of all republicans in Europe, and in denigrating it, Lucien is implicitly repudiating republicanism. His objections are identical with those Stendhal in his other writings constantly puts forward as his own opinion. Firstly, American society being wholly geared to self-enrichment, the arts, including the social art of graceful conversation, are neglected. Secondly, where every man is a voter, no man is free. 'A New-York, la charrette gouvernative est tombée dans l'ornière opposée à la nôtre. Le suffrage universel règne en tyran, et en tyran aux mains sales. Si je ne plais pas à mon cordonnier, il répand sur mon compte une calomnie qui me fâche, et il faut que je flatte mon cordonnier.'[4] And keeping one's shoemaker sweet is not only difficult but can be, as Sydney Smith said of poverty, 'confoundedly inconvenient'.

me dit: "Vous tendez vos filets trop haut" (Thucydide)' (*Vie de Henri Brulard*, i. 173). The attribution to Thucydides appears to be spurious, and the source of the expression has never been discovered. It is more important to know what Stendhal meant by it. The clue may be the following marginal note (undated, but probably belonging to the year 1814): 'Un homme tendait un filet, il s'étonnait de n'y prendre que des grives. C'est que quand les aigles y entrent, lui dit-on, ils le déchirent et en sortent' (*Mélanges intimes et Marginalia*, i. 296).

[3] *Lucien Leuwen*, i. 113–15.
[4] Ibid. iii. 369. Stendhal's anti-American prejudices, visible in all his writings from the *Promenades dans Rome* onwards, were epitomized in a review of Basil Hall's *Travels in North America*, published in *Le National*, 10 Mar. 1830, in which he talks glibly of 'les centaines de volumes que j'ai parcourus, en bâillant, afin de me faire une idée de la seule véritable république qui marche bien au XIXe siècle' (*Mélanges de littérature*, iii. 319). While writing *Lucien Leuwen*, he appears to have perused the first part of Tocqueville's *La Démocratie en Amérique* which came out in 1835; it did not alter his preconceived views.

On the other hand, Lucien reveals himself only a lukewarm supporter of the régime he serves, judging it to be a plutocracy entirely lacking in dignity. 'Qu'est-ce qu'on estime dans le monde que j'ai entrevu? L'homme qui a réuni quelques millions ou qui achète un journal et se fait prôner pendant huit ou dix ans de suite... Mais, d'un autre côté, faire la cour aux hommes du peuple, comme il est de nécessité en Amérique, est au-dessus de mes forces.'[5] Just as Stendhal himself was at heart an aristocrat, however much his reason inclined him to democratic principles,[6] so too Lucien is tempted to conclude in favour of a chimerical restoration of the *ancien régime*. 'Je ne puis vivre avec des hommes incapables d'idées fines, si vertueux qu'ils soient; je préférerais cent fois les mœurs élégantes d'une cour corrompue. Washington m'eût ennuyé à la mort, et j'aime mieux me trouver dans le même salon que M. de Talleyrand. Donc, la sensation de l'estime n'est pas tout pour moi; j'ai besoin des plaisirs donnés par une ancienne civilisation...'[7] And Lucien has no scruples and he experiences no inner conflict even when he decides, since there is no other passport to the drawing-rooms of the local nobility, to feign attachment to the cause of the exiled royal family and to pretend to desire the re-establishment of the privileges of the aristocracy. He advertises his conversion by attending mass at a fashionable church and subscribing handsomely to a fashionable charity.

The complacency with which Stendhal portrays the various decayed or still sprightly ladies and gentlemen of ancient lineage whose acquaintance Lucien is thereupon privileged to make, betrays in itself where his sympathies lie—his human if not his political sympathies. His hero is introduced first to the dowager Comtesse de Commercy who, in spite of her great age, sits very upright and wears lace which, as Lucien notes with satisfaction, is not yellow. She is restrained in gesture and soft in speech: a relic, he decides, of the age of politeness. She invites him back to dinner, where he meets a delightful *ménage à trois*; the Marquis d'Hocquincourt,

[5] *Lucien Leuwen*, i. 116–17.

[6] Cf. *Rome, Naples et Florence*, ii. 147–8: 'J'ai cru jusqu'à ces derniers temps détester les aristocrates; mon cœur croyait sincèrement marcher comme ma tête. Le banquier R*** me dit un jour: "Je vois chez vous un élément aristocratique." J'aurais juré d'en être à mille lieues. Je me suis en effet trouvé cette maladie: chercher à me corriger eût été duperie... Je me soumets à mon penchant aristocratique, après avoir déclamé dix ans, et de bonne foi, contre toute aristocratie.'

[7] *Lucien Leuwen*, i. 114.

his lady, and her *cavaliere servente* M. Antin. Mme d'Hocquincourt has everything to commend her in Lucien's eyes: she is
beautiful, pleasure-loving, nonchalant, and devoid of all hypocrisy. At the same table he meets Théodelinde de Serpierre, who
is plain and ill dressed, but sensible and unaffected, and, to Lucien's
surprise, not sharp-tongued. She is the eldest of six girls; Lucien
meets the rest of the family while paying duty visits. M. de Serpierre, an old royalist officer reduced to near-penury, makes the
best of impressions because he is so clearly not bent on making
any sort of impression. Then there is the Marquise de Puylaurens,
who had spent her youth (she is now in her mid-thirties) at the
court of Charles X. An inimitable *raconteuse*, vivacious yet urbane,
she spares no one but is universally liked. The story of how at
church she rebuffed a priest who ventured to remonstrate with her
for talking too loud during divine service illustrates not only the
lady's imperturbable *hauteur* but also a disrespect of the clergy
which smacks more of the golden age of Louis le Bien-Aimé than
of the times of Charles X. And lastly—not that with him the catalogue would be complete, but our space is limited while Stendhal's
inventive fecundity is apparently inexhaustible—there is the
Marquis de Sanréal, the richest of them all, corpulent, loud-
spoken, vain and pretentious, habitually drunk, and flaunting the
most reactionary opinions when in his cups. But Lucien finds
something to admire even in Sanréal: 'celui-ci ne manque pas
d'énergie et ne tendrait pas le cou à la hache de 93.'[8] The majority
of these legitimists live in dread of a new revolution which will send
them to the scaffold; this fear, together with envy of the people
who enjoy the privileges and power they think are theirs by right,
poisons their outlook: 'à cause de ces deux aimables passions [envy
and fear] ils oublient de vivre.' This is how, back in Paris, Lucien
retrospectively sums up the provincial aristocracy with its touching
though foolish devotion to a lost cause;[9] but at Nancy, though
occasionally irritated by the emptiness of their conversation and the
perversity of their opinions, Lucien finds them charming. Not all
of them reciprocate: the younger squires in particular find it hard
to forgive Lucien for wearing what they regard as a usurped uniform; but his indulgence can extend even to them. It is, after all, in
a quixotic but honourable devotion to their political creed that they
have forgone their army pay and condemned themselves to kick

[8] Ibid. 238.   [9] Ibid. iii. 348.

their heels in shabby idleness. The 'Henriquinquistes'[1] are the counterpart, in *Lucien Leuwen*, of the Jacobites in the Waverley Novels, and Stendhal, in unconscious imitation of Scott, sheds over them the same lustre of poetic sympathy which is imagination's tribute to the martyrs of history.

The autobiographical element in *Lucien Leuwen* is strongest where Stendhal is dealing with Lucien's courtship of Bathilde de Chasteller, which in mood and circumstance transposes with disarming frankness his own relations with Mathilde Dembowski between 1818 and 1821. The introduction of this painful but exalting love-affair of his late thirties into the novel written in his early fifties was pointed out as long ago as 1918 by Henri Delacroix,[2] is confirmed by a number of marginal notes in the manuscript, and can be further corroborated by a comparison between the text of certain passages in the novel and that of drafts of letters written by Beyle to 'Métilde' in the summer of 1819. Victor Brombert, who has made this comparison,[3] concludes that *Lucien Leuwen* must be interpreted as simultaneously and conjointly Stendhal's defence against Mathilde's accusations of indelicacy and calculation (a defence pleaded across the bar of the grave, for Mathilde had died in 1825), and a re-interpretation of events in a guise more soothing to the rejected lover's vanity: Mathilde Dembowski had crossly refused to respond to Beyle's devotion, Bathilde de Chasteller shyly longs, but does not dare, to yield.

The parallel is so well documented, and so fully discussed elsewhere, that it is unnecessary to dwell much on it. Mme Dembowski (*née* Viscontini) had been separated from her husband some years before Stendhal met her; Mme de Chasteller has lost her husband; both husbands were generals. Stendhal, in laying siege to Mathilde's virtue, was encouraged by the report that she had once formed a liaison with the poet Ugo Foscolo; modern research has shown that here rumour lied,[4] but Stendhal's state of uncertainty was duly transferred to Lucien who has been told that Mme

---

[1] 'Henry V' was the name given to Charles X's grandson and heir by his supporters; his official title was Comte de Chambord, and at this time he was residing at Holyrood. Hence his portrayal as a young Highlander in the painting displayed at the legitimist ball given by Mme de Marcilly (chapter xv).

[2] *La Psychologie de Stendhal*, pp. 159 et seq.

[3] *Stendhal et la voie oblique*, pp. 118–25.

[4] See A. Caraccio, *Variétés stendhaliennes* (1947), pp. 120–38 ('Stendhal, Foscolo, et leur amie Métilde Dembowski').

de Chasteller had shown favour to a certain M. Busant de Sicile, lieutenant-colonel in a regiment formerly stationed at Nancy. Mathilde was a liberal in politics, and in fact was arrested and interrogated in 1822 on suspicion of abetting the *carbonari*; Bathilde is a legitimist, which means that she belongs to a faction bent, like the *carbonari*, on upsetting the *status quo*. Most important of all is the bashfulness, prudery, or else frigidity, which keeps Mme de Chasteller from responding to Lucien's usually mute appeals. It hardly crosses his mind to propose marriage, though the match would not have been a misalliance and, in any case, they are both of age and free. This small implausibility has its roots, no doubt, in the situation that Stendhal was remembering: for Mathilde when he knew her was legally tied to her absent husband.

Lucien Leuwen contains the lengthiest and most meticulous analysis of a love-affair to be found anywhere in Stendhal's fiction: a love-affair ending not in fulfilment but in a separation which is regretted on both sides but proves eternal. Behind the narrative lies a whole philosophy of love—one which he had enunciated long before in *De l'amour*, a work started in Milan in 1819 and written under the immediate influence of his wounded bafflement. The philosophy can be summed up in a sentence: it is better, if the choice has to be made, to be ravished in mind than to be sensually satisfied; a doctrine of the purest hedonism, notwithstanding the ascetic dress it wears. In *De l'amour* the two alternatives are embodied in the figures of Werther and Don Juan. Don Juan is called successful by the world, but the pleasures Werther enjoys, if less 'real' than Don Juan's, are more intense. 'Le plus grand bonheur que puisse donner l'amour, c'est le premier serrement de main d'une femme qu'on aime.' This implies no apologia for platonic worship. Consummation has its place, but not at the end of the process; it is a climacteric and probably necessary stage in the establishment of an ideal harmony. We are paraphrasing, since Stendhal's terseness borders here on obscurity, a sentence on the same page of *De l'amour* (at the beginning of chapter xxxii): 'Dans l'amour-passion, l'intimité n'est pas tant le bonheur parfait que le dernier pas pour y arriver.' Essentially, this treatise is a plea for the restoration of warmth in passion; what Stendhal is attacking is a certain cold libertinage (of which many of his contemporaries took him to be the apostle) which reduced love to a succession of campaigns and conquests, a mere question of generalship.

Lucien Leuwen dramatizes the thesis argued in *De l'amour*. For all Mme de Chasteller's misgivings (there are moments when she regards him as 'un Don Juan terrible et accompli'), Lucien knows himself to be a Werther.

Eh! grand Dieu! [he exclaims ruefully] ai-je le talent qu'il faut pour séduire une femme vraiment vertueuse? Toutes les fois que j'ai voulu m'adresser à quelque femme un peu différente du vulgaire des grisettes, n'ai-je pas échoué de la façon la plus ridicule?... Au lieu de profiter de mes petits succès et de marcher en avant, je reste comme un benêt, occupé à les savourer, à en jouir. Un serrement de main est une ville de Capoue pour moi; je m'arrête extasié dans les rares délices d'une faveur si décisive au lieu de marcher en avant.

All the pleasures of Capua in a hand pressing his—decidedly, Rome will never fall to such a Hannibal. 'Enfin, je n'ai aucun talent pour cette guerre...'[5] This gloomy prognosis is strikingly confirmed, or so it seems, later when Lucien discovers that Mme Grandet became his mistress not because she found him irresistible but simply to keep her side of an ignoble bargain struck with his father. He laments then that he is 'un nigaud incapable d'obtenir une femme par mon esprit et de la gagner autrement que par la méthode plate de la *contagion de l'amour*'.[6] To obtain a woman's favours by appealing to her sympathy and compassion is vulgar; the real buck uses his brains and conquers her by calculation. Intellectually at least, Lucien is the sceptical child of the eighteenth century, when seduction was practised as a fine art. His trouble is that he cannot translate his scepticism into action.

Neither could Stendhal. Experience had taught him that (as he wrote in 1811 when he was ruminating his failure to make any impression on Alexandrine Daru) 'j'ai trop de sensibilité pour avoir jamais de talent dans l'art de Lovelace'.[7] Subsequently he became reconciled to this deficiency or rather ceased to regard it as one. Schooled by his far deeper passion for Mathilde, he concluded that 'the art of Lovelace' was incompatible with love properly understood, and informed her, with unquestionable sincerity, that: 'j'aurais le talent de vous séduire, et je ne crois pas ce talent possible, que je n'en ferais pas usage.'[8]

These conflicting attitudes to love are, in the earlier part of the novel, characteristically expressed in the form of author's

---

⁵ *Lucien Leuwen*, i. 345–6.   ⁶ Ibid. iii. 364.
⁷ *Journal*, iv. 187.   ⁸ *Correspondance*, v. 233.

commentary. Stendhal's practice when commenting on the action in *Lucien Leuwen* is curious and disconcerting, though there are precedents in the earlier novels. Siding, as we know, with Werther against Don Juan, privately he endorses Lucien's behaviour, however unenterprising it may appear. The commentary, however, is not delivered from this defensive standpoint but in the main from that of some robust, sarcastic, cynical *roué* who, Stendhal feigns, is holding the pen. In the main; but here and there the real Stendhal pencils in a word or two, slyly refuting the worldly wise cynic, and the irony, from being directed against the hero, is abruptly switched round and trained on to the hero's biographer.

Thus one evening Mme de Chasteller accedes to Lucien's modest request that she should dispense with a chaperone at his next visit. He finds her, when he arrives, in a disposition debonair and unconstrained. 'S'il avait eu un peu plus d'expérience,' writes Stendhal, or rather the pseudo-Stendhal before whom Stendhal has temporarily effaced himself, 'il se serait fait dire qu'on l'aimait. Avec de l'audace, il aurait pu se jeter dans les bras de madame de Chasteller et n'être pas repoussé. Il pouvait du moins établir un traité de paix fort avantageux pour les intérêts de son amour. Au lieu de tout cela, il n'avança point ses affaires et fut parfaitement heureux.'[9] The martial metaphor in the penultimate sentence is reminiscent of the libertine vocabulary of an earlier literature: military imagery of this sort besprinkles the pages of Louvet de Couvray and Choderlos de Laclos and typifies the *roué's* frigidity and superficiality. But with the last three words sincerity flows back.

It happens occasionally that Lucien violates the tacit agreement between Mme de Chasteller and himself. Once, in the course of another of these evening tête-à-têtes, he ventures to touch her hand. For this Stendhal, writing now in his authentic character, condemns him: for Lucien is not, on this occasion, acting spontaneously, in response to an irresistible passionate impulse, but is modelling himself on some mental image of the dashing gallant. 'Ce n'était pas pour le bonheur de serrer la main d'une femme qu'il aimait qu'il prenait celle de madame de Chasteller, mais parce que je ne sais quoi en lui lui disait qu'il était ridicule de passer deux heures tête à tête avec une femme dont les yeux montraient quelquefois tant de bienveillance, sans au moins lui prendre la main

[9] *Lucien Leuwen*, ii. 90–91.

une fois.' His education, once more, is to blame: 'Ce n'est pas impunément que l'on habite Paris depuis l'âge de dix ans.' He gets his deserts, for Mme de Chasteller rebukes him angrily and Lucien, abashed and tongue-tied, bows himself out without a protest. What else could he have done? Why, intervenes Stendhal's *alter ego*,

il aurait dû se lever, saluer froidement madame de Chasteller, et lui dire:
'Vous exagérez, madame. D'une petite imprudence sans conséquence, et peut-être sotte chez moi, vous faites un crime in-folio. J'aimais une femme aussi supérieure par l'esprit que par la beauté, et, en vérité, je ne vous trouve que jolie en ce moment.'
En disant ces belles paroles, il fallait prendre son sabre, l'attacher tranquillement, et sortir.

But even having made the mistake of allowing himself to be treated like a small boy caught stealing jam, he might at least, instead of raging with humiliation, he might at least have felt amused, suggests Mr. Worldly Wiseman . . . and returned the following evening as though nothing had happened, prepared to tender his apologies if the lady still wanted to show indignation. Any eighteen-year-old stripling would have had the sense to do that much, 'pour peu qu'il eût eu quelque sécheresse d'âme et un peu de ce mépris pour les femmes, si à la mode aujourd'hui… Mais Leuwen était bien loin de ces idées…', and, in the next sentence, the derisive tone continues unchecked and unchanged so that one hardly notices at first that the line of fire of the irony has swept round once more and that it is now Mr. Worldly Wiseman who is the target. 'Au point de bon sens et de vieillesse morale où nous sommes, il faut, j'en conviens, faire un effort sur soi-même pour pouvoir comprendre les affreux combats dont l'âme de notre héros était le théâtre, et ensuite pour ne pas en rire.'[1] Who would laugh? Not Stendhal: it would be the sourest self-mockery, Lucien's agony was Henri Beyle's fifteen years before, when he was wandering in misery outside the Palazzo Belgiojoso, hoping to see a certain hand lift a curtain at the window. Only the reader, then, who will know, if he accepts the invitation to scoff, that he is the wrong reader, and has no business to be reading, since he is at one with Chrysale, the middle-aged man of sense whom Stendhal detests.

[1] *Lucien Leuwen*, ii. 99–100, 104, 119–20.

No fictional character is ever an exact mirror image of the author and, relative age and personal attractiveness apart, there are two vital differences between Lucien and Stendhal. Lucien has no sense of artistic vocation; and he has no need to earn his living. No great purpose lures him forward as Beyle at his age was magnetized by the ambition 'to make chef-d'œuvre'. No spectre of poverty snaps at his heels. Since his life has no aim, he has to invent one, if only to keep his self-respect and have some answer ready to Dévelroy's jibe that he cannot even keep himself in cigars. At Nancy he is reasonably successful for a time. True, peace-time soldiering offers little excitement beyond ignoble squabbles with his superiors, in which his father's influence with the Minister for War ensures him rather easily the upper hand. He might have subsided into an aimless lethargy, had not his vanity suggested to him the task of conquering the good graces of mesdames d'Hocquincourt, de Puylaurens, &c.; while later, Mme de Chasteller's beauty challenges him to win her love. In the first object he is, for a while, entirely successful; and in the second, too, more successful than he realizes. But this flimsy scaffolding of achievement tumbles to pieces at a stroke, and Lucien returns to Paris with a broken heart, doffs his uniform, and is put on the retired list. In all this Stendhal follows quite closely, if one makes allowances for the inevitable adjustments (which included the fusion of his third sojourn at Milan with his first), his own career in his late teens and early twenties. He too had accepted a commission in the army (in 1800) procured by the influence of well-placed relatives (the Darus); had, in his second lieutenant's uniform, worshipped from afar a supposedly unapproachable beauty (Angela Pietragrua[2]); had tired of the military life and resigned. In 1804-5 he was planning to associate himself with his friend Fortuné Mante in a banking enterprise; and Lucien, on his return to Paris, considers, but turns down, a place in his father's banking house. In 1806, Beyle became an official in Napoleon's administration; this corresponds to the job Lucien elects, that of secretary in the Home Office.

[2] If Métilde is the primary model for Mme de Chasteller, Angela is a secondary one. In particular, the way Stendhal was finally disabused of his love for her has some analogy with Du Poirier's staging a false confinement which Lucien has to witness, hidden in Mme de Chasteller's house. One of Mme Pietragrua's maids, angry at having been dismissed, offered to give Beyle proof of his mistress's infidelity; unwisely he accepted, was smuggled into the house, and had to watch her in the very act of love with his rival.

It is his 'third career'; the first, as a student at the École Polytechnique, ended before the novel opened; the second was abruptly terminated by his inglorious flight from Nancy; and, in his depression, he wonders whether it is worth his while to embark on a fresh occupation—'quand on possède une âme comme la mienne, à la fois faible et impossible à contenter, on va se jeter à la Trappe'.[3] In the event, the job he chooses or is pushed into involves him in a number of shady adventures, but does at least succeed in maturing him, and by the time he leaves it Lucien can be said to be a man at last. His hard-won independence is symbolized by two events, happening at the very end of the novel: his father's death, which removes the most potent of the directive influences on his life, and the discovery that, after all, he inherits no millions, his father's assets only just covering his liabilities. The debilitating waters of Pactolus which had borne him along all his life abruptly recede; the last time we see Lucien, he has crossed the Alps and is breathing the unladen air of Italy.

In this second part of *Lucien Leuwen* the position the hero occupies, very near the centre of the web of power, gives Stendhal the opportunity of displaying the workings of government with a savage candour which even Balzac could not emulate and which makes the work undoubtedly the most searching 'political novel' of the first half of the nineteenth century. One Marxist critic has indeed singled it out as being 'perhaps the most violent critique of capitalist society any novelist has made';[4] other commentators, who cannot be suspected of reading into it a particular political message, have stressed its value and interest as a social document.[5] Its importance, so regarded, cannot be denied; but it must be said at the outset that if the panoramic picture of the Orleanist régime which *Lucien Leuwen* provides is accurate, Stendhal must have arrived at this accuracy more by divination or intuition than by close personal

---

[3] *Lucien Leuwen*, ii. 247. It is curious how the monastic life fascinates Stendhal's heroes. For a long time, we are told in the first chapter of *Armance*, 'Octave avait pensé à se retirer du monde et à consacrer sa vie à Dieu', while Fabrice, of course, ends his days as a recluse in a Carthusian monastery.

[4] R. Andrieu, 'Soixante ans après *Lamiel*', *La Pensée*, no. 26 (1949), p. 35.

[5] e.g. R. Boylesve, *Réflexions sur Stendhal*, pp. 55–56: 'Il y a dans ce remarquable, cet exceptionnel roman de *Lucien Leuwen*, une partie objective prédominante... Il me semble que Stendhal y a porté sur la société française, et sur ce qui la constitue essentiellement, un jugement d'une extraordinaire lucidité.' G. Blin similarly takes the view that *Lucien Leuwen* is an irreplaceable piece of social history (*Stendhal et les problèmes du roman*, p. 69).

observation. For, apart from the leave he spent in Paris from 11 September to 4 December 1833, he had been living outside France almost all the time since Louis-Philippe ascended the throne, and for his knowledge of conditions in the capital and the provinces must have relied on what he could glean from the newspapers and on what his friends reported to him.[6]

Moreover, those who so confidently expound Stendhal's satiric intentions overlook the fact that, except in *Lucien Leuwen*, he rarely expresses hostility to the July Monarchy. He presents this régime in the novel as not unlike certain neo-Fascist administrations of our own times, those, for example, that linger on in the Iberian peninsula. The machinery of government is designed solely for self-perpetuation; for that reason, foreign adventures are shunned, but every kind of gerrymandering, corrupt practice, and oppression flourishes. Any trace of popular support is totally absent. Bribery and rigged elections secure the return of a sufficient number of incompetent or suborned legislators to ensure the passage of whatever bills the ministry judges fit to promote. The magistracy takes orders from the executive. The sovereign authority, too discredited to command an old-fashioned loyalty, can keep its supporters satisfied only by continual and mounting cash rewards. Hence real power has passed to the financial magnates, the bankers and the entrepreneurs: Leuwen senior and M. Grandet.

This analysis may not have been incorrect; the point is that Stendhal gave a very different picture of the France of the reign of Louis-Philippe when, in 1837, he wrote his *Mémoires d'un touriste* which were, unlike *Lucien Leuwen*, based on first-hand knowledge: he had journeyed around France and resided in the capital for a period of eighteen months (from the middle of 1836 to the end of 1837) before he sent his first batch of copy to the printer. It is true that the *Mémoires* were written with a view to publication, that Beyle was still in government service, that it behoved him therefore to mind what he said; but it was not required of him that he should go out of his way to paint what is after all a remarkably

---

[6] As an example of the sort of remote documentation Stendhal attempted when writing *Lucien Leuwen*, cf. the curious letter of 27 Sept. 1835 to Albert Stapfer, in which he asks for information about life in a small town in France. 'Connaissez-vous un bourgeois de La Rochelle garni de 8000 francs de rente et âgé de 40 ans? A quelle heure se lève-t-il, et que fait-il heure par heure? Que pense-t-il de Voltaire, de Rousseau, de M. de Lamennais, et de Louis-Philippe?...' (*Correspondance*, ix. 292–3).

favourable picture of the France of the times. At the start of his tour his road south takes him through Essonnes: an ugly town, but in the context political considerations are doubtless more important than aesthetic ones, and the Tourist's political reflections are extraordinarily flattering to the régime. 'Le sage gouvernement d'un roi homme supérieur n'autorise pas les insolences des riches envers les pauvres comme en Angleterre, ou les insolences et prétentions des prêtres, comme du temps de Charles X. Ainsi, me disais-je, en voyant Essonnes devant moi, voici peut-être le bourg du monde où le gouvernement fait le moins de mal aux gouvernés...' Steaming down the Rhône, 'je ne sais où trouver des termes prudents', writes Stendhal, 'pour peindre la prospérité croissante dont la France jouit sous le règne de Louis-Philippe. J'ai peur de passer pour un écrivain payé.' There is new building in the towns, there are improvements in the countryside. None of this took place under the two preceding Bourbon monarchs, when the rich were paralysed by the fear of a new revolution and the poor uneasy lest what they had gained in the first was to be filched from them.[7] Truly, in 1837 the French had never had it so good; and for once there appear to be no ironical reservations in Stendhal's panegyrics.

Consequently it would be safer to consider the political satire in *Lucien Leuwen* as being directed less against the abuses of a particular régime, than against the imperfections, defects, and villainies of any and every administration. 'Tout gouvernement est un mal,' Coffe tells Lucien, 'mais un mal qui préserve d'un plus grand.'[8] His long years of experience in administrative work, beginning at Brunswick and ending at Civitavecchia, gave Stendhal full authority to analyse this lesser evil. There is a further point. *Lucien Leuwen* is after all a novel, and the 'imaginary biography' of the hero; it was therefore essential, if he was to gain any moral firmness, that Lucien should encounter the particular moral turpitudes which Stendhal, through M. de Vaize, introduces him to. Lucien must at last take off his gloves and get his hands dirty. 'Do you imagine', Hoederer asks Hugo in Sartre's play, 'that anyone can govern innocently?'

Lucien becomes a state employee in full awareness of the risks his niceness runs. When he announced his intention of entering the service, his father had expressed a comical misgiving: 'Serez-vous

---

[7] *Mémoires d'un touriste*, i. 22, 320.   [8] *Lucien Leuwen*, iii. 195.

assez coquin pour cet emploi?' Before introducing Lucien to his superior he had warned him: 'laissez le sens moral à la porte en entrant au ministère.'⁹ M. de Vaize is an energetic and gifted administrator but, like everyone else, bent on feathering his own nest. Lucien finds his duties include acting as liaison officer between the Minister and his father, there being an arrangement between the two that M. Leuwen should use secret information passed on to him by M. de Vaize in order to speculate in government stocks: the profits are then shared. But since, for an amateur economist like Lucien, it is not clear who is being robbed by these transactions, he plays his part with relative equanimity, though his opinion of His Excellency's integrity goes down and the services he is called on to perform deepen his misanthropy: 'il avait le sentiment de s'enfoncer dans la boue.' His father's cynical admonishments do little to dispel this impression. 'Tu vois les choses par le côté utile et, ce qui est pis encore, par le *côté honnête*. Tout cela est déplacé et ridicule en France... Il faut voir d'instinct les choses par le côté plaisant, et n'apercevoir l'*utile* ou l'*honnête* que par un effort de volonté.'¹

The first real test of Lucien's principles comes when De Vaize asks him to handle the Cortis affair. Cortis, an *agent provocateur* employed by the War Ministry, had been instructed to disguise himself as a drunken workman and pick a quarrel with a conscript on sentry duty on the Pont d'Austerlitz. The incident was part of a secret campaign to sow dissension between the workers and the military whom the government is sometimes compelled to use against them. Unluckily on this occasion the conscript shot the *agent provocateur*. Cortis is now in hospital with a bullet in his stomach and has not long to live. Already the opposition press has wind of the scandal, and a suggestion has been made that Cortis might be kept under drugs so that he cannot talk. Lucien is asked to visit the hospital and ensure, in whatever way he thinks fit, that the man lets nothing out that might embarrass the government. At first he hesitates. Ought he to risk his reputation dabbling in such an unsavoury business? it could mean that his name would be associated for the rest of his days with the poisoning of an innocent man who had only been acting under orders. But, thinks Lucien, 'si j'ai du courage, qu'importe la forme du danger?... je suis las de reculer devant le danger... Puisque la vie, au XIXᵉ siècle, est si

⁹ Ibid. ii. 239, 256.   ¹ Ibid. 296, 317.

pénible, je ne changerai pas d'état pour la troisième fois.' So he accepts the mission and with a blend of diplomacy and bribery fulfils it. Nothing leaks, nor is Cortis's death intentionally hastened. After a day of frantic activity Lucien is surprised to find himself elated: 'il avait supposé au contraire qu'il serait horriblement malheureux jusqu'à la fin de cette affaire. "Je côtoie le mépris public, et la mort, se répétait-il souvent, mais j'ai bien mené ma barque."'[2]

The lesson he is learning is humdrum and melancholy. A man should not look to do more than exert himself disinterestedly in whatever task lies to hand; and if this task is to mop up the filth that others have spilt, provided the mopping up is efficiently done, all is well. The idealistic boy in Lucien wanted at first to draw back and let the muck lie; that he took up the swab notwithstanding shows him to be growing to man's estate.

The crucial test for the hero comes when the filth bespatters him. This happens to Lucien, literally, in the course of an electoral mission which he accepts, again with the deepest reluctance. At Blois he and Coffe, his secretary and travelling companion, are recognized as ministerial agents by a group of angry townsfolk, who start pillaging the coach while the two Parisians are at dinner. The luggage boot is stuffed with pamphlets intended for distribution at Caen, where the opposition candidate has every chance of being elected, and the calumnies these pamphlets contain add to the crowd's fury. Lucien, darting out of the inn with some headstrong notion of quelling the riot, is stopped dead by a handful of mud thrown in his face. Someone on the inn balcony shouts: 'Voyez comme il est sale; vous avez mis son âme sur sa figure!'[3] A burst of laughter greets this sally. Lucien, fuming, talks of finding the man who has insulted him, but Coffe bundles him into the coach, and they are run out of town, pursued by hooligans hurling more mud and cabbage stalks and threatening to duck them as they cross the bridge that leads away from Blois.

The incident is the most vivid, undoubtedly, in a novel which may be judged a little lacking in incident. It marks a culminating point in Lucien's career: it is his Gethsemane. The code of honour he has inherited teaches that a bodily injury such as he has received

---

[2] *Lucien Leuwen*, ii. 343-4, 368.

[3] Ibid. iii. 47. Giraud (op. cit. 60-62) has pointed out that the terms of the insult are probably a reminiscence of something said of Mme de Merteuil when smallpox ruins her beauty: 'que la maladie l'avait retournée, et qu'à présent son âme était sur sa figure' (*Les Liaisons dangereuses*, last letter).

must be wiped out in blood; he had fought a duel at Nancy for far less—merely to silence those who insisted on calling him a republican—and at Paris had threatened to leave the service and challenge the Minister for Foreign Affairs who, he judged, had spoken to him impertinently. Choking now with mortification, he tells Coffe he will hand in his resignation on the spot and return to Blois a week later to search out the mud-slinger. Coffe will not hear of it. Lucien has taken service under the government which has commissioned him to procure the defeat of the opposition candidate at Caen; to give up before they have even got to Caen would be desertion on the battlefield, the treachery of the Saxons at Leipzig. Coffe's disillusioned sagacity reads Lucien the moral of the adventure. 'Dans l'extrémité du malheur, et surtout du pire des malheurs, de celui qui a pour cause le mépris de soi-même, faire son devoir et agir est... la seule ressource.' And Lucien has not reached this pitch of misery, since he has done nothing for which he should despise himself. The rabble at Blois is far from constituting a court from which there is no appeal; a man should be his own judge. 'Vous n'avez pas la peau assez dure pour ne pas sentir le mépris public. Mais on s'y accoutume, on n'a qu'à mettre sa vanité ailleurs.' Greater men than he have had to suffer worse affronts: the Cardinal de Retz, thrashed by his own groom, the Duke of Wellington.... Ah, cries Lucien, the English, what do they know of honour?[4]

Stendhal noted in the margin of the manuscript hereabouts that this lengthy colloquy, Lucien's lamentations, Coffe's sermon, does not advance the action. 'Lucien est comme un clou exposé aux coups de marteau du sort.' Jean Prévost may have been thinking of this observation of the author when he wrote of Lucien's 'lack of initiative' and suggested that the novel

incurred the risk of being less firmly organized around the hero than *Le Rouge et le Noir* was around Julien. Not that Lucien is less constantly present, but the events in the story are less often created by his own will; he is more acted on than acting: his posting as second lieutenant, his flight from Mme de Chasteller, his activities and travels as principal private secretary, his financial ruin and his departure for Rome, are imposed on him by his enemies, his father, or his superiors.[5]

All of which is true enough, except for the implied distinction between *Lucien Leuwen* and *Le Rouge et le Noir*. When one starts

4 *Lucien Leuwen*, iii. 60–62.   5 *La Création chez Stendhal*, p. 306.

thinking along these lines it is surprising how many of the decisive events in Julien's life are similarly 'imposed on him' by others or are due to the promptings and advice of others. His father and his future employer arrange between themselves, almost behind his back, for him to enter the Rênal household as tutor. Chélan arranges for him to enter the seminary. Pirard arranges for him to leave the seminary and become M. de La Mole's secretary. Mathilde arranges her own seduction by Julien and Korasoff tells him what to do to win her back after she has discarded him. It is scarcely an exaggeration to say that the only occasion on which Julien truly acts of his own free will is when he shoots Mme de Rênal; and we have seen how here he has been judged by various competent critics to be acting out of character.

The very conditions of the novel perhaps require a protagonist who is 'more acted on than acting': one is reminded of the distinction Goethe made between the hero of drama who is active and the hero of a novel who must needs be passive. Even Don Quixote, who nominally rides in search of adventures, in effect undergoes whatever adventures he chances to encounter.

The vital question to be asked is: into what shape is Lucien hammered by the blows of fortune? This is no more than a rephrasing of the question propounded earlier, whether Lucien is really an unheroic hero—one undeserving of admiration.

The answer is there in the last few chapters of the novel, but diffused and needing to be sifted from a medley of miscellaneous subsidiary anecdotes—François Leuwen's election to the Chamber and his series of devastating attacks on the ministry, Mme Grandet's ambitious intriguing on behalf of her husband, the reappearance of Du Poirier, &c. Lucien's mission at Caen fails, but not for want of strenuous and even inspired efforts on his part. Chapters lviii and lix show him back at his desk in the Home Office, involved in paper work which, however, reveals him as capable of the right kind of initiative: saving an innocent man from the consequences of a slander, attempting to stop other acts of injustice and, when he cannot prevent them, ensuring at least that those who have committed them do not go altogether unpunished. His father, who had regarded him too long as a handsome simpleton, revises his opinion and gives his wife a glowing account of their son's administrative talents. More important still, his historian, never indulgent hitherto, marks the points.

Depuis quelques mois, notre héros était devenu beaucoup plus hardi, il avait vu de près les motifs qui font agir les hommes chargés des grandes places. Cette sorte de timidité, qui à un œil clairvoyant annonce une âme sincère et grande, n'avait pu tenir contre la première expérience des grandes affaires. S'il eût usé sa vie dans le comptoir de son père, il eût peut-être été toute la vie un homme de mérite, connu pour tel d'une personne ou deux. Il osait maintenant croire à son premier mouvement, et y tenir jusqu'à ce qu'on lui eût prouvé qu'il avait tort. Et il devait à l'*ironie* de son père l'impossibilité de se payer de mauvaises raisons.

Such a passage, awkward and inartistic though it is, makes clear the *Bildungsroman* aspect of *Lucien Leuwen*. Later in the same chapter (the 65th) Lucien is shown in his box at the Opera, letting the music stimulate his thoughts and reverie according to the thoroughly unmusical habit which was Stendhal's own.

Ce stupide travail de bureau me prouve au moins que je suis capable de gagner au besoin ma vie et celle de ma femme [i.e. Bathilde: Lucien's confident fancy has projected him into the future]. 'A qui l'a-t-il prouvé?' dit le parti contraire. Et à cette objection le regard de Lucien devint hagard. 'A ces gens-ci que peut-être tu ne reverras jamais, qui, si tu les quittes, te calomnieront...'

'Eh! non, parbleu, il l'a prouvé à moi, et c'est là l'essentiel. Et que me fait l'opinion de cette légion de demi-fripons qui regardent avec ébahissement ma croix et mon avancement rapide? Je ne suis plus ce jeune sous-lieutenant de lanciers partant pour Nancy afin de rejoindre son régiment, esclave alors de cent petites faiblesses de vanité... Faisons comme le monde, laissons de côté la moralité de nos actions officielles. Eh bien! je sais que je puis travailler deux fois autant que le chef de bureau le plus lourd, et partant le plus considéré, et encore à un travail que je méprise, et qui à Blois m'a couvert d'une boue méritée peut-être.'

Ce fonds de pensées était à peu près le bonheur pour Lucien...

Life has purged Lucien of vanity but left intact and fortified his self-respect. The words used by Scott Fitzgerald to describe Anthony Patch (in *The Beautiful and the Damned*) could well be applied to Stendhal's hero in this final stage: 'opinionated, contemptuous, functioning from within outward—a man who was aware that there could be no honour and yet had honour, who knew the sophistry of courage and yet was brave.' Lucien, at the end of his odyssey, is perhaps a less engaging figure than he was at the beginning, but he has not foundered, and if on the road he has

lost his innocence and much of his charm, he has gained in robust-
ness and stature, yet without any coarsening of fibre. This last is
perhaps the saving clause. Balzac's Lucien de Rubempré goes
morally and spiritually soft in the course of *Illusions perdues*;
Frédéric Moreau, at the end of Flaubert's *Éducation sentimentale*,
is shrivelled and hardened. But Lucien Leuwen is allowed to go
forward with the secret springs of poetry and gaiety still bubbling
in his soul's depths, unsullied and unimpaired. On the last page of
the book, as he crosses the Alps and rides down into the plain of
Lombardy, his spirits soar irrepressibly. Milan, Bologna, Florence,
'le jetèrent dans un état d'attendrissement et de sensibilité aux
moindres petites choses qui lui eût causé bien des remords trois
ans auparavant. Enfin, en arrivant à son poste, à Capel [i.e. Rome],
il eut besoin de se sermonner pour prendre envers les gens qu'il
allait voir le degré de sécheresse convenable.'

VI ⁎ A HERO UNAWARE

THE promised land which, on the last page of the novel just discussed, opens up before Lucien, is Fabrice del Dongo's birthplace and home, which he leaves only once, to 'lend Napoleon the aid of his invincible arm' as Mosca later puts it with indulgent irony. The episode of Waterloo apart, *La Chartreuse de Parme* has an exclusively north Italian setting: the scenes of action are Milan, Parma, Bologna, Lake Como, and Lake Maggiore, 'i luoghi ameni', to use Ariosto's words adopted as an epigraph for the first volume of the novel. Those who people these scenes are as Italian as the characters of *I promessi sposi* or *Il gattopardo*. Their very speech sounds as though it had been translated from the Italian: passionate and matter-of-fact by turns, but never epigrammatic, never witty. What Frenchwoman would ever have welcomed her lover with the noble simplicity of Clélia's invitation: 'Entre ici, ami de mon cœur'? Against her words Stendhal wrote, in his private copy, the Italian phrase which he had had in mind: 'Di quà, amico del cuore.'[1] Though the book opens with the entry into Milan of the victorious French troops in 1796, these foreign liberators soon depart. One of them, the young Lieutenant Robert, wins the heart of the Marchesa del Dongo whose hateful husband had fled for safety to his country estate. Fabrice is the fruit of this union; but the French blood that flows in his veins hardly shows as he grows up, and Stendhal never refers to him except as an Italian. His mother's clandestine affair that the Bonapartist officer figures at the very beginning of the novel as an emblem, perhaps, of the author's lifelong love intrigue with the nymph for whom he invented the punning cryptogram *1000 ans* (Milan). Thereafter we are allowed to forget about France; or reminded only of the French for the purpose of ironic confrontation. Only one other foreigner puts in an episodic appearance in the later pages of the novel: he is a carroty-haired Englishman, a medieval historian of uncertain temper researching in the libraries of Parma.

[1] For a detailed study of Italianisms used in *La Chartreuse de Parme*, see S. Ullmann, *Style in the French Novel*, pp. 44–52.

There exists doubtless no other major work of fiction, in French or any other literature, so purely exotic as *La Chartreuse de Parme*. The prince of expatriate novelists, Henry James, never attempted anything like it: Roderick Hudson was the American in Italy, Christopher Newman the American in Paris. An imaginative tale set in a foreign country, and introducing no characters that are not nationals of that country, rarely runs to more than a few score pages: Balzac's most Stendhalian of short stories, *Massimilla Doni*, is an apt example. The reason is obvious: the reader's interest may be attracted by an unfamiliar setting and alien characters, but can with difficulty be lastingly attached, the novel having developed essentially as a commentary on the known scene.

The exotic short story had tempted Stendhal about the time he was composing *Le Rouge et le Noir*. *Vanina Vanini*, which he published in the *Revue de Paris* in December 1829, has a purely Italian cast, the heroine being a Roman Mathilde de La Mole, the hero an idealistic *carbonaro* with something of Julien Sorel in him and something of Ferrante Palla.[2] In the same magazine there appeared the following year *Le Coffre et le revenant*, an atrocious story of jealousy and murder of which the setting was Granada and the three principal characters Spaniards to the backbone.

At the same period Stendhal was experimenting with one of the principal variants of the exotic story as it has been practised for centuries: that which starts from the device we may conveniently denominate as 'the stranger in our midst', a device put to effective use by the eighteenth-century satirists—Montesquieu conducted his noble Persians round Paris at the time of the Regency, as did, at a later period, Voltaire his ingenuous Huron. For such writers, fiction was mainly a pretext for social criticism. With Stendhal, the reverse holds, and though, in a story like *Mina de Vanghel* (written about the turn of the year 1829–30), his intention may have been to show the foibles of the French through the observations of the Prussian heiress who was his heroine, this intention was only meagrely realized; the author, after the first few pages had been written, became absorbed in the character of Mina herself, imperious, self-willed, and reckless, and in her catastrophic career. Using the same starting-point and the same name for his heroine, Stendhal tried again some years later, in *Le Rose et le*

---

[2] The parallel between *Vanina Vanini* and the later *Chartreuse de Parme* has been drawn in detail by L. F. Benedetto, *La Parma di Stendhal*, pp. 169 et seq.

Vert, to present the Parisian scene through the sharp but not unkindly eyes of an observant foreigner. Earlier than either *Le Rose
et le Vert* or *Mina de Vanghel* was the brief fragment entitled *Le
Journal de Sir John Armitage*. An innocent young Englishman
with a passion for France comes into some money and is able to
gratify his longing to visit the country of his election. Stendhal
accompanies him as far as an hotel in Calais, where he makes friends
with a party of commercial travellers, passing himself off as a groom,
and getting cheerfully drunk in their company. The only observation the young baronet has time to make is neither novel nor profound: 'On voit les passions se succéder comme les images d'une
lanterne magique dans ces âmes françaises; les passions, j'ai tort,
c'est toujours la vanité.'[3]

The formula applied in these earlier fictional experiments is
used in *La Chartreuse* for the anecdote which was in all likelihood
one of the two starting-points of Stendhal's last novel: the episode
of Fabrice's excursion to France, including his adventures on the
field of Waterloo. The hero, who is sixteen (Mina's age at the start
of *Le Rose et le Vert*) is not simply what most readers take him for:
the 'young innocent' encountering the grown-up world for the first
time; nor is he just a generalized *outsider*. Sir John Armitage had
not been conspicuously English, any more than Mina very recog-
nizably German; but Stendhal does not forget that Fabrice is an
Italian, and has him fall into all the errors, experience all the
bewilderment, of an Italian thrown for the first time into the
company of a group of Frenchmen. Their sense of values being
quite different from his, unintentionally he insults them by an idle
remark, is rebuked, and later, when he finds himself in a position
of superiority, tries to take his revenge by repeating the insult,
only to find to his astonishment that they remain unmoved.
During the rout that follows the defeat, Fabrice attaches himself
to a Corporal Aubry who with a handful of infantrymen is making
a fighting retreat towards Charleroi. Imprudently Fabrice remarks
in their hearing that the fleeing troops are like a flock of sheep.
The corporal, greatly shocked, tells him to hold his tongue, and
his comrades glower at him: he has insulted the nation. 'Avec ces
Français il n'est pas permis de dire la vérité quand cela choque leur
vanité', reflects Fabrice. After marching a league or so, he finds a
cavalryman willing to sell him his horse. Mounted, Fabrice catches

---

[3] *Mélanges de littérature*, i. 40.

up with his companions and, rising in his stirrups, the reins in one hand and a sabre in the other, firmly repeats that the French army look like nothing so much as a flock of frightened sheep. 'Fabrice avait beau appuyer sur le mot *mouton*, ses camarades ne se souvenaient plus d'avoir été fâchés par ce mot une heure auparavant. Ici se trahit un des contrastes des caractères italien et français; le Français est sans doute le plus heureux, il glisse sur les événements de la vie et ne garde pas rancune.' A few pages farther, Stendhal slips in a similar didactic observation on the dissimilarities between the two nations. Fabrice falls in with the *vivandière* who had befriended him before the battle; she presses him to relate the various adventures that have befallen him, and puzzles him by insisting on hearing certain details over and over again. 'Pourquoi répéter si souvent, se disait Fabrice, ce que nous connaissons tous trois [the corporal is included] parfaitement bien? Il ne savait pas encore que c'est ainsi qu'en France les gens du peuple vont à la recherche des idées.'[4] Exceptionally, in these passages, Stendhal identifies himself with the French, in opposition to his hero, a foreigner: the Italian is vindictive, the Frenchman, more lucky, forgets offences; the *vivandière* is the humble representative of French intellectual curiosity and that delight in an oft-told tale which, ever since the time when those of her nation gathered to listen to the *chansons de geste*, has made France the motherland of story and romance.

Stendhal's normal attitude, his invariable attitude when his hero is in Italy, is a sly hostility to 'French' values and standards, a secret admiration for everything that can be attributed to the Italian temperament and way of life. This is altogether to be expected. 'Arrigo Beyle Milanese' as he is described, in accordance with his own instructions, on his tombstone, had conceived in childhood a passion for the country of Dante and Ariosto which later experience fortified and which not even the tedium of sweltering dog-days at Civitavecchia could weaken. To console himself for his unambiguously French name, he invented a fictitious descent on his mother's side from a family of Italian emigrants who had settled at Avignon about 1650; Guadagni or Guadaniamo becoming, by phonetic attrition, Gagnon, his grandfather's name. The pure rapture with which, at seventeen, he first set eyes on the plain of the Po still made his heart beat faster when, at fifty odd, he tried

[4] *La Chartreuse de Parme*, i. 100–1, 108.

to recapture it in the last pages of the *Vie de Henri Brulard*. The young traveller's letters to his sister in the year 1800 betray, however, a somewhat temperate enthusiasm.

J'ai pris des Italiens une bien meilleure idée qu'on n'en a en France; je me suis lié avec deux ou trois qui, vraiment, m'étonnent par la sagesse de leurs idées et le sentiment d'honneur qui règne dans leur cœur. Une chose à laquelle j'étais bien loin de m'attendre, c'est la charmante amabilité des femmes de ce pays. Tu ne me croiras pas, mais vraiment en ce moment je serais au désespoir de retourner à Paris.

There was a dark side to this picture: 'Je n'ai jamais vu et je ne m'étais pas formé l'idée d'hommes aussi abrutis que le bas peuple italien. Ils joignent à toute l'ignorance de nos paysans, un cœur faux et traître, la plus sale lâcheté et le fanatisme le plus détestable.'[5] Absence effaced those of his memories that were disagreeable. Writing to Pauline in 1804, he told her of a travelling companion with whom he had fallen into conversation in the coach from Grenoble to Paris; this man had just returned from a seven-year stay abroad and, exchanging impressions with him, Stendhal felt, as he said, that 'j'aime l'Italie de passion'. In the same year he noted in his diary an anecdote very much in the manner of those he was later to incorporate in the *Promenades dans Rome*: a young man shoots his fifteen-year-old mistress in a fit of jealousy, flees, but returns at midnight, breaks into the chapel where her body is laid out for burial, and sends a bullet through his own heart. Stendhal added laconically: 'Voilà qui me prouve de plus en plus que la douce Italie est le pays où l'on sent le plus, le pays des poètes.'[6]

'Milan m'offre des souvenirs bien tendres', he confided to a correspondent in 1811, a little before he left for Italy on furlough. 'J'y ai passé les douces années de l'adolescence. C'est ici que j'ai le plus aimé. C'est ici aussi que s'est formé mon caractère. Je vois tous les jours que j'ai le cœur italien, aux assassinats près, dont, au reste, on les accuse injustement.'[7] It is enough for him to sit next to an Italian girl at the opera house in Paris (it was a performance of *Le Nozze di Figaro*) for his blood to be stirred—not by the girl, but by her speech. 'L'Italie est pour moi la patrie, tout ce qui me la rappelle touche mon cœur.'[8] The following year, on the point of leaving for Russia, he wrote: 'Si je puis, à mon retour, I will see again my dear Italy. It is my true country. Non pas que j'y aime

---

[5] *Correspondance*, i. 15, 25–26.   [6] Ibid. 177; *Journal*, i. 162–3.
[7] *Correspondance*, iii. 325.   [8] *Journal*, iv. 23.

excessivement tel ou tel objet; mais ce pays est d'accord avec mon caractère.'⁹ And in 1813, travelling east once more, he declared ih a letter written from Erfurt that if, as he hoped, his services in the current campaign were rewarded by a more lucrative position, he would rather administer Florence (contenting himself with a mere 20,000 francs a year) than be appointed to a prefecture in France.

No one who has studied his life and works could accuse Stendhal of lacking proper affection for his native land, or of failing to give proper credit to the achievements of its people. But he was no chauvinist, and would rather have been considered unpatriotic than agree to admit to fellowship with a bombastic reactionary (Chateaubriand) on the grounds that he spoke and wrote the same language. So Stendhal declared that for him Chateaubriand was an undesirable alien, and the Milanese doctor Rasori a fellow countryman. 'L'étranger n'est pas celui que sépare de nous le hasard d'une rivière ou d'une montagne. Mais celui dont les principes, les vœux et les sentiments sont en guerre avec vos principes, vos vœux et vos sentiments.'¹ One's motherland is the country where most of the inhabitants are members of one's own tribe— one's spiritual, not one's racial tribe, however. For most men, the distinction would be meaningless: they are most at home with the people among whom they were born; Stendhal, like Conrad, was an exception. In calling Italy his 'true country' he meant, of course, rather more than that he got on better with Italians than with the people of any other nation, and felt more at home in Milan than in any other city. It was of no small importance to Stendhal that it was only at the Scala that he could hear the sort of music he loved, performed and sung in the manner he loved; that his favourite painters were, one and all, Italians; that the cities of the Peninsula were crowded with examples of that romanesque architecture which again he preferred to all other styles. His passion was nourished on all these things, and on much else besides.

J'éprouve un charme, dans ce pays-ci, dont je ne puis me rendre compte: c'est comme de l'amour; et cependant je ne suis amoureux de personne. L'ombre des beaux arbres, la beauté du ciel pendant les nuits, l'aspect de la mer, tout a pour moi un charme, une force d'impression qui me rappelle une sensation tout à fait oubliée, ce que je sentais à seize ans, à ma première campagne. Je vois que je ne puis rendre ma pensée, toutes les circonstances que j'emploie pour la peindre sont faibles.

---

⁹ *Correspondance*, iv. 53.   ¹ *Pages d'Italie*, p. 108.

Toute la nature est ici plus touchante pour moi; elle me semble neuve: je ne vois plus rien de plat et d'insipide. Souvent, à deux heures du matin, en me retirant chez moi, à Bologne, par ces grands portiques, l'âme obsédée de ces beaux yeux que je venais de voir, passant devant ces palais dont, par ses grandes ombres, la lune dessinait les masses, il m'arrivait de m'arrêter, oppressé de bonheur, pour me dire: Que c'est beau! En contemplant ces collines chargées d'arbres qui s'avancent jusque sur la ville, éclairées par cette lumière silencieuse au milieu de ce ciel étincelant, je tressaillais, les larmes me venaient aux yeux. — Il m'arrive de me dire à propos de rien: Mon Dieu! que j'ai bien fait de venir en Italie![2]

No foreign visitor to Italy, however inadequate his culture, can ever look at the country with a vision quite unclouded by the golden haze in which twenty-two centuries of the most chequered history and the allusions of a score of poets in half a dozen literatures— from Du Bellay to Goethe, from Browning to Pound—have steeped it. Italy is condemned, much more even than England, to be seen never as it is but always as it has been, and Stendhal in his turn has helped the process, compelling us to look at Lake Como a little through the eyes of Fabrice, and to spend time in a visit to Parma searching its alleyways for a door in the Via San Paolo bearing the number 19, which should lead into the orange-orchard of the Palazzo Crescenzi where Clélia received Fabrice.[3] The Italy that Stendhal evoked in La Chartreuse de Parme is, strictly, a product of the imagination stimulated by memories of the past, as contemporary Italian critics are careful to point out.[4] Zola who, when he wrote his essay on Stendhal, had never visited the land of his forefathers, was guided by a sure instinct when he expressed scepticism of the reality that was presented in La Chartreuse. 'I must confess', he wrote, 'that I have the utmost difficulty in accepting Stendhal's Italy as the Italy of contemporary time; in my opinion, he depicted rather fifteenth-century Italy, with its large-scale poisonings, its sword-play, its spies and masked bandits, its extraordinary adventures in which love would blossom sturdily in the midst of bloodshed.'[5]

---

[2] *Rome, Naples et Florence*, iii. 96–97.

[3] P. Martino claimed to have identified the spot: see 'La Parme de Stendhal', *Le Divan*, no. 242 (1942), pp. 75–86.

[4] e.g. G. Macchia, who calls it 'questa particolarissima, illocalizzabile "Italia di Stendhal" che non è solo un'Italia fantastica, ma, proprio come il mondo ariostesco, quasi un dono o una trovata spirituale' (*Il paradiso della ragione*, p. 301).

[5] *Les Romanciers naturalistes*, p. 107. Zola, the occasional acuity of whose

This Italy that Stendhal created for his own delectation and for the purposes of his art, was indeed a strange fusion of the present which he knew and the past he sentimentally admired and yearned after. For the present was a sadly shrunken spectre of a splendid past. Even over the years Stendhal had known the country, he marked—or thought he marked—a continuous decadence. 'L'Italie n'est plus comme je l'ai admirée en 1815', he wrote to Sainte-Beuve at the end of 1834.[6] Humiliation at being kept in the tutelage of a foreign power was a canker at the heart of the nation, turning men's thoughts away from art and from the supreme *arte di godere*. Contemporary Italy interested Stendhal mainly in so far as he could discover in it vestiges of the distant past—the ruined Colosseum, the buried city of Pompeii then being excavated, the bust of Tiberius dug out of the ground and presented to his patron Molé—or study its more recent past, recorded in oils on canvas or in printed books. In 1817 he was reading with the keenest pleasure Verri's *History of Milan*. 'Les passions gigantesques du moyen âge y éclatent dans toute leur féroce énergie; nulle affectation ne vient les masquer.'[7] The Italy that De Brosses knew, the suave, immoral society of the early eighteenth century, appealed to one side of Stendhal's nature, but the fiercely primitive soul of the man was stirred by what he could read of an earlier age. 'Il faut chercher toute l'Italie naturelle dans le moyen âge. Tous les usages que nous voyons ne sont que des conséquences. C'est un vieillard glacé par les ans, et presque retombé en enfance, et qui conserve encore, sans s'en douter, les habitudes des heureux jours de son enfance.'[8]

During the early days of his consulship at Civitavecchia, Stendhal had the good fortune to light on a number of hand-written histories of old crimes and scandals which had occupied Rome in the sixteenth and early seventeenth centuries. Some of these manuscripts were preserved in the family archives of impoverished nobles; for a small payment, the consul was permitted by their owners to peruse them and have a copyist transcribe them. He told Sainte-Beuve on 21 December 1834 that he had so far filled eight folio volumes; his idea at this stage was, if he fell on evil days again and needed to live by his pen, to translate them faithfully.

remarks about Stendhal is seldom recognized these days, observed on the following page, with equal truth, that *La Chartreuse de Parme* was 'le seul roman français écrit sur un peuple étranger, qui ait l'odeur de ce peuple'.

[6] *Correspondance*, ix. 82.   [7] *Rome, Naples et Florence*, i. 96.
[8] *Mélanges intimes et Marginalia*, ii. 170. The note is dated 2 June 1818.

This he never did: what he eventually settled on was a free adaptation of the originals which indeed, couched as they often are in a clumsy and ambiguous style, scarcely lend themselves to direct rendering. A few months later the eight volumes have become twelve, and these twelve, he claimed, were condensed from a hundred that he had consulted. 'J'ai négligé la valeur de vingt volumes *purement historiques*; j'ai cherché ce qui me plaît, comme peignant le cœur humain.'[9] On some of the tomes that he pored over the dust had become encrusted to the thickness of three crown pieces, so that when he rose from his desk his shirt was grey.

All this labour and expenditure were undertaken as an intelligent literary speculation. The narratives were to provide the material for a series of volumes (six were originally projected) of short stories. The first generic title that occurred to him, and which he used in his letter to Sainte-Beuve, was *Historiettes romaines*; Stendhal was thinking of Tallemant des Réaux's *Historiettes* which were currently being edited by Monmerqué and Taschereau and published by Levavasseur. It seemed reasonable to propose them first to this publisher. In the event it was François Buloz, editor of the recently founded *Revue des Deux Mondes*, who bought the publication rights. *Vittoria Accoramboni* and *Les Cenci* appeared in the pages of this periodical in 1837, *La Duchesse de Palliano* in 1838, *L'Abbesse de Castro* in 1839. Others were started, but Stendhal's sudden death prevented their completion.[1]

The manuscript copies, annotated by Stendhal, were bound up in fourteen volumes, the sale of which was negotiated after his death by Mérimée. The director of the British Museum, given the option to purchase, declined, and they were bought instead (for 600 francs) by the Bibliothèque Nationale.[2] Only a tiny proportion of their contents was worked up by Stendhal into finished stories. Often a few lines were sufficient to stimulate his imagination, and although he preferred to give his reader the impression that he had condensed material which, in the original, ran to several volumes, in reality his task was normally to give flesh to the bare

---

[9] *Correspondance*, ix. 122.
[1] The title *Chroniques italiennes*, now universally used, was adopted by Colomb for a posthumous collected edition issued in 1855.
[2] Manuscript Department, *fonds italien*, nos. 169–79, 296–7, 886. Casimir Stryienski was the first to examine them and publish his findings ('Source des *Chroniques italiennes*', pp. 214–66 in *Soirées du Stendhal Club*, 2ᵉ série, 1908).

narrative bones which the Roman scriveners provided him with. Thus, at a point near the end of *L'Abbesse de Castro*, Stendhal apologizes for the 'inevitably much abbreviated extract' which he proposes to give of Hélène's trial for violation of her vow of chastity. He alleges he has studied a transcript of the proceedings, couched in a mixture of Italian and Latin, which stretched to no fewer than eight folio volumes. In reality the narrative that he used covers thirty-five pages in one of the volumes found in his possession at his death.[3] Moreover, the account of this trial constitutes but an episode in *L'Abbesse de Castro*: the remainder of Stendhal's story sprang, apparently, from his own imagination, tempered and controlled by his sense of historical probability.

La Chartreuse de Parme, according to all the available evidence, started in very much the same way as any of the *Chroniques italiennes*; but at an early stage in its drafting, an obscure diversionary impulse caused Stendhal to turn it into something quite different. The historical setting was abandoned and the background became the Italy not of the *Rinascimento* but of the Holy Alliance; and instead of being a short story like *La Duchesse de Palliano* or a short novel like *L'Abbesse de Castro*, *La Chartreuse* developed into a very long novel, originally, perhaps, even longer than it is in the form it has come down to us. It is as though, by some extraordinary freak of genetic mutation, what was planted as a holly bush grew up as a vast forest tree.

The known facts are as follows. The year 1838 found Stendhal enjoying a prolonged spell of leave from his consular duties. Between March and July he was travelling extensively in the south of France, in Switzerland, in the Rhineland and the Low Countries. On his return to Paris his first task was to compose *La Duchesse de Palliano* which appeared in the *Revue des Deux Mondes* for 15 August. The following day, hunting through his Italian manuscripts, he happened on a particular story of some 700 words, reread it, and wrote in the margin of the first page: 'To make of this sketch a romanzetto' [*sic*]. He dated this note, after his usual custom.

The story in question was an anonymous, ill-written, malicious,

---

[3] *Successo occorso in Castro, città del Duca di Parma, nel monastero della Visitazione, fra l'abbadessa del medesimo e il vescovo di detta città l'anno 1572 . . .,* B.N. MS. *fonds italien* no. 171, fols. 134–68. See Ch. Dédéyan, *Stendhal et les 'Chroniques italiennes'*, pp. 44–45, 48–51.

and, from the point of view of an historian, garbled account of the
early life of the man who eventually became Supreme Pontiff under
the name Paul III. It was entitled *Origine delle grandezze della
famiglia Farnese*.[4] Alexander Farnese, who at the age of sixty-
seven became pope in succession to Clement VII, was the son of
a poorly circumstanced gentleman, and according to the author of
the *Origine* owed his immensely successful career initially at least
to the intrigues of his father's beautiful but unprincipled sister,
Vanozza or Vandozza Farnese. Among her lovers was counted
Rodrigo Borgia (surnamed Lenzuoli), nephew of Pope Calixtus III
and the richest of the Roman cardinals: this was the man destined
to become, in 1492, Pope Alexander VI, the notorious nepotist and
enlightened patron of Raphael and Michelangelo. At the age of
twenty Alexander Farnese entered this prelate's household where,
as a close relative of Vandozza, he enjoyed extraordinary favour.
In this atmosphere of debauchery and licence no check was put on
his violent and lustful humours, until on one occasion he over-
stepped the bounds of what was considered permissible to men of
rank and power even in those lawless days. This was when he
engineered the kidnapping of a young noblewoman on the highroad
outside Rome. He caused her to be taken to a house he owned and
there seduced or ravished her. The reigning pope, Innocent VIII,
to whom complaint was made, had the young man arrested and
imprisoned; but after some months his patron Rodrigo procured
his escape *per mezzo di una corda*, by means of a rope. (Benvenuto
Cellini is more specific about this incident: the future Pope
Paul III was let down from the window of his cell in a laundry
basket.) Having recovered his liberty, Alexander went into hiding,
at least for the remainder of the pontificate of Innocent VIII. But
when this pope died Cardinal Rodrigo was elected by the assembled
conclave and the fortunate young offshoot of the Farnese family
returned to Rome. Hereafter his career was assured: cardinal at
the age of twenty-four, living lavishly on the revenues of many a
fat see, he saw no reason to curb his lascivious instincts; the
chronicler mentions the name of one of his mistresses, Cleria, with
whom he maintained close relations during the latter part of his

[4] B.N. MS. *fonds italien*, no. 170, fols. 11–18. The text was transcribed and
published by Benedetto, op. cit., pp. 92–94. There have been various French
renderings, the most readily available being the translation printed by Martineau
in his annotated editions of *La Chartreuse de Parme* (Garnier, 1954, pp. 481–3,
and Gallimard (Bibliothèque de la Pléiade), 1956, pp. 499–500).

life, but with such secrecy that no scandal resulted. When in his turn he was elevated to the throne of St. Peter, he created his eldest son, Pierluigi, Duke of Parma; this dukedom remained in the family thereafter.[5] In such wise, concludes his biographer coldly, a princely family may owe its greatness originally to the good offices of a gifted whore.

Such was the 'sketch' of which Stendhal proposed, on 16 August 1838, 'to make . . . a romanzetto'. The Italian word was doubtless intended to be the equivalent of the French *historiette* which, as we have seen, was the term he originally thought of applying to the stories we now call his 'chroniques italiennes'. By great good fortune, this *romanzetto*, *historiette*, or *chronique*, has come down to us,[6] or at any rate the opening part of it, for Stendhal seems not to have pursued his narrative farther than Alexander's imprisonment by Innocent VIII. In places he follows quite closely the text of his source, but elsewhere, as was his custom, he embroiders, invents incidents, subtly modifies the characterization, and tones down or touches up the atmosphere of the original. Thus he elaborates on the beauty of Vandozza and confers on her an additional quality which the rude memorialist had forgotten: her intelligence, which shows itself in an admirable versatility in the invention of amusements. We are told how she electrified the pleasure-loving courtiers of Rome by appearing in the costume of a naiad, swimming in the waters of the Tiber by moonlight, and reciting verses by the leading local poet of the day. Rewritten by Stendhal, the sordid incident of the ravishing of an unnamed gentlewoman is transformed into a story of love at first sight. Attributing to his hero one of his own hobbies, digging for Roman remains, Stendhal describes how Alexander, while supervising some peasants he had hired to make an excavation, descried the lady in her coach and, fired by her beauty, attacked single-handed and put to flight the three armed men who were escorting her. The vulgar thug becomes, in this adaptation, an intrepid if unprincipled pursuer of beauty.

[5] Until 1731, when the eighth Duke of Parma, and the last in direct line of descent from Alexander Farnese, died without issue.

[6] It is printed, in the Divan edition, in *Mélanges de littérature*, i. 275–91. P. Arbelet was the first to compare it with the text of the *Origine delle grandezze della famiglia Farnese*. His conclusion, which we have adopted, was that it is in fact 'un premier essai du petit roman, du *romanzetto*, que Beyle, le 16 août 1838, voulait tirer de la chronique italienne' ('Les Origines de *la Chartreuse de Parme*', *Revue de Paris* (1922), vol. ii, pp. 356–79). It should be added, however, that Arbelet's view has not gone unchallenged.

Why did he discontinue the work? The life of this particular Renaissance pope was far from edifying, and Stendhal was still exercising diplomatic functions within the Papal States; it may have occurred to him that to rake up these ancient scandals was not the best way of ensuring smooth relations with the Vatican. Equally, he may have decided on purely aesthetic grounds that this was the wrong sort of story. The 'chroniques italiennes' which he did complete and publish have one element in common: they all end as bloodily and tragically as any melodrama by Webster. The Abbess of Castro, condemned to life-imprisonment, stabs herself. Beatrice Cenci is, with her brother and stepmother, sentenced and executed for the murder of her father. The Duke of Palliano stabs his wife's lover, then strangles the Duchess, only to be arrested, tried, and executed for the crime, when a new pope hostile to his house ascends the throne. But Alexander Farnese escapes the consequences of all his misdeeds and in his old age assumes the triple tiara. 'Il faut convenir', wrote Stendhal on the first page of his *romanzetto*, 'que cet Alexandre Farnèse fut un des hommes les plus heureux du XVIᵉ siècle.' His life was eminently a 'success story' which would have jarred with the sombre tone of the rest of the series.

Stendhal required, therefore, to do two things: to break the link which identified his hero with an historical pope; and to invent a tragic ending. He attained these two objects successively in the fortnight or so that followed his decision to work on the *Origine delle grandezze della famiglia Farnese*.

Since the well-known story of Alexander Farnese could not reasonably be tampered with, Stendhal had the luminous idea of simply transferring the events to modern times. The decision to do this was taken some time before 1 September (as we know from an inscription at the top of a particular page in a volume of Shakespeare's works which belonged to him).[7] Then on 3 September there occurred to him what he called, in two separate notes, the 'idea' of *La Chartreuse*.[8] The Charterhouse, or Carthusian monastery, in which Fabrice ends his days, was to provide if not a tragic, at any rate a sadly subdued ending in place of Alexander's triumphal elevation to the papal throne. The reader hears nothing of the

[7] For fuller details, see L. F. Benedetto's brochure, *La Chartreuse noire*.

[8] 'The 3 septembre 1838, I had the idea of the Char.' (note on the Chaper copy of *La Chartreuse de Parme*); 'The idea and some few sheets the third of September' (note on the Primoli copy of the *Vies de Haydn, de Mozart et de Métastase*): *Mélanges intimes et Marginalia*, ii. 366, 55.

Charterhouse until the very last page of the novel; but it was per-petually present in the author's mind, 'drawing towards itself, like a motionless engine, the whole plot and all the ramifications of the novel of Fabrice'.[9]

As soon as he had been visited by this final flash of illumination, Stendhal pushed all his papers into a drawer and left Paris for a short tour of Normandy and Britanny. It was normal with him, as we have had occasion to observe already, that some weeks or months should intervene between the moment of a novel's concep-tion and its execution. He returned to Paris on 3 November and the following day began writing and dictating *La Chartreuse de Parme*. By 26 December it was all finished, in fifty-two days of brilliant improvisation. The achievement was even more remark-able than at first appears, since cuts had to be made in the final part to placate the publisher, appalled at the uneconomic length of Stendhal's novel.[1] For once it seems proper to apply the over-used word 'miraculous' to this extraordinary eruption of a dense, intri-cate, dazzlingly poetic masterpiece: for sheer speed of composition at least, the feat has few parallels in the history of literature.[2]

How much of the character of Alexander Farnese passed into Fabrice del Dongo, and how much of his life-story did Stendhal preserve when inventing the imaginary biography of the hero of *La Chartreuse de Parme*? The lecherous ruffian portrayed in the *Origine* is totally different from the high-spirited but dreamy youth whom Stendhal conjures up for us. Certain incidents were trans-posed: most obviously, of course, the episode of the imprisonment and escape 'by means of a rope'. The *dramatis personae* of *La Chartreuse* can be traced back, *grosso modo*, to those of the Italian 'chronicle': Vandozza, Alexander's aunt, corresponds to Gina, Fabrice's aunt; her lover, Cardinal Rodrigo, to Gina's lover, Count Mosca; Cleria to Clélia; Pope Innocent VIII to Prince Ranuce-Ernest IV. If we turn from the original Italian text to Stendhal's first attempt at adaptation a few other connexions become apparent.

---

[9] G. Durand, *Le Décor mythique de la 'Chartreuse de Parme'*, p. 195.

[1] This is at any rate how we would interpret certain statements made by Stendhal in the form of marginal notes in the Crozet-Royer copy of *La Char-treuse*: 'Ceci a été *sabré* après [la page] 300 à peu près: le libraire Dupont trouvait le volume énorme'; and: 'M. Dupont me fit sabrer en mars 1839.' *Mélanges intimes et Marginalia*, ii. 367, 370.

[2] *Guy Mannering*, *César Birotteau*, Lawrence's *Kangaroo*, were written in as short a space of time; but this is, perhaps, the only respect in which they are comparable to *La Chartreuse*.

Alexander was supervising excavations when he observed the coach carrying the lady whose beauty so struck him; to secure her person he rushed to attack the escort. In chapter xi of *La Chartreuse* Fabrice is keeping an eye on workmen engaged by Mosca to dig up Roman antiques in a trench near the road leading from Parma to Casal-Maggiore; a dilapidated carriage approaches, the occupants of which are Marietta, an actress with whom Fabrice had spent some delightful hours in Parma, and Giletti, her protector; the latter, seeing his rival in a lonely spot, leaps on him with a sword and a rusty pistol ready cocked. There has been a change of aggressors and, of course, Fabrice is stirred by no impatient lust for Marietta; but the filiation between the two scenes is clear.

There are a few other details that Stendhal remembered and used in his novel; but far more important is the transposition of the peculiar ethos which the story of Alexander and Vandozza Farnese seemed to Stendhal to illustrate, into the context of the contemporary society which *La Chartreuse de Parme* purported to mirror. It is this moral anachronism, more than anything else, that gives the novel its specific savour.

The two or three pages with which Stendhal introduced his version of the life of Alexander Farnese are partly taken up with a discussion of the question, as he puts it, of how Italians about the year 1515 conducted their private *chasse au bonheur*. One particular passage in this preface is indispensable for a proper understanding of the moral substructure of *La Chartreuse de Parme*.

Au XVIe siècle, on mettait moins d'importance à donner et à recevoir la mort. La vie *toute seule*, séparée des choses qui la rendent heureuses, n'était pas estimée une propriété si importante. Avant de plaindre l'homme qui la perdait, on examinait le degré de bonheur dont cet homme jouissait; et, dans ce calcul, les femmes tenaient une place bien plus grande que de nos jours; il n'y avait point de honte à faire tout pour elles. La vanité et le *qu'en dira-t-on* naissaient à peine; et, par exemple, on ne prenait point au sérieux les honneurs décernés par les princes; l'opinion ne les chargeait point d'assigner les rangs dans la société; lorsque Charles-Quint fit le Titien comte, personne n'y prit garde, et le Titien lui-même eût préféré un diamant de cinquante sequins. J'achèverai le tableau en rappelant qu'on avait alors une sensibilité extrême pour la poésie, et que la moindre phrase, contenant un peu d'esprit, faisait, pendant une année entière, l'entretien de la ville de

Rome. De là tant d'épigrammes célèbres qui, aujourd'hui, paraissent dénuées de sel: le monde était jeune.

Notre pruderie n'a pas la plus petite idée de la civilisation qui, à cette époque, a régné dans le royaume de Naples et à Rome. Il faudrait un courage bien brutal pour oser l'expliquer d'une façon claire. Mais, par compensation, toutes nos vertus *momières* eussent semblé complètement ridicules aux contemporains de l'Arioste et de Raphaël; c'est qu'alors on n'estimait dans un homme que ce qui lui est personnel, et ce n'était pas une qualité personnelle que d'être comme tout le monde; on voit que les sots n'avaient pas de ressource.[3]

Stendhal gives us here a veritable breviary of Renaissance Italian ethics, embracing, if we may recapitulate for the sake of clarity, five articles, every single one of which contradicts modern assumptions. Life, having no value in itself, was not regarded as sacred; a man's life acquired value in proportion to the happiness he enjoyed; the love of women was reckoned much higher in the assessment of this happiness; worldly honours much lower; and finally, poetry, or even mere verbal dexterity, was held in universal esteem. In short, the sixteenth century was the age of personal distinction, in contrast to the nineteenth century which is the age of conformity to the norm.

Each of these generalizations may be reduced to a particular moral principle which is amply illustrated in the behaviour and outlook of the characters of *La Chartreuse de Parme*, or rather, of certain characters in this novel, for they fall into two distinct categories, the sympathetic and the antipathetic, the elect and the damned: Mosca is opposed to Rassi, the Duchessa Sanseverina contrasts with the Marchesa Raversi, Clélia, even, is of a different species from her father Fabio Conti. The moral divisions in *La Chartreuse de Parme* are established with pitiless rigour: there is no mingling of good and evil, but vice calls to vice, and no character is heroic in part. Those who devote their lives to enlarging their personal fortunes, like the elder Del Dongo, also tremble for their lives—misers are necessarily cowards. The *élite* rate love higher than wealth or political power and are ready at any point to renounce the latter for the former: witness Mosca; the snobs, Fabio Conti, Rassi, are not merely loveless but on occasion villainous. A poet, Ferrante Palla, may be embraced by a duchess; and the nobly born Fabrice does not disdain to correct the

3 *Mélanges de littérature*, i. 277–9.

ill-spelt compositions of his servant Ludovic who is a homespun sonneteer.

What Stendhal did in *La Chartreuse* was to transfer to modern times the values which, according to his reading of history, had guided the society of early sixteenth-century Italy. These obsolete values form the secret code of a limited group of characters, a loose freemasonry of generous spirits evolving amid the reefs and shoals of envy and persecution. The author himself, fearing, or feigning, that the moral outlook of his hero and his hero's adherents might appear bizarre, unacceptable, if not downright perverse to his French readers in 1839, adopts his usual ironical stance, pretending to blame, but blaming with such clumsy philistinism that no reader could mistake his intention. His usual 'excuse' for his characters is that they are Italians *and know no better*. The contrast between Italian immorality and French pseudo-morality is a constant discreet refrain; and such contrasts are always accompanied by an ironical pirouette.

J'avouerai [Stendhal wrote in the brief *avertissement* placed at the beginning of *La Chartreuse de Parme*] que j'ai eu la hardiesse de laisser aux personnages les aspérités de leurs caractères; mais, en revanche, je le déclare hautement, je déverse le blâme le plus moral sur beaucoup de leurs actions. A quoi bon leur donner la haute moralité et les grâces des caractères français, lesquels aiment l'argent par-dessus tout et ne font guère de péchés par haine ou par amour? Les Italiens de cette nouvelle sont à peu près le contraire.

In the novel proper, there is an early instance of an infringement of conventional morality, treated in the lightly ironical mode, in Stendhal's account of the 'arrangement' by which Gina Pietranera is persuaded by Count Mosca to settle in Parma (chapter vi). Since Mosca has a wife living, he cannot offer her marriage. On the other hand, court conventions would not allow a lady of her station to live openly as his mistress in the capital city of the state which, under the prince, he administers. He can, of course, resign and together they could live at Milan on the count's exiguous personal fortune. A minister on the French side of the Alps might have boggled at handing in his portfolio on so trumpery a pretext as wanting to live with the woman he loved; but, Stendhal reminds us, we are not on the French side of the Alps. However, if the young widow with whom he has fallen so violently in love is reluctant to agree to a penurious existence with an unemployed admirer, the Count has an alternative proposal. Let her contract, for form's sake, a marriage with a certain Duke Sanseverina-Taxis, a Parmesan subject of vast wealth but obscure lineage who, if she consents to bestow her hand on him, will be happy to accept an embassy in a far country and a certain coveted decoration awarded by the sovereign. Since he is already well stricken in years, his bride may hope to mourn him before she is much older.[4] Gina raises—but how seriously?—the question of the immorality of this arrangement. It would be an arrangement, replies Mosca, no more immoral than many a similar one at the court of Parma or a dozen others. Whatever is sanctioned by public opinion, is moral; morality has no other basis or reality; and in an absolute monarchy public opinion responds to the signals given by the ruler's smile or frown. 'Soyez bien convaincue que ce mariage ne semblera singulier chez nous que du jour où je serai disgracié. Cet arrangement n'est une friponnerie envers personne, voilà l'essentiel, ce me semble.' Never was a violation of the seventh commandment so elegantly and persuasively proposed.

Not, indeed, that Gina needs much persuasion, even though she has not the excuse of being passionately in love with Mosca: Fabrice, already, has first place in her heart. Stendhal does not even trouble to record her agreement to Mosca's proposition; he dismisses the matter with a brief paragraph registering disapproval— a disapproval which, however, dissolves halfway through the second sentence into amused irony:

Pourquoi l'historien qui suit fidèlement les moindres détails du récit qu'on lui a fait serait-il coupable? Est-ce sa faute si les personnages, séduits par des passions qu'il ne partage point malheureusement pour lui, tombent dans des actions profondément immorales? Il est vrai que des choses de cette sorte ne se font plus dans un pays où l'unique passion survivante à toutes les autres est l'argent, moyen de vanité.

Reading *La Chartreuse de Parme*, we are periodically reminded (but not so frequently that Stendhal can be accused of a vexatious mannerism) of the differences that mark off these Italians from their

---

[4] Stendhal's sketch of this episodic figure, 'joli petit vieillard de soixante-huit ans, gris pommelé, bien poli, bien propre, immensément riche, mais pas assez noble', seems to be a reminiscence of Figaro's description of Bartholo in *Le Barbier de Séville*: 'un beau gros, court, jeune vieillard, gris pommelé, rusé, rasé, blasé...'

more 'civilized' counterparts. In some ways they are more realistic: they are, as we have seen, less liable to be distracted from the all-important pursuit of happiness by trivial considerations of conventional morality. In certain circumstances, however, they could be better described as romanticists, possessing as they do to a high degree the faculty of imaginative response to the beauties of nature. They find the happiness they seek where the ambitious materialists of Paris would never look for it—for example in a solitary midnight walk along the wooded banks of a placid lake. Stendhal describes the scene with an effortless restraint which is more picturesque in its results than the most luxuriant of Scott's set-pieces.

Les arbres des bouquets de bois que le petit chemin traversait à chaque instant dessinaient le noir contour de leur feuillage sur un ciel étoilé, mais voilé par une brume légère. Les eaux et le ciel étaient d'une tranquillité profonde; l'âme de Fabrice ne put résister à cette beauté sublime; il s'arrêta, puis s'assit sur un rocher qui s'avançait dans le lac, formant comme un petit promontoire. Le silence universel n'était troublé, à intervalles égaux, que par la petite lame du lac qui venait expirer sur la grève. Fabrice avait un cœur italien; j'en demande pardon pour lui: ce défaut, qui le rendra moins aimable, consistait surtout en ceci: il n'avait de vanité que par accès, et l'aspect seul de la beauté sublime le portait à l'attendrissement, et ôtait à ses chagrins leur pointe âpre et dure. Assis sur son rocher isolé, n'ayant plus à se tenir en garde contre les agents de la police, protégé par la nuit profonde et le vaste silence, de douces larmes mouillèrent ses yeux, et il trouva là, à peu de frais, les moments les plus heureux qu'il eût goûtés depuis longtemps.[5]

There is irony even in this passage, but here it is much muted. In any case, nowhere in *La Chartreuse de Parme* is it obtrusive, or ferocious.

Besides being Italian, these characters are also Catholics, and the younger they are, the more devout. Of all Stendhal's heroes, Fabrice alone is a believer,[6] though the manner of his life will not edify the pious. Octave's religion is, to say the least, suspect; Julien is as obdurate a non-Christian as the great Apostate his name-sake; Lucien harbours a gentlemanly scepticism; Lamiel, when

---

[5] *La Chartreuse de Parme*, i. 269–70.

[6] Together with Jules Branciforte, the hero of *L'Abbesse de Castro*, who, for instance, when he thinks his mistress is lost to him, is restrained from suicide by the thought that divine justice might punish him in the hereafter by forcing him to witness Hélène's marriage to another.

her turn came, was to prove a pure pagan. But Fabrice needs to do no violence to his convictions when he embarks on an ecclesiastical career. Even as a child he had frightened his mother by the fervour of his faith: 'Fabrice avait pris au sérieux toutes les choses religieuses qu'on lui avait enseignées chez les jésuites. Quoique fort pieuse elle-même, le fanatisme de cet enfant la fit frémir.'[7] Throughout, he firmly believes himself to be in the hand of God, he looks forward to a life beyond the grave, he knows there must be atonement and forgiveness for his transgressions. 'Il avait trop d'esprit', writes Stendhal almost on the last page of his novel, 'pour ne pas sentir qu'il avait beaucoup à réparer.' In these words no mephistophelian irony is detectable. Fabrice's logic is impeccable; that he should start from false premisses is not something that should lower him in the novelist's esteem or in the reader's, for how, given his origins and upbringing, could he have grown up anything other than a faithful son of the Church? 'Religion is an ironic device in [Stendhal's] novels, not something true or false in itself. So that, like Proust, Joyce James and others who use religion for fictive ends, *inside his work* he is neutral towards it.'[8] Outside, of course, he was relentless: 'a passionate atheist', Brandes called him; 'an honest atheist', said Nietzsche, who added that he was even a little envious of Stendhal for having got in first with an excellent irreligious quip which he, Nietzsche, would have been delighted to have coined: 'God's only excuse is that he does not exist. . . .'[9]

From his viewpoint of a sturdy non-participant, Stendhal, looking in on the cloudy whirlpool of religious commitment, was able to draw certain distinctions which would hardly occur to a believer: that, for instance, frontiers change the quality of faith, and that, despite etymology, the Catholics of France are not to be identified with those of Spain or Italy; the Irish kern and the Sicilian peasant, alike ruled by the parish priest, manifest striking differences in outlook and customs. The Italian Catholic is a special breed of which Fabrice del Dongo is a fair representative specimen. His belief in the direct intervention of providence in human affairs is carried to extreme lengths in the regard he pays to portents and oracles:'sans

[7] *La Chartreuse de Parme*, i. 27.

[8] A. Cook, 'Stendhal's irony', *Essays in Criticism*, vol. viii (1958), p. 366.

[9] *Ecce Homo: Warum ich so klug bin*, 3. The aphorism which Nietzsche quotes is not to be found in Stendhal's published work, but was reported by Mérimée as one of his sayings.

manquer d'esprit, Fabrice ne put parvenir à voir que sa demi-croyance dans les présages était pour lui une religion.'¹ In Stendhal's other writings there may be found curious confirmation of the prevalence of superstition among the Italians of his day, whatever their rank. Few of them were unbelievers. In the country-side every natural calamity (hail-storm, flood, or epidemic) was regarded as a punishment from on high. 'Cette superstition pro-fonde des gens de la campagne se communique aux classes élevées, par les nourrices, les bonnes, les domestiques de toute espèce.' There are, in Italy, stone or plaster madonnas who turn their eyes or heave sighs. 'Nous remarquons que la haute société de Rome croit à ces miracles, ou, du moins, a peur d'offenser la Madone, en se permettant d'en plaisanter.'²

Fabrice sets down as a miraculous favour every circumstance which turns unexpectedly to his advantage. After he has killed Giletti he makes for the Austrian frontier with the dead man's passport. The personal particulars given on this document corre-spond in no way to Fabrice's; but the passport officer, after some hesitation, lets him across. A true miracle, thinks Fabrice, and enters the first church he sees at Bologna to give thanks. In reality the official had been a personal friend of Giletti's and had assumed that the strolling player had sold his passport for a good sum: to arrest this unknown young man on a charge of travelling with false papers might have brought serious trouble on Giletti.

Kneeling before the altar, Fabrice recites the list of sins which has been taught him, stopping wherever he comes to one of which he thinks he should make confession. The list includes *simony*, which he interprets in the literal sense, as meaning to procure office in the Church in return for money.

Si on lui eût proposé de donner cent louis pour devenir premier grand vicaire de l'archevêque de Parme, il eût repoussé cette idée avec horreur; mais, quoiqu'il ne manquât ni d'esprit ni surtout de logique, il ne lui vint pas une seule fois à l'esprit que le crédit du comte Mosca, employé en sa faveur, fût une *simonie*. Tel est le triomphe de l'éducation jésuitique: donner l'habitude de ne pas faire attention à des choses plus claires que le jour. Un Français, élevé au milieu des traits d'intérêt personnel et de l'ironie de Paris [as it might be, Lucien Leuwen], eût pu, sans être de mauvaise foi, accuser Fabrice d'hypocrisie au moment

¹ *La Chartreuse de Parme*, i. 274.
² *Promenades dans Rome*, i. 10, 116.

même où notre héros ouvrait son âme à Dieu avec la plus extrême sincérité et l'attendrissement le plus profond.[3]

This time it is with no idea of endorsing his hero's attitude that Stendhal contrasts him with his stock Parisian. The passage quoted is only the conclusion of a long development in which Stendhal insists—and insists, for once, too much—on how Catholicism, as inculcated by Fabrice's Jesuit teachers, '*ôte le courage de penser aux choses inaccoutumées*, et défend surtout l'*examen personnel*, comme le plus énorme des péchés; c'est un pas vers le protestantisme'.[4] Now one of the most widely accepted assumptions about the heroes of Stendhal is that typically they spend their lives striving to live up to a private image of themselves; they believe, or act as though they believe, that 'a man owes a duty to his own definition of himself', in the words of R. M. Adams which we have quoted already.[5] Fabrice is the outstanding exception to this rule. Having accepted that self-examination is sinful, he never asks where he is going, he never wonders what sort of a man he is; unlike the others, he has no ideal image of himself which he is striving to realize. In psychological parlance, Fabrice is 'integrated'. His life is as unorientated as Lucien's but, unlike Lucien, he is completely untroubled by the fact. He watches, amused and barely concerned, the various events that befall him, the different passions that pull at him. Always himself, he never acts a part (whereas Julien is rarely off the stage). 'Il avait l'âme trop haute pour chercher à imiter les autres jeunes gens et, par exemple, pour vouloir jouer avec un certain sérieux le rôle d'amoureux.' This is said of Fabrice when he is living at Naples, having been packed off to that city by Mosca with instructions to follow lectures in theology and choose a mistress from some noble Neapolitan house. When, the four years' purgatory at Naples having been completed, he arrives at Parma, it is Mosca who reads on the young man's countenance his serene unawareness that anything

---

[3] *La Chartreuse de Parme*, i. 359.

[4] Ibid. 358. The words echo the account given in *Lucien Leuwen* (i. 329) of Mme de Chasteller's education: 'Au Sacré-Cœur, une religieuse qui s'était emparée de son esprit en caressant tous ses petits caprices d'enfance, lui faisait remplir tous ses devoirs avec une sorte de religion par ces simples mots: "Faites cela par amitié pour moi." Car c'est une impiété, une témérité menant au *protestantisme*, que de dire à une petite fille: "Faites telle chose parce qu'elle est raisonnable." *Faites cela par amitié pour moi* répond à tout, et ne conduit pas à examiner ce qui est raisonnable ou non.'   [5] p. 88 above.

in the world is of the least importance except happiness, and expresses this idea in a phrase which tells us all we need to know about Fabrice: 'Tout est simple à ses yeux parce que tout est vu de haut.'[6]

Seeing everything from above makes everything seem simple but also makes everything seem slightly unreal. The celebrated scene in the ninth chapter when Fabrice, hiding at the top of a tower in his native Grianta, watches a religious procession in the village street below, symbolizes aptly his whole progression through life: at every stage he is a non-participant, looking on from a lofty vantage-point, and has as it were to pinch himself to be convinced he is really there. At Waterloo he asks himself periodically, whenever he has a moment for reflection, whether this is a real battle he is involved in; and when he is finally locked up in the highest cell in the redoubtable Citadel of Parma, again he asks himself, vaguely astonished: 'Mais ceci est-il une prison? est-ce là ce que j'ai tant redouté?... Serais-je un de ces grands courages comme l'antiquité en a montré quelques exemples au monde? *Suis-je un héros sans m'en douter?*'[7]

A hero unaware that he is one is perhaps the perfect specimen of his kind. The risk Stendhal incurred, especially in the first part of his novel, was that Fabrice's imperturbable remoteness from events, the innocent gaiety of his non-involvement, tend to affect the whole novel with unreality. There is, certainly, danger for Fabrice: danger from the Austrian police, for whom he is a marked man; danger from Rassi's minions, who also want him under lock and key. He stands in peril from Mosca's stiletto; should he drive the minister's jealousy beyond a certain point, and from Giletti's pistol, when jealousy does goad this other offended male to murderous rage. But all these threats are like the ploughed field at Waterloo which Fabrice crosses with Ney's escort, observing curiously how the muddy earth in the furrows keeps leaping unaccountably three or four feet into the air. Only when two hussars immediately behind him fall from their horses with a sharp groan, does he realize that the mud is spurting because cannon-balls are striking it. Yet the unreal appearance of danger does not lessen the sinister fact of its existence.

It means, however, that *La Chartreuse de Parme* is bathed in an

---

[6] *La Chartreuse de Parme*, i. 229, 252.
[7] Ibid. ii. 127, 133–4. My italics.

atmosphere of such bland serenity that we read the first dozen chapters at any rate as we might one of the more benign fairy-tales of childhood. It is a fact that we tremble less for Fabrice when he is on the run than we do for Jean Valjean in *Les Misérables*. And a hero who bears a charmed life is perhaps not fully acceptable in a modern novel. Certainly this criticism has been levelled against *La Chartreuse*, and by a practitioner of the art of fiction. 'Everything is too easy', comments Frank O'Connor; 'there is no harsh reality that stops anyone dead. Imaginative freedom, the quality for which the dramatist has to struggle, is only a burden to the novelist. His characters are best determined and delimited; his prisons are best bolted and barred.'[8]

The criticism may be widened to include other than the purely narrative aspects of the work. It is, for instance, arguable that a great novel requires a certain moral density, which is not, of course, conferred by the spectacle of virtue rewarded and wickedness confounded, but rather, perhaps, by the introduction of critical moral conflicts, either between the individual characters or within a single character's conscience. Of any such thing there is hardly a trace in this book, for the characters have no conscience. 'In *La Chartreuse de Parme*, where everyone is grossly immoral, and the heroine a kind of monster' (Henry James's words[9]), what room is there for moral doubts or scruples? We have seen with what little compunction Gina consented to contract a marriage intended as a mere cloak for adultery. The struggles of conscience Clélia endures when she finds herself torn between her duty to her father and her love for Fabrice are not of the kind to wring our hearts: Fabio Conti is so odious, and the young prisoner so devoted and so charming. The force of her resolution is in any case so weak that she needs to bind herself by a religious vow to make it effective—a vow in the subsequent violation of which she employs all the resources of a fond woman's casuistry.[1] As for Fabrice, the nearest he comes to the anguish of moral decision is when he tries to make up his mind

---

[8] *The Mirror in the Roadway*, p. 57.

[9] *Literary Reviews and Essays*, p. 156.

[1] Clélia and Fabrice fall in love with one another when Fabrice is a prisoner in the fortress of which Clélia's father, Fabio Conti, is the commandant; the latter risks disgrace and perhaps court-martial if Fabrice escapes. Gina and Mosca plot this escape, which can be contrived only if Clélia co-operates. She swears to the Virgin that if the plan succeeds she will never set eyes on Fabrice again. The Virgin, it would seem, acquiesces, for Fabrice secures his liberty, but she is finally frustrated, for Clélia admits her lover to her bed *in the dark*.

how to deal with the too amorous duchess, his father's younger sister. He would not for the world hurt her feelings; he is filled with a proper gratitude for the benefits she has showered on him—he owes his brilliant position in the world entirely to her. On the other hand he feels for her no more than the affection a nephew might normally be expected to feel for an indulgent, good-looking aunt; and he would hate to disturb Mosca's happiness. But again, how does one avoid playing the ridiculous part of Joseph with Potiphar's wife? Fabrice reaches no firm decision and in his conduct wavers between a frigidity which he feels is ungracious and demonstrations of tenderness of which he later repents. In the category of grave moral dilemmas, George Eliot and Henry James have accustomed us to something rather different. There is a particular 'great tradition' to which *La Chartreuse de Parme* can emphatically not be attached.

It would be unfair, nevertheless, to say that the characters in this book are entirely ruled by unreflecting hedonism. There are one or two occasions when they almost succeed in giving the impression of being concerned about the rights and wrongs of a specific course of action. Here, for instance, is Fabrice, in desperate need of a mount to escape from the Austrian gendarmerie; from the hollow trunk of a chestnut tree in which he is hiding he espies a groom leading a fine hunter along the highroad. He recollects an aphorism of Mosca's, according to which the dangers that threaten a man are always a proper measure of the rights he may assume over his neighbour's life and property. In his position, therefore, Fabrice would be justified in firing a bullet at the groom's head and galloping off on his horse. 'A peine de retour à Parme, j'enverrais de l'argent à cet homme ou à sa veuve... mais ce serait une horreur.' Instead, by a combination of threats and largess, he frightens the groom into giving up the horse, and returns to safety without burdening his conscience with murder on top of highway robbery. But, as he anticipated, Mosca chides him for his folly: 'puisque ce valet de chambre tenait votre vie entre ses mains, vous aviez droit de prendre la sienne.' The first principle of statecraft, applied by everyone from Prince Ernest IV downwards, is epitomized in the maxim: 'It is better to kill the devil than let the devil kill you.' Fabrice promises to bear this in mind in future, but he is not altogether convinced. 'Aurais-je dû tirer un coup de pistolet au valet de chambre qui tenait par la bride le cheval maigre? Sa raison lui disait oui, mais son cœur ne pouvait s'accoutumer à l'image sanglante du beau jeune homme tombant de cheval dé-figuré.'[2] The conflict of principles is rendered a little suspect by Stendhal's phrasing. Would it have made any difference if the horse had been in the possession of a pot-bellied, pock-marked, surly ruffian, instead of a slim, neatly dressed adolescent who when Fabrice noticed him was cheerfully and tunefully singing a well-known air from a Neapolitan opera? Is Fabrice the possessor of a delicate conscience, or is he merely squeamish?

If questions of right and wrong are settled on such adventitious or, morally speaking, frivolous grounds, how can Stendhal escape the charge of a lack of high seriousness in *La Chartreuse de Parme*? When we turn from the domain of ethics to that of politics, the scandal is, if anything, greater. The virulent social criticism of the earlier novels is absent from *La Chartreuse de Parme*; perhaps because the vast stage of a great and powerful country which had dominated Europe politically for a generation has here shrunk to the closet dimensions of an insignificant principality; perhaps again because the power-hungry are necessarily, in the value-system of *La Chartreuse*, regarded as poor dupes who have not realized that power is at best one of the compensation prizes of life. Power cannot release the holder of it from the bonds of the very etiquette which his dignity obliges him to uphold. His subjects may attend the delightful evening gatherings organized by Gina at the Palazzo Sanseverino, but not the prince: it would be unheard of for a sovereign to pay a social call on a private citizen. The misery of unlimited power is borne in on Ernest IV one cold wet Thursday evening as he watches the carriages of Gina's guests roll up to her door: 'D'autres s'amusaient, et lui, prince souverain, maître absolu, qui devait s'amuser plus que personne au monde, il con-naissait l'ennui.'[3] The prince is bored, the prince is frightened too:

---

[2] These incidents are recounted at the end of chap. ix and in chap. x.

[3] *La Chartreuse de Parme*, i. 222. 'Quelque condition qu'on se figure, si l'on assemble tous les biens qui peuvent nous appartenir, la royauté est le plus beau poste du monde; et cependant, qu'on s'en imagine accompagné de toutes les satisfactions qui peuvent le toucher,... s'il est sans ce qu'on appelle divertisse-ment, le voilà malheureux, et plus malheureux que le moindre de ses sujets, qui joue et se divertit' (Pascal, *Pensées* 139 (Brunschvicg edition)). Who would think to find Pascal illustrated in *La Chartreuse de Parme*? But in 1804 Stendhal had noted: 'Quand je lis Pascal il me semble que je me relis... Je crois que c'est celui de tous les écrivains à qui je ressemble le plus par l'âme' (Pensées, *Filosofia nova*, ii. 353-4).

when he decides to cast formality to the winds and join the party,
it takes his aide an hour to ensure that the street from the palace of
His Serene Highness to that of the Duchess is cleared of possible
regicides. There are evenings when this monarch, whose manners
are an imitation of Louis XIV's but whose humour is often nearer
that of Philip II of Spain, dares not retire for the night until his
apartments have been searched by the only man he trusts, Count
Mosca della Rovere. 'Si une feuille du parquet vient à crier, il
saute sur ses pistolets et croit à un libéral caché sous son lit.'[4] Earlier
in his reign he had ordered the hanging of a couple of conspirators
and had never had a quiet moment since.

Balzac, misled by his reverence for crowned heads, said of
Ernest-Ranuce that he had in him the stuff of a great administrator, a tsar of all the Russias; Zola, surely, made a saner estimate in
calling the portrait 'a biting caricature of royalty by a man of
infinite intelligence, and nothing more'.[5] His terror of assassination
is none the less grotesquely pathetic for being well founded. In
the end he dies a violent death, but as the victim of a private ven-
detta, and not—or only indirectly—for any political reasons. These
'liberals' who, he thinks, are thirsting for his blood are a purely
imaginary bugbear. They are, for the time being, the opposition
party, waiting in the wings for a change in the sovereign's mood.
The label is in any case meaningless: Mosca, the most liberal-
minded of men, is nominally a conservative, while Fabio Conti,
mean-souled, slippery, and vindictive, is a leading light of the
liberal party. Possibly Stendhal's intentions were satirical; in party
politics, policy counts for nothing, the temporary favour of the
ruling monarch, or, in a parliamentary democracy, of the elec-
torate, is all that matters. But there is nothing in the novel to
enforce such an interpretation; the disabused reader may spell it
out, if he chooses.

Rather, Stendhal is. at pains to play down the portentousness of
the political engine he displays to us. Spies, prison-warders, and
hangmen are there, but, for the moment, so allusively there as to
be almost inoffensive. The prince's writ runs only so far, with a
good team of horses and if needs be a supply of false passports one
is soon across the frontier; the occasional barbed epigram shot off
in the drawing-rooms of Naples or Rome, the odd anecdote dropped

---

[4] *La Chartreuse de Parme*, i. 171.
[5] *Les Romanciers naturalistes*, p. 113.

in the ear of a Parisian journalist, will make the Prince of Parma the laughing-stock of Europe; and this he knows, and dreads. Tyranny, then, is clipped, unreal. Political life is a game of skill, with a strong element of hazard, in which the stakes do not appear to be ruinously high. 'Une cour, c'est ridicule,' Gina tells her sister-in-law the Marchesa del Dongo, 'mais c'est amusant; c'est un jeu qui intéresse, mais dont il faut accepter les règles. Qui s'est jamais avisé de se récrier contre le ridicule des règles du whist? Et pourtant une fois qu'on s'est accoutumé aux règles, il est agréable de faire l'adversaire *chlemm*.'[6]

The sophisticated reader, turning the first hundred or two hundred pages of *La Chartreuse de Parme*, would be justified in asking whether this is anything more than an elaborate, brightly coloured fable. And it is undeniable that the first part of the novel is, or seems to be, a harmless fairy-story: the memoirs of Saint-Simon in a Ruritanian setting; Bardèche's definition of *La Chartreuse* as a 'picaresque-poetic novel'[7] is wholly applicable . . . to the first thirteen chapters. But there is a second part. The twofold division had been used before, in *Le Rouge et le Noir* and in *Lucien Leuwen*, but not to the same end. There, it corresponded simply to a change in geographical location, from the provinces to the capital, with all that that implied. In *La Chartreuse* the theatre of action, apart from Fabrice's dash across the Alps during the 'Hundred Days', remains the same throughout (Parma and the adjoining states and territories); the change is one of tone. A dramatic shift in the lighting turns the ropes of tinsel into iron chains; an infernal magic converts the cardboard daggers into actual stilettos; the stagey world of *opera buffa*[8] is brusquely transformed

---

[6] *La Chartreuse de Parme*, i. 181–2. This passage is transcribed not from the text of the first edition (reproduced in the Divan works) but from the text as emended for the Garnier edition. In the original version, Gina confused the terms used in two different games, whist and piquet.

It is worth noting that she uses exactly the same metaphor in advising Fabrice how to comport himself at his theological college: 'Crois ou ne crois pas à ce qu'on t'enseignera, *mais ne fais jamais aucune objection*. Figure-toi qu'on t'enseigne les règles du jeu de whist; est-ce que tu ferais des objections aux règles du whist?' (i. 215). Thus, for Gina at any rate, religion and politics exist on the same level of meaningless triviality.

[7] *Stendhal romancier*, p. 396.

[8] A major aspect of the 'dévaluation du réel dans *la Chartreuse de Parme*' of which J. D. Hubert writes (article in *Stendhal Club*, no. 5 (1959), pp. 47–53) is the perpetual play that Stendhal makes with analogies between the world of the theatre and court life.

into a hard, hateful reality. Nowhere has any novelist achieved a similar aesthetic *coup de théâtre*, by startling his reader out of the dream of false security into which he has been lulled by a smooth tale of adventure and intrigue, and surrounding him thereafter with the harsh clamour of urgent passion and authentic tragedy.

The thirteenth chapter, the last of the first part, relates Fabrice's maddest and most pointless escapade—his undercover return to Parma (risking arrest for the murder of Giletti) in pursuit of an opera-singer called La Fausta of whom he is only very moderately enamoured. After this prank he bolts back to Bologna and safety. In the first chapter of the second part, Gina learns that the proceedings which have been initiated against Fabrice in his absence are on the point of conclusion, and that the sentence of death or life-imprisonment will be presented very shortly for the Prince to sign. Even signed, this sentence will represent no threat to Fabrice's life or liberty, so long as he remains outside the principality; but it will spell the end of a promising career in the Church, with the ultimate prospect of becoming archbishop of Parma.

In the ensuing pages Stendhal is at his most inimitable: every clause is at once graphic and dynamic; the scene, the characters, are sparkling with life, and the current of the narrative flows without a word that clogs. It is the hour, perhaps, of Gina's greatest triumph. The Prince is sure that she will come in tears to plead for her nephew's life; when she is announced, he orders his aide to ask her to wait; and for the next twenty minutes savours the exquisite pleasure of *reigning*, with the power of life and death. The Duchess is then ushered in; she is dressed as for a journey, and her eyes are sparkling with gaiety. She has come, she announces, to take her humble leave. The Prince, who has for longer than consorts with his dignity cherished the hope of succeeding Count Mosca in her favours, is reduced to stammering and squirming in his chair. For three or four reasons, he cannot afford to let her go. Gina, forgetting none of the required formulae of respect, speaks her mind with cheerful candour about the venality of the judges of Parma, and renews her parting homages. Her success is complete: the Prince capitulates abjectly and gives her what she asks for: a written promise not to sign the sentence that has been pronounced against Fabrice, and not to permit the proceedings to be taken any farther; he also, at her request, exiles the Marchesa

Raversi, whom she suspects of being the principal instigator of the plot against her nephew.

Once more it seems that nothing more serious is being played than a rubber of whist, in which the Duchess, producing an unexpected trump, wins the vital trick. But in the next few pages the narrative races on into a totally different climate. We are in a kind of *Alice in Wonderland* in reverse, where the pack of cards turns on the heroine, and 'off with his head' rings out no longer as a meaningless ejaculation. Mosca had warned the other two a long time before: 'nous ne sommes pas ici en France, où tout finit par des chansons ou par un emprisonnement d'un an ou deux.'[9] The *élite* can, with boldness and intelligence, foil their base adversaries the first time, and the second time; but sooner or later they are tripped up, 'de tous temps les vils Sancho Pança l'emporteront à la longue sur les sublimes don Quichotte'.[1] Gina imagines she has tied the Prince's hands and sent her chief enemy, Mme Raversi, where she can do no more mischief; in any case, Fabrice is out of harm's way, whatever sentence is pronounced, signed, and sealed. The events that precipitate themselves upset every one of her calculations. By antedating the sentence which Rassi presents him for signature, the Prince evades the obligation she had forced him to contract. Mme Raversi, stung into action, decoys Fabrice on to Parmesan territory and informs the police; he is arrested at the frontier post and sent under heavy guard to the capital. At seven in the evening, loaded with chains, he passes beneath the portals of the infamous Citadel of Parma.

Stendhal chose a peculiarly effective device to show how the Duchess's spirit is broken by these tidings. He introduces a character whose previous appearances had been brief and on the whole insignificant: this is Clélia Conti, who from this point on plays a major part in the story. The daughter of the prison governor, she has watched, with compassion and even indignation, Fabrice's consignment to prison. The same evening she attends a social gathering in the house of Count Zurla, who as Minister of the Interior had dispatched the squad which arrested Fabrice. The Duchess Sanseverina is also there, radiant, unsuspecting, and her

---

[9] *La Chartreuse de Parme*, i. 308. Another reminiscence of Beaumarchais; 'tout finit par des chansons' is the last line of the song that concludes *Le Mariage de Figaro*.
[1] Ibid. 310.

vivacity is observed by the pensive girl with a sort of anguish. At length the terrible moment of illumination arrives: Clélia sees a friendly informant whisper in her ear—and sees the Duchess make her departure, the smile on her lips now frozen into a polite grimace, too sick at heart to pronounce the conventional leave-taking to her hostess. 'Jamais je n'oublierai', reflects Clélia, 'ce que je viens de voir; quel changement subit! Comme les yeux de la duchesse, si beaux, si radieux, sont devenus mornes, éteints, après le mot fatal que le marquis N... est venu lui dire!'[2]

In the harrowing account of Gina's despair the barbarity of an absolute despotism impinges on the reader for the first time; the exiguity of the territory, the insipidity of the court are forgotten, for these do not alter the reality of the grief and the cruelty. The Duchess is now as much a prisoner in Parma as Fabrice himself; she cannot leave him to his fate and must remain where there is a possibility she may be of help to him. If she takes the most drastic vengeance—the idea occurs to her even as early as this—and has the Prince assassinated, his successor will hang Fabrice as her accomplice. As for engineering his escape from the sinister Tower, this would call for a magic carpet. Gina, whom we have never seen save as a brilliant strategist and woman of action, is reduced to mumbling pointless lamentations or indulging in hopeless flights of fancy, pathetic daydreams of a safe life in Paris, with Fabrice an officer in a French regiment. The only decision she reaches is to break, ostensibly, with Mosca—for a variety of reasons, but chiefly because the danger besetting Fabrice has quickened or brought more into the open her love for him and this, correspondingly, makes Mosca's faithful adoration merely irritating to her.

The irruption of a disastrous reality has no more tragic effect than this: to destroy the admirable, unsentimental attachment which had hitherto linked in fragile harmony these three nonchalant hedonists, the cynical middle-aged minister of state, the glittering duchess, and the harum-scarum youth. Fabrice's imprisonment begins the process by driving a wedge between Gina and Mosca; the exclusive passion for Clélia which he develops in prison con-tinues the work of destruction, for when at last he is delivered, Gina realizes he is lost to her. The strenuous, hazardous, and heart-breaking efforts she has made for months to secure his freedom prove ultimately unavailing to her, for it is a changed Fabrice who

2 Ibid. ii. 61.

emerges and with whom she drives through the night to Piedmont and safety.

Cet être adoré, singulier, vif, original, était désormais sous ses yeux en proie à une rêverie profonde; il préférait la solitude même au plaisir de parler de toutes choses, et à cœur ouvert, à la meilleure amie qu'il eût au monde. Toujours il était bon, empressé, reconnaissant auprès de la duchesse, il eût comme jadis donné cent fois sa vie pour elle; mais son âme était ailleurs. On faisait souvent quatre ou cinq lieues sur ce lac sublime sans se dire une parole...

Voilà ce qui devait arriver tôt ou tard, se disait la duchesse avec une tristesse sombre. Le chagrin m'a vieillie, ou bien il aime réellement, et je n'ai plus que la seconde place dans son cœur.[3]

One day she enters his room at Locarno and finds the walls covered with views of the tower in which he had been imprisoned and of the governor's lodge—Clélia's dwelling.

Mathilde's jealousy of Mme de Fervaques, Armance's of Mme d'Aumale, had been real to Mathilde and to Armance; but the reader, knowing Julien and Octave to be merely acting the part of faithless lovers, cannot take this jealousy very seriously. Stendhal had never before attempted to depict the jealousy of a woman who knows herself irrevocably supplanted, though a few sentences of analysis in De l'amour shows the quality of his intuition. 'Une femme se sent avilie par la jalousie... elle doit pencher à la cruauté, et cependant elle ne peut tuer légalement sa rivale.' (A man, Stendhal means, can obtain satisfaction by a duel.) 'Chez les femmes la jalousie doit donc être un mal encore plus abominable, s'il se peut, que chez les hommes. C'est tout ce que le cœur humain peut supporter de rage impuissante et de mépris de soi-même, sans se briser.' And this, in particular, anticipates the chapters of La Chartreuse we are considering: 'Les femmes fières dissimulent leur jalousie par orgueil. Elles passent de longues soirées silencieuses et froides, avec cet homme qu'elles adorent, qu'elles tremblent de perdre, et aux yeux duquel elles se voient peu aimables. Ce doit être un des plus grands supplices possibles...'[4] The particular piece of cruelty that her jealousy suggests to Gina is to use all her influence at Parma to promote Clélia's marriage to Crescenzi.

[3] La Chartreuse de Parme, ii. 278–9.

[4] De l'amour, i. 190, 192. We have italicized the phrases which correspond most closely to Gina's state of mind. In writing this passage of De l'amour, Stendhal was thinking chiefly of Diderot's Mme de Pommeraye (Jacques le Fataliste).

C'était donc avec la conscience d'avoir cherché à hâter, autant qu'il était en elle, le mariage qui mettait Fabrice au désespoir, que la duchesse le voyait tous les jours. Aussi passaient-ils quelquefois quatre ou cinq heures à voguer ensemble sur le lac, sans se dire un seul mot. La bienveillance était entière et parfaite du côté de Fabrice; mais il pensait à d'autres choses, et son âme naïve et simple ne lui fournissait rien à dire. La duchesse le voyait, et c'était son supplice.[5]

The most extravagant of dithyrambs have been sung for Gina, Angelina-Cornelia-Isola Valsera del Dongo, duchessa Sanseverina, as she signs herself when she wants to gratify a snob. She is, wrote James Huneker, 'the queen of Stendhal women'. And, he added, 'a more vital woman has not swept through literature since the Elizabethans'. For Balzac it was obvious that she was the centrepiece of the book. 'The Duchess is one of those magnificent statues which make you at once admire art and curse nature for being so niggardly with such models.' Racine's Phèdre 'is not so fine, nor so full, nor so living'.[6] Criticism is all but unanimous in judging her one of the major character creations of literature; she is, indeed, so much more compelling a figure than Fabrice that *La Chartreuse de Parme* could almost be considered, like *Vanity Fair*, a heroine's novel. This is not the only sign of a trend in Stendhal, as his literary career drew to a close, towards replacing the male by the female protagonist. Lamiel is Gina rejuvenated and, as it were, made airy: wild rather than savage, the tigress turned gazelle.

But Lamiel, had Stendhal finished the work, would have died young, in a spectacular gesture of self-immolation: like Mina, and also like Julien Sorel. Gina Sanseverina outlives her splendour, declines, and is broken—which stamps *La Chartreuse de Parme* with the quality of true human tragedy, whereas *Lamiel* would have been merely melodramatic in its ending. Nowhere else, except in *L'Abbesse de Castro* which was written at the same time as *La Chartreuse*, did Stendhal venture on this painful theme of the slow degradation of a human being. One may suppose that awareness of the decline of his own vigour partly accounted for his preoccupation with this theme.

Gina grows old. She is the first of his heroines to do this. If one counts age by the years that have passed since birth, she is not

[5] *La Chartreuse de Parme*, ii. 300.
[6] Huneker, *Egoists, a Book of Supermen*, p. 60; Balzac, *Œuvres diverses*. iii. 381-2.

much older at the end than Mme de Rênal; but can one imagine Mme de Rênal ageing? The Count, received by her the day after she heard of Fabrice's capture, 'fut atterré à la vue de la duchesse. — Elle a quarante ans! se dit-il, et hier si brillante! si jeune!' During the ensuing interview between the two lovers, she asks Mosca to bear in mind that, as she puts it, 'la jeune femme est morte en moi, je ne puis plus m'exagérer rien au monde, je ne puis plus aimer'.[7] Here she is being less than honest with Mosca: had Fabrice been restored to her, even not loving her, provided he were heart-whole as before, then, perhaps, the young woman in Gina would have sprung to life again. The conviction, borne in on her at Belgirate, that Fabrice has lost his heart to Clélia, kills all hope of rejuvenescence. Stendhal epitomizes her unhappiness in one terrible sentence: 'La vieillesse et l'affaiblissement de l'âme étaient arrivés pour elle avec la perspective d'une illustre vengeance.' In a state of listlessness foreign to her nature, she awaits the news of the Prince's assassination—plotted by her earlier, with one accomplice, the half-crazed poet Ferrante Palla. 'Avilie, atterrée par ce plus grand des chagrins possibles, la duchesse se disait quelquefois: Si le ciel voulait que Ferrante fût devenu tout à fait fou ou manquât de courage, il me semble que je serais moins malheureuse. Dès ce moment ce demi-remords empoisonna l'estime que la duchesse avait pour son propre caractère.'[8] Wrinkles and white hair are less significant, as tokens of decline, than the waning of energy and of the power of resolution, which in Gina had been invincible: never once before, in all her erratic, wilful, unreflecting career, had she allowed herself to repent of any action which a spontaneous impulse had prompted.

One final humiliation is reserved for her—the humiliation of the flesh. The sexual charm to which, like her predecessor and original Vandozza Farnese, she owed her worldly success and the fortune of her nephew, proves her final undoing. She is forced into the ultimate degradation of having to choose between Fabrice's life and her own prostitution. Ernest IV, having succumbed to a draught of poison, is duly succeeded by his son, a naïve and timid adolescent, overawed by the Duchess and yet in love with her. He sends her a charming letter, inviting her to return to Parma; this she does, and works skilfully a whole winter to restore Mosca's credit, destroy Rassi's, and rehabilitate Fabrice. At last matters

---

[7] *La Chartreuse de Parme*, ii. 84. 92.   [8] Ibid. 279.

seem to have reached the point where a trial could be held at which the young man would be certain of an acquittal. But it is necessary for him first to give himself up to justice. Mosca had intended he should occupy a cell in the town jail; instead, Fabrice recklessly surrenders himself at the Citadel, delighted to be once more in Clélia's proximity, but running immense risks of being poisoned by Fabio Conti. The commandant of the fortress bears Fabrice a deadly grudge, for his impertinence in escaping, curiously, and not for his intrigue with his daughter, about which he knows nothing. Gina is distraught with anxiety: something of the unrepentant woman of passion she had been re-emerges with Stendhal's observation that 'elle ne fit point cette réflexion morale, qui n'eût pas échappé à une femme élevée dans une de ces religions du Nord qui admettent l'examen personnel: j'ai employé le poison la première, et je péris par le poison. En Italie, ces sortes de réflexions, dans les moments passionnés, paraissent de l'esprit fort plat, comme ferait à Paris un calembour en pareille circonstance.'⁹ Time presses; it is essential to persuade someone to act before the midday meal is served to Fabrice. After a parley of agonizing length, the young prince yields to her entreaties; on conditions. So early in his reign, he has little to learn of the uses of absolute power.

Gina cannot break the promise he has exacted from her. She postpones paying this debt of dishonour as long as she can, but the young man presses her, has his way, and she leaves Parma immediately afterwards, never to return. Mosca, who at some unspecified point has become a widower, resigns his portfolio, joins her, and the two middle-aged lovers are married at last.

The shadow of misfortune and disillusion extends over Fabrice too in these concluding chapters; but, perhaps because he is cast in a less terrestrial mould than Gina, his sufferings deject without debasing him. Clélia's marriage, every obstacle to which is carefully removed by Gina, drives him not to despair but to a mood of elegiac resignation—and to deepening piety. He goes into a first religious retreat; the mortifications to which he subjects himself age him prematurely, exactly as the mental agonies which his aunt had earlier endured on his behalf aged her. When he revisits her, 'elle le trouva tellement changé, ses yeux, encore agrandis par l'extrême maigreur, avaient tellement l'air de lui sortir de la tête, et lui-même avait une apparence tellement chétive et malheureuse,

---

⁹ Ibid. 370.

avec son petit habit noir et râpé de simple prêtre, qu'à ce premier abord la duchesse, elle aussi, ne put retenir ses larmes'[1]—though a little later, when she realizes the reason for his misery, she enters into a cold fury and deliberately tortures him by recounting in great detail the ceremonies which had marked Clélia's marriage to Crescenzi. Clélia, when she sees him, does not even recognize him to begin with, taking him to be some person resembling Fabrice, perhaps his elder brother, but much older: she judges him to be a man of forty.

This is at the court reception, the poignant scene which we had occasion to analyse in an earlier chapter. Stendhal allows his lovers, a little before the close, a clandestine idyll which, although it lasts three years, is passed over in a single sentence. As has been remarked already, Stendhal was compelled by a barbarous publisher to slash the final part of La Chartreuse; much though one may regret the loss, which Stendhal did not live long enough to make good in a later edition, it may perhaps be thought that the acceleration of the narrative in the last pages of the novel confers on them something of the fascination of a phantasmagoria. The story does not so much end as vanish, in a tenuous, iridescent vapour. A theory in modern astronomy states that the more remote the galaxies are from our point of observation, the faster in fact they are speeding away from us: only part of the spectrum of their light reaches us, and there is, perhaps, some analogy with the Doppler effect in the abridged and schematic presentation of the last end of Stendhal's characters, as rapidly they recede from view. There is no happy ending, but the further misfortunes are related so summarily that the impact is barely felt. Fabrice persuades Clélia to allow him to have charge of their child, Sandrino (the name, a diminutive of Alessandro, is one of the few indications in the text of the novel of the original link between the hero and Alexander Farnese). Fabrice, like Julien—but, as far as can be known, unlike their creator—longs for a son; but, if the child is to be truly his son, he must bring him up. The two-year-old boy is given out as dead, but secretly removed to a nearby house; unluckily he pines and dies a few months later. Clélia, heart-broken, follows him into the grave, and Fabrice, renouncing all the dignities and wealth that have accrued to him (he has been raised to the archbishopric of Parma and, his father and brother

[1] La Chartreuse de Parme, ii. 403.

having both died, has inherited the vast estates of the Del Dongos),
retires to the 'Charterhouse of Parma', which is thus mentioned,
for the first time in the book, in the antepenultimate paragraph.
Death takes him after a year of austerities. A little later Gina too
dies, and the stage is empty, the players all departed.

> Ils ont fondu dans une absence épaisse,
> L'argile rouge a bu la blanche espèce.

Only Mosca remains to administer Parma and enlarge his private
fortune, pursuing both occupations with immense success.

After a first reading, or even after the first two or three readings,
the impression *La Chartreuse de Parme* is apt to give is one of
formlessness, or of what has been called, more indulgently, 'an art
which laughs at art'.[2] This apparently uncalculated narrative, like
a dragonfly in flight, could finish up anywhere; the Charterhouse
of Parma happens simply to emerge at the very end, arbitrarily,
almost whimsically. It is too clear, surely, that the work was un-
planned—the author himself declared that he never knew, when
writing one chapter, what he was going to put in the next. There
is no unity of subject: is this a political novel, a love-story, a tale
of adventure? all three by turns, sometimes all three together. No
one theme either: Bardèche tentatively suggested the formula
'gaiety in the midst of danger',[3] but, as we have seen, the gaiety
evaporates after the thirteenth chapter and never returns. More
credibly, an Italian critic[4] finds the essential leitmotiv to lie in a
series of conjugated opposites, heroism versus machiavellianism,
passion versus intelligence, beauty and courage versus cleverness
and guile. There is incoherence in the plotting. Stendhal sometimes forgets to mention an important detail in its place, and introduces it belatedly with some such apologetic formula as: 'We have
omitted to inform the reader. . . .' Worse still, he inverts in the
telling the sequence of events, and for no apparent reason; the
most unfortunate instance being the episode of Fabrice's narrow
escape from death by poisoning, thanks to Clélia's devotion and
presence of mind, which Stendhal relates *before* telling us of the
frantic efforts made by the Duchess to persuade some official and,
in the last resort, the Prince himself, to send for Fabrice before

---

[2] Jacoubet writes of 'l'art qui se moque de l'art — l'art qui domine ses moyens
en négligeant ses vaines ressources, l'art suprême de *la Chartreuse de Parme*,
œuvre d'art' (*Curiosités et récréations littéraires*, p. 150).

[3] *Stendhal romancier*, p. 375.   [4] A. Momigliano, *Studi di poesia*, p. 5.

he can eat. The suspense which might have been built up is thus destroyed in advance, since we know that the hero is safe and that Gina's alarm is unnecessary. So ill contrived has the plot seemed to certain critics that they have not hesitated to redraft it. Balzac was the first to do this, as a gesture of genuine friendship to a fellow novelist who might have profited from his counsels in a second edition. A British professor of French literature not long ago went to considerable trouble to outline two alternative plots either of which, in his view, would be preferable to the hotchpotch of stories which jostle with each other in *La Chartreuse* as it stands.[5] This time Stendhal had been in his grave for rather more than a century, which made the advice even more disinterested than Balzac's.

Despite all this, the general consensus of critical opinion has for a long time now assigned *La Chartreuse* a high place among the masterpieces of European fiction in the nineteenth century. And the general consensus of critical opinion, at any rate when passing a positive judgement, is not often at fault. Where, then, does one look for that structural unity which is invariably a feature of the true work of art?

The traditional vocabulary of criticism is of little help as a guide to the qualities that confer on *La Chartreuse de Parme* the excellence which the discerning mind divines in it. For once, it is better to discard the old framework of concepts—theme, characterization, plot—and look elsewhere for the unity underlying this intricate diversity. This unity is undoubtedly organizational. Almost any great canvas will provide an analogy for the kind of wholeness of pattern which can be sensed in *La Chartreuse*. Like certain paintings of Titian, in particular, it is crowded, vividly coloured, pulsating with life, but not on that account dispersed:

---

[5] A. Lytton Sells, '*La Chartreuse de Parme*. The problem of composition', *Modern Language Quarterly*, vol. xii (1951), pp. 204–15. Lytton Sells's criticism centres on the supposed incompatibility of a plot involving Gina and Mosca with one involving Fabrice and Clélia. For this reason he would have liked Fabrice to be rescued from the Tour Farnèse by his real father, the former Napoleonic general, instead of by Gina, Mosca, and Clélia in collusion. Another suggestion he makes is that after Clélia's death Fabrice should join his father in the Dauphiné where the general might be supposed to be spending his retirement. 'A retreat on some high Alpine platform, from which, while awaiting the hour of death, he [Fabrice] would have surveyed the world as from the eyrie of an eagle, would have been more appropriate . . . than an old *certosa* by the banks of the Po.' Considering that all it requires is infinite presumption, this particular type of emendatory criticism could well be practised more frequently than it has been.

grouped on the contrary, unified, gathered into a closed system. If one were to be more precise, one would have to say that the whole novel gives the impression of being balanced at the intersection of two inclined planes: the one rising with the rising sun from the warm mists of the morning of life, the other dipping with the lengthening shadows of evening towards the chilly darkness of cloister and tomb. The exact point of convergence can be plotted to a hair's breadth: it is the moment when an unnamed marquis whispers to Gina, in Count Zurla's drawing-room, that Fabrice has been taken. One may speak alternatively, using a term of Baudelaire's coining, of two *postulations*: the one towards youth, sunlight, and that 'gaiety in the midst of danger' of which we have heard; the other towards the enfeeblement of age and the encroaching shadow of cares, fears, grief, and loss.

Recalling, in the *Vie de Henri Brulard,* with what feelings and with what fervour he used to read novels as a boy, Stendhal said that he studied them as *predictions. La Chartreuse de Parme,* in spite of the exoticism, the extravagance, the frothy unreality, is essentially a prediction. This is how youth ends—or so Stendhal believed, taught by his own experience—this is what life leads to: disillusion, degradation, compromise, and extinction. But this prediction is made not, as for example in *L'Éducation sentimentale,* in the mode of realism, but rather in the mode of the allegorical poem; which is why the temper of the work is elegiac but not pessimistic.

Pessimism is held at bay too by a kind of gentleness in the tone of the latter half of *La Chartreuse* (exemplified particularly in the long chapters, of which we have said nothing, devoted to Fabrice's wooing of Clélia through his prison bars) which may well reflect the conclusion Stendhal had reached that neither sunlight nor shadow corresponds absolutely or permanently to good or to evil. As time passes, the heat and the brightness of day end by becoming a burden; the drawing on of evening can be anticipated with gratitude. For the ageing consul, the cloudless skies of an Italian summer, in their unbroken procession, were sometimes felt as unbearably oppressive. A cry charged with infinite lassitude was once wrung from him in those last years at Civitavecchia: 'j'ai trop vu le soleil', he wrote, in conscious or unconscious imitation of Hamlet's 'I am too much i' the sun'. Perhaps too he was remembering the dirge sung in another of Shakespeare's plays, a favourite of his, *Cymbeline*: it is consolation to Imogen that she should 'fear no more the heat of the sun'. Though none of his vitality had left him, Beyle could find it in him in these years to wish he had done with the incessant sunlight, and to decide that in the lengthening of the shadows there was no cause for repining.

Sunlight and shadow, morning and evening, these are, tinting this fresco that is *La Chartreuse de Parme*, the elemental tonalities. An early scene in the novel, which impresses the mind with a vivid sensation of the heat of an August mid-morning and the dust of a highroad white under the sun, is a memorable instance of the first of these two tonalities; it is the scene where Fabrice and Clélia meet for the first time, she being only twelve, though she looks two or three years older, and he sixteen. If the passage is analysed, it will be found that the impression of brilliant sunshine is rendered with a bare minimum of notation and no description properly speaking. The Countess Pietranera (Gina), who is travelling to Milan with her sister-in-law, Fabrice's mother, and Fabrice himself, asks the sergeant in command of the police detachment who have arrested them, whether the coachman might be allowed to move a few paces forward under the shadow of a tree: 'la chaleur était accablante, quoiqu'il ne fût que onze heures du matin. Fabrice, qui regardait fort attentivement de tous côtés, cherchant le moyen de se sauver, vit déboucher d'un petit sentier à travers champs, et arriver sur la grande route, couverte de poussière, une jeune fille de quatorze à quinze ans qui pleurait timidement sous son mouchoir.' A long deliberation ensues (the police were looking for Fabio Conti and had arrested the three Del Dongos in error). The countess, having engaged Clélia in conversation, and struck by her beauty, invites her into the coach: 'le soleil va vous faire mal, mademoiselle', she says.[6]

The undertones of this sunlit scene consist in the extreme youth of Fabrice and Clélia, corresponding to the morning hour; in the danger which is real enough but quickly averted by Gina's presence of mind; in the dust and the heat, material elements, together with the shadow which, here, is beneficent, refreshing, not sepulchral. A counterpart to these two or three pages may be found in chapter xxvi, when Fabrice takes it on himself to visit Clélia, who is staying at the Palazzo Contarini, a little before her marriage. The melancholy of the scene is attenuated by the joy the two lovers find in this secret reunion; but it is, after all, the last time they will see

[6] *La Chartreuse de Parme*, i. 141–3.

each other before Clélia passes into the arms of an unworthy stranger. In terms of the symbolism which Stendhal can be seen distilling in *La Chartreuse de Parme*, the significance of the episode lies in the fact that Fabrice presents himself at the palace door *at nightfall*; Clélia, when he is admitted to her presence, is sitting at a little table with a single candle burning on it; on seeing him, she hides her face in her hands (for she has vowed never to look at him), and Fabrice can calm her only by blowing out the candle, so that the talk, the kisses, and whatever else Stendhal refrains from recording, take place in complete darkness.

The morning sunlight and the shadows of evening: these are the poles of Stendhal's symbolism, but over and above and beyond stretches the night sky, the 'glittering' sky of Italy which he had conjured up so feelingly in the pages of *Rome, Naples et Florence*. One starlit scene we have evoked already: Fabrice's midnight walk along the banks of Lake Como. He is on that occasion on his way to his native Grianta to revisit his old tutor, the astrologer-priest Blanès. He arrives at dawn to find Blanès awaiting him, his coming having been announced by some conjunction of planets. The astrologer reveals to the young hero what he had read in the stars concerning his future: that he will be thrown into a prison; that he will escape, but that his escape will be the occasion of a crime; and finally that, provided he does not burden his own conscience with this crime, he will end his days in serenity of soul, seated on a wooden bench and dressed in white.

The visit to Blanès in his observatory allows Fabrice an indistinct vision of his own future: the nine months he will spend in a cell in the Citadel of Parma, the assassination of Ernest IV which Gina Sanseverina will order as soon as he is liberated, his last days spent in cloistered quiet, these are foretold, but as events the realization of which will be conditional on his withstanding certain temptations.[7] Moreover, the return to his birthplace is not merely

---

[7] 'Si tu as la faiblesse de tremper dans ce crime,' says Blanès, 'tout le reste de mes calculs n'est qu'une longue erreur' (*La Chartreuse de Parme*, i. 281). The reservation which hedges these predictions weakens the force of the criticism which is sometimes made of Fabrice, that his belief in Blanès's prophecies turns him into an apathetic fatalist: 'Par les prédictions, que le superstitieux Fabrice ne rejette pas, l'avenir est comme fermé' (Prévost, *Les Épicuriens français*, p. 115; cf. also F. Michel's essay, 'Les Superstitions de Fabrice del Dongo', in *Études stendhaliennes*). In a later work (*La Création chez Stendhal*, pp. 361–2) Prévost took up a much more acceptable view, viz. that the predictions serve

the occasion for glimpses into the future; it is also a pilgrimage into the past and as such, affords Fabrice a more-than-sentimental happiness. As a boy he had spent long hours with Blanès in his observatory; this room at the top of the church belfry tower is, he finds, exactly as it always had been: the priest's little lantern burns where it used to on the second floor, the planisphere is laid out on a great terracotta vase, with a small lamp burning at the base of it. 'Tous ces souvenirs de choses si simples inondèrent d'émotions l'âme de Fabrice et la remplirent de bonheur.' He spends the night in the tower (there is a strong element of risk in this return to Grianta, which is on Austrian territory, so that he needs to remain strictly concealed). The following morning he descries the sparrows looking for bread-crumbs on the balcony of the dining-room of his father's castle, and reflects that they must be the progeny of the birds he used to catch and tame when a child. At several leagues' distance he has a view of the shimmering waters of Lake Como, 'et cette vue sublime lui fit bientôt oublier toutes les autres; elle réveillait chez lui les sentiments les plus élevés. Tous les souvenirs de son enfance vinrent en foule assiéger sa pensée; et cette journée passée en prison dans un clocher fut peut-être l'une des plus heureuses de sa vie.'[8]

These pages are significantly reminiscent of the last chapters of *Le Rouge et le Noir*, where Julien's situation and state of mind are close forecasts of Fabrice's. Both heroes are prisoners—the one a prisoner at law, the other a prisoner for fear of the law. For both of them the prison is a tower, allowing a sublime, wide-ranging view. Each has an interview with an aged priest (Chélan, like Blanès, is on the brink of the grave). Both look back on life as though from the ultimate bourn (which Julien has, of course, reached, but not Fabrice, of whom nevertheless Stendhal writes: 'Le bonheur le porta à une hauteur de pensées assez étrangère à son caractère; il considérait les événements de la vie, lui si jeune, comme si déjà il fût arrivé à sa dernière limite'). Both turn their backs on the lures of the world and declare their longing to embrace a simple life, Julien 'dans un pays de montagnes comme Vergy', Fabrice somewhere on the banks of the lake that stretches before him. Julien reflects: 'J'étais heureux alors... Je ne connaissais pas

to link the reader to the author who is improvising his story and therefore knows only in broad outline what events are to come.

[8] *La Chartreuse de Parme*, i. 278, 287.

mon bonheur', and Fabrice: 'A quoi bon aller si loin chercher le bonheur, il est là sous mes yeux!'

The resemblances are instructive because of the one great difference: Julien's life is ending, while for Fabrice the end is still distant. In these two chapters, the eighth and the ninth of *La Chartreuse de Parme*, which plunge at once into the future and the past, time is caught for a moment in the eye of eternity.[9] In his other novels Stendhal was concerned only to capture the brief red hours of youth. The old men were there, yes, but buffoons, wise-acres, tyrants; and the old women, scarecrows or, at best, dignified ghosts. In *La Chartreuse de Parme* he had the courage to let his people grow old, break up, and die; he allowed a sincere, virile friendship between the young and the old, between Fabrice and Mosca, where formerly he had admitted, with rare exceptions (Julien and Pirard) only open antagonism or smouldering rebellion. For the first and last time, the whole pageant of human life was displayed, as in *War and Peace*: childhood, youth, the terrors and the raptures of love, the multifarious activities which absorb a man's prime; the battlefield and the political arena, the altruistic crusade and the egoistic game of power; and the heartbreak of defeat, defeat after ignominious defeat, souring the soul; the loss of one's heart's desire, despair, retreat, withdrawal; the sudden blossoming of a brief, belated happiness when hope of happiness had fled; and the disappearance of life's companions, and final extinction. *La Chartreuse de Parme* has something of the scope of *War and Peace*, but is unimaginably different in mood and treatment. The Russian novel stretches on endlessly, like the Russian steppes, and one travels slowly; the Franco-Italian novel which was Stendhal's legacy to Tolstoy[1] darts forward like a stream of quicksilver. Tolstoy's epic resolves itself ultimately into a paean to the forces of life, while Stendhal wrote an elegy. Natasha's son Petya is

[9] One must recall here Alain's glowing commentary on Fabrice's meditation in the belfry at Grianta: 'Il semble que Fabrice interrompe ici sa vie, et presque la recommence. Tout est souvenir en ce grand examen; tout y est prévision, par l'artifice de l'horoscope; tout y est contemplation, et invisible, et immobile, par cette prison du clocher. Aussi c'est là que je trouverai le plus haut sommet de la poésie stendhalienne' (*Stendhal*, pp. 107–8).

[1] Tolstoy's acknowledgement of his literary debt to Stendhal (particularly in respect of the treatment of battle scenes in the Waterloo passage of *La Chartreuse de Parme*) was made in a conversation with Paul Boyer, who reported it in *Le Temps*, 28 August 1901. See A. Paupe, *Histoire des œuvres de Stendhal* (1903), p. 326, and T. S. Lindstrom, *Tolstoï en France* (1952), pp. 107–10.

a healthy infant on the last page, with three older sisters in the house. Clélia's son Sandrino dies. There is no possibility for Fabrice of survival in his posterity, and the reunion elsewhere that he looks to is doubtless no more than the pious illusion of a credulous mind.

.   .   .   .   .   .

With *La Chartreuse de Parme* we have reached the climax, but not the close, of Stendhal's career as a novelist, since after its completion he went on to map out and compose in part that most disturbingly perverse work, *Lamiel*, the history of a girl who, early in life, achieves a startling emancipation; Lamiel emerges in this rough-hewn and unfinished study as a more charming Mme de Merteuil whose intellectual brilliance is at the service of her intellectual curiosity instead of being—as had been the case with Laclos's heroine—devoted to demolishing the moral fabric of society. But the temptation to look at *Lamiel* must be resisted, for if in these pages no thesis is argued, the intention has been to explore certain distinguishable themes, and Stendhal's last novel, whatever else it may illuminate, can shed no further light on these.

We have chosen to examine four novels as specimens of the 'imaginary biography'. All four present an attractive young man whose apprenticeship to society and initiation to the life of the emotions provides the story-teller with a solid and unvarying framework. All four heroes are in one way or another exceptional or, to use Stendhal's word, *singular*: burdened by an exceptional misfortune, driven by an exceptional ambition, handicapped by an exceptional position in the world, or, finally, reserved for an exceptional destiny. All four are in one way or another, again, self-projections on the author's part or, perhaps, instances of wish-fulfilment. If little has been said in the preceding pages about this particular way of looking at Stendhal's fiction, the reason is partly because it has so frequently been adopted in the past as to constitute by now a commonplace in Stendhal criticism.[2] So much so, indeed, that it is perhaps necessary rather to draw attention to its limitations as an interpretative approach. In the first place, none of Stendhal's heroes springs from quite the same social stratum as he did. Then, more important, none is a creative artist or has any ambitions to become one. Herein lies a fundamental difference between Stendhal's novels and Proust's in their autobiographical aspect.

[2] See above, p. 47.

The point has now been reached when it should be possible to provide some answer to the question put at the beginning of this study: whether these four heroes represent simply variants on Stendhal's conception of modern youth in France and Italy, or whether, on the other hand, they can properly be regarded as embodying varying approximations to an ideal of living—in which case they would be not simply social types but moral prototypes.

If we may refer back to an earlier discussion of the failings of Octave de Malivert as Stendhal may be thought to have seen them, it will be recalled that we summarized the situation by saying that the hero of his first novel was suffering from an excess of *egotism* unredeemed by *egoism*. The exact meaning attached to these terms is important enough to justify a fuller elucidation at the stage we have now reached.

Egotism may be defined as a rooted tendency to speak—and hence to think—exclusively of one's own self.[3] It may easily be combined with an acute and indeed painful concern for other people's opinions of oneself; and in the process of deserving their good opinion, the egotist may be punctilious in discharging what he considers to be his duties towards them. He may even practise altruism to the point of self-abnegation, for this too will tend to enhance his own opinion of himself. But his egotism is none the less, in Stendhal's view, irrational, however morally desirable the by-products it may give rise to: for (if we are to judge by Octave) it makes for dissatisfaction, discomfort, irritability, and unhappiness, in place of the self-satisfaction, tranquillity, and happiness which the egotist, like all other men, would understandably prefer to have as his lot.

The word *egoism*, as we are using it, calls for a more special definition, since in normal usage it is, morally speaking, a question-begging term. Let us call it attunement to one's own nature and readiness to follow its promptings regardless of the world's approval or disapproval. It may be supposed that Stendhal was urging egoism on his sister when he put it to her that 'il faut se faire un bonheur solitaire, indépendant des autres'. Such withdrawal means curbing the natural expansiveness of a generous spirit; but *the*

---

[3] The word was an English importation (it is usually traced back to Addison), but it existed in the French language before Stendhal began to use it. Martineau quotes the definition given in Rivarol's Dictionary (1827 edition): 'habitude blâmable de parler de soi' (*L'Œuvre de Stendhal*, p. 441).

others can never respond, and are best left to their chilly fate: 'on perd son feu à vouloir le communiquer à ces morceaux de glace: il faut jouir de soi-même dans la solitude...' Stendhal found confirmation of this disillusioned philosophy in the *Letters* of Mme du Deffand. He wrote to Pauline again: 'Mme du Deffand me fait sentir encore mieux tout le bon de mon système: de ne rendre son bonheur dépendant de personne... Pour goûter tous les fruits de ce système, il faut qu'il soit tourné en habitude.'[4]

His pose of dandified disdain was perhaps more theoretical than real; otherwise, logically, Stendhal would have had to consign these statements to his diary or his private notebooks; by confiding in his sister he tacitly admits the flaw in his self-sufficiency. Pauline Beyle was, over the years these letters were written (1807–12), the one person from whom Henri had no secrets: she was the Armance to his Octave. The egoist is never totally closed in on himself, being, against appearances, no misanthropist (misanthropy he leaves to the egotist); and there has to be a dialogue, with a preferably passionate interlocutor. When Pauline, sinking into domestic mediocrity, ceased to qualify as Stendhal's *âme-sœur*, others took her place—his various mistresses, Mme Curial and Giulia di Rinieri in particular, and certain friends of his later years like Domenico Fiore and Abraham Constantin.

Somewhere in each of Stendhal's novels there is a sentence spoken by the hero by which can be measured with some accuracy the degree to which his soul has been invaded by the canker of egotism. The key to Octave's spiritual condition is the assertion: 'Tout ce que j'ai pu faire, c'est de me connaître.' How damning this modest disclaimer of all knowledge but self-knowledge! And doubtless there is no exaggeration here: it would have been hard indeed on Octave if his perpetual concern with self had not enabled him to know himself. Among Julien's utterances, we would single out the exclamation beginning: 'Et moi, jeté au dernier rang par une Providence marâtre, moi à qui elle a donné un cœur noble et pas mille francs de rente...' Julien too is preoccupied with himself, but specifically with himself as a discontented commoner. He is finally cured of this preoccupation and, as one might expect, the cure coincides with his acquisition of a title and a settled income. In the last chapters his egotism has evaporated and his egoism finds significant expression in his outburst: 'Que m'importent

---

[4] *Correspondance*, ii. 242, 240; iv. 8.

les autres?'—by which time he and his charming mistress have achieved a happiness 'independent of the others', short-lived though it inevitably is. Lucien reveals his egotism with the question he puts his father on his return from Caen: 'Quelle opinion dois-je avoir de moi-même?'[5] It is not until his father has disappeared from the scene that Lucien can finally reach an opinion as to what he should think of himself, and only when he has reached it can he forget about himself and start in pursuit of his own happiness: appropriately, he leaves for Italy.

Thus, Octave never rids himself of egotism, Julien succeeds in doing so a few weeks before execution, Lucien not until the end of the novel (but Lucien still has his life before him). It can be seen that, progressively, in each of his novels, Stendhal approximates ever more closely to his ideal hero, one who would live his whole life along lines directly opposed to those of an egotist, a man, in other words, supremely indifferent to the opinion his neighbours choose to have of him and, what is more important and more diffi-cult, to the opinion of that importunate, censorious mentor whom we all carry within ourselves: conscience. Fabrice del Dongo is this ideal hero, Fabrice whose most characteristic utterance is the ques-tion he puts himself during the first hour of his captivity: 'Suis-je un héros sans m'en douter?' The naïveness of this reflection is proof enough that to question his own nature, even to attempt to see where he stands in any moral order of merit, is something this unegotistical hero has never considered doing before.

At every point Fabrice is seen to be as little given to interro-gating himself on his motives, as unconcerned about the possible results of his own actions, as uncalculating, in a word, as a child. Where Lucien Leuwen, returning from his election campaign, asks what opinion he should have of himself, Fabrice, returning from his campaign (Waterloo), is anxious only to know whether he has been present at a real battle. In contrast to the great majority of men, who allow themselves to be guided by a combination of social pressures and acquired standards, Fabrice is unaware that social pressures exist and he has no standards. When, on his return from Locarno to Parma (chapter xxiv), he calmly delivers himself into the power of his most embittered enemy, Fabio Conti, it is certainly not with any notion of accomplishing a spectacularly

5 *Armance*, p. 14; *Le Rouge et le Noir*, ii. 172–3, 435; *Lucien Leuwen*, iii. 210. See above, pp. 79, 56, 129, 144.

heroic gesture, like Regulus giving himself up to the vindictive Carthaginians; quite simply, Fabrice wants to be near Clélia. And when a few hours later Clélia bursts into his cell and dashes to the floor the plate of poisoned food which has been brought to him, Fabrice takes a most ungentlemanly, not to say unheroic, advantage of her wrought-up state and scanty dress. At one moment, Fabrice is the sublime romantic lover, at the next, a cad. Both roles meet in his egoism, that is, in his uncritical acceptance of the promptings of his own nature.

Herein, no doubt, lies a more prosaic explanation of his faith in omens than any that the ingenuity of Stendhal's commentators has offered: they are merely an exteriorization of the directives of his own instincts. An eagle flying north overhead is taken as a sign that he should cross the Alps and join Napoleon; but to fight under the French flag is, of course, just what his generous idealism and sense of adventure urge him to do. No omen would ever be construed as bidding him follow any course against which his deeper nature would rebel. Never does Fabrice force himself to anything, never does he make any attempt at self-transcendence: the hypocrite's mask will not fit him; he cannot invent cheerful chatter to allay Gina's jealous suspicions, and has no need to impose on himself the austerities to which he submits after Clélia's marriage—his grief translates itself naturally into such macerations.

If Stendhal's novels had any underlying didactic purpose, the moral implicit in the story of Fabrice's career might well be epitomized in the single clause of the rule of the Abbey of Thélème: *Do what thou wilt*. But it must be added that Rabelais's gloss is just as valid for the *élite* of Stendhal's imaginary world: '*Fay ce que vouldras*, parce que gens liberes, bien nez, bien instruictz, conversans en compagnies honnestes, ont par nature un instinct et aiguillon qui tousjours les pousse à faictz vertueux, et retire de vice: lequelz ils nommoient honneur.' Less optimistic than Rabelais, Stendhal did not suppose, perhaps, that every act of Fabrice, Gina, Mosca, or Clélia was strictly *honourable*: but nothing of what they do is ever common or mean.[6]

---

[6] However, the following passage is not without significance: 'Le comte n'avait pas de vertu; l'on peut même ajouter que ce que les libéraux entendent par *vertu* (chercher le bonheur du plus grand nombre) lui semblait une duperie; il se croyait obligé de chercher avant tout le bonheur du comte Mosca della Rovere; mais il était plein d'honneur... De la vie il n'avait dit un mensonge à la duchesse' (*La Chartreuse de Parme*, ii. 83–84).

As it happens, the novels are not didactic literature, however clearly the author's values are established and conveyed. *Beylisme* is not a practical philosophy intended for universal application, since it degenerates into anarchic hedonism unless the *beyliste* happens to be endowed with a native fineness which unfortunately is the appurtenance of few (of those *happy few*, no doubt, to whom *La Chartreuse de Parme* is dedicated). The novels, nevertheless, are not to be dismissed as utopian rhapsodies, any more than as 'profound immoralities'.[7] In recounting these four careers, Stendhal had another, deeper, and less contentious purpose: to convey through his fables a heightened awareness of the inexpressible depth and richness of the individual life. And this is poet's work. His object is to communicate to his reader something of the delicate poetry which is, or which can and should be, woven into the fabric of the individual life, not so much in order that the reader should admire the clarity and power of the communication, as that he should pursue on his own, the book being closed, that tender meditation, that *rêverie* which is, as he remarked in *De l'amour*, 'le vrai plaisir du roman', but which is also, alas, 'innotable', defying formulation by the written word. Stendhal seeks neither to edify nor to instruct, neither to denounce, nor simply to entertain; he wants more than to beguile an idle hour, less than to alter the social order. In the final analysis his purpose is just to bring a certain happiness to those few chosen spirits who resort to him. A curiously modest, unexpected, and, in these times, a most unfashionable doctrine. But fashions change.

---

[7] This phrase is used of Stendhal's work by Andrew H. Wright, *Jane Austen's Novels*, p. 24 of the Peregrine Books edition.

BIBLIOGRAPHY

A. STENDHAL'S WORKS

1. Published during his life

Lettres écrites de Vienne en Autriche, sur le célèbre compositeur Jh. Haydn, suivies d'une Vie de Mozart et de Considérations sur Métastase et l'état présent de la musique en France et en Italie. 1814. Subsequently republished as: *Vies de Haydn, de Mozart et de Métastase*, the title by which the work is now generally known.

Histoire de la peinture en Italie. 1817.

Rome, Naples et Florence en 1817. 1817. A new edition, much altered and enlarged, was published in 1826, the date having been dropped from the title.

De l'amour. 1822.

Racine et Shakspeare. 1823. *Racine et Shakspeare No. II.* 1825.

Vie de Rossini. 1824. (Actual date of publication: November 1823.)

Armance, ou Quelques scènes d'un salon de Paris en 1827. 1827.

Promenades dans Rome. 1829.

Le Rouge et le Noir, chronique du XIXe siècle. 1831. (Actual date of publication: November 1830.)

Mémoires d'un touriste. 1838.

La Chartreuse de Parme. 1839.

L'Abbesse de Castro. 1839. The volume included also *Vittoria Accoramboni* and *Les Cenci.*

2. Published after his death

A few volumes consist of collected articles or stories which had appeared in contemporary newspapers and magazines; but the majority are transcriptions from Stendhal's manuscripts (at present housed in the Grenoble Municipal Library). The fullest edition of his complete works is that edited by Henri Martineau and published under the imprimatur Le Divan between 1927 and 1937. All references in the present study are to this edition which comprises 79 volumes. It includes, of course, all works published during Stendhal's lifetime (as noted above) together with the following:

Chroniques italiennes (2 volumes).

Correspondance (10 volumes).

Courrier anglais (5 volumes). Contributions to various English periodicals, translated back into French.

Écoles italiennes de peinture (3 volumes). Material for a continuation of the *Histoire de la peinture en Italie.*

Journal (5 volumes). Covers the years 1801–18.

Lamiel. Composed mainly October–December 1839.

Lucien Leuwen (3 volumes). Composed June 1834–November 1835.

Mélanges d'art.

Mélanges de littérature (3 volumes). The first volume contains *Une Position sociale* and various other uncompleted novels.

Mélanges de politique et d'histoire (2 volumes).

Mélanges intimes et Marginalia (2 volumes).

Molière, Shakspeare, la Comédie et le Rire.

Napoléon (2 volumes).

Pages d'Italie.

Pensées. Filosofia nova (2 volumes).

Romans et nouvelles (2 volumes). A collection including *Le Rose et le Vert, Mina de Vanghel, Le Philtre, Féder,* &c.

Souvenirs d'égotisme. Composed June–July 1832.

Théâtre (3 volumes).

Vie de Henri Brulard (2 volumes). Composed November 1835–April 1836.

Voyage dans le midi de la France.

3. Additional recently published material

Since the completion of the Divan Edition, some additional material has been embodied in the following volumes:

R. D'ILLIERS, *Un Inédit de Stendhal. Guide à l'usage d'un voyageur en Italie.* Paris, 1951. 51 pp.

J. F. MARSHALL (ed.), *Henri III. Un Acte inédit.* Urbana, 1952. 85 pp.

V. DEL LITTO, *En marge des manuscrits de Stendhal. Compléments et fragments inédits (1803–1820).* Paris, 1955. 434 pp.

M. A. RUFF, *Feuillets inédits de Stendhal.* Paris, 1957. 91 pp.

Y. DU PARC, *Quand Stendhal relisait les 'Promenades dans Rome'. Marginalia inédits.* Lausanne, 1959. 130 pp.

4. Letters

Letters of Stendhal continue to come to light. A number were published in the quarterly journal *Le Divan* until its demise in 1958. A new collection, fuller than that contained in the Divan Edition, is being published currently in the 'Bibliothèque de la Pléiade' series; the first volume came out in 1963.

A huge literature has grown up around Stendhal—only a proportion being devoted to the evaluation of his creative work. The list that follows is in principle restricted to books, essays, and articles which deal, wholly or partly, with some aspect or other of his work as a novelist; but we have noted, in the first section, a few of the more recent and important studies of the life of Henri Beyle, together with some collections of documents relating to his career or personality. In the remaining sections, critical and interpretative material has been grouped under what headings seemed most convenient.

B. BIOGRAPHIES AND BIOGRAPHICAL MATERIAL

ARBELET, PAUL. *La Jeunesse de Stendhal.* Paris, 1919. 2 vols., xviii+403, 244 pp.

BILLY, ANDRÉ. *Ce cher Stendhal: récit de sa vie.* Paris, 1958. 282 pp.

DEL LITTO, VITTORIO (ed.). *Lettres à Stendhal (1803–1806).* Paris, 1943. 2 vols., xxxv+200, 256 pp.

JOURDA, PIERRE. *Stendhal raconté par ceux qui l'ont vu. Souvenirs, lettres, documents.* Paris, 1931. x+233 pp.

MARTINEAU, HENRI. *Petit dictionnaire stendhalien.* Paris, 1948. 501 pp.

—— *Le Calendrier de Stendhal.* Paris, 1950. 408 pp.

—— *Le Cœur de Stendhal: histoire de sa vie et de ses sentiments.* Paris, 1952–3. 2 vols., 448, 486 pp.

—— (ed.). *Cent soixante-quatorze lettres à Stendhal (1810–1842).* Paris, 1947. 2 vols., 293, 329 pp.

MÉRIMÉE, PROSPER. *Portraits historiques et littéraires,* ed. P. Jourda. Paris, 1928. ('Stendhal', pp. 153–92: the text of *H.B.*, a pamphlet first published, in an edition limited to 25 copies, in 1850; together with *Notes et souvenirs,* an essay which served as introduction to the 1855 edition of Stendhal's *Correspondance inédite.*)

C. GENERAL STUDIES

1. *Earlier period*

BOURGET, PAUL. *Essais de psychologie contemporaine.* Paris, 1885. ('Stendhal (Henri Beyle)', pp. 253–323.)

BRANDES, GEORGE. *Main Currents in Nineteenth-Century Literature. Vol. V. The Romantic School in France.* London, 1904. ('Beyle', pp. 205–38.)

BRUN, PIERRE. *Henry Beyle—Stendhal.* Grenoble, 1900. 145 pp.

BUSSIÈRE, AUGUSTE. 'Poètes et romanciers modernes de la France. XLVIII. Henry Beyle (M. de Stendhal)', *Revue des Deux Mondes,* 13ᵉ année (1843), nouvelle série, tome I, pp. 250–99.

CHUQUET, ARTHUR. *Stendhal—Beyle.* Paris, 1902. 548 pp.

COLLIGNON, ALBERT. *L'Art et la vie de Stendhal.* Paris, 1868. 535 pp.

COLOMB, ROMAIN. *Notice sur la vie et les ouvrages de M. Beyle (de Stendhal). Deuxième édition.* Paris, 1854. civ pp.

FAGUET, ÉMILE. *Politiques et moralistes du dix-neuvième siècle, 3ᵉ série*. Paris, 1903. ('Stendhal', pp. 1–64.)

JAMES, HENRY. *Literary Reviews and Essays*. New York, 1957. ('Henry Beyle', pp. 151–7. Reprinted from *The Nation*, 17 Sept. 1874.)

PAUPE, ADOLPHE. *Histoire des œuvres de Stendhal*. Paris, 1903. 446 pp.

—— *La Vie littéraire de Stendhal*. Paris, 1914. viii+227 pp.

ROD, ÉDOUARD. *Stendhal*. Paris, 1892. 160 pp.

SAINTE-BEUVE, CHARLES-AUGUSTIN. *Causeries du lundi. Tome IX*. Paris, 1854. ('M. de Stendhal', pp. 301–41.)

STRYIENSKI, CASIMIR. *Soirées du Stendhal Club*. Paris, 1905. xx+352 pp.

—— and ARBELET, PAUL. *Soirées du Stendhal Club, 2ᵉ série*. Paris, 1908. 290 pp.

TAINE, HIPPOLYTE. *Nouveaux essais de critique et d'histoire*. Paris, 1894. ('Stendhal (Henri Beyle)', pp. 223–57.)

2. Later period

ALAIN (i.e. Émile-Auguste Chartier). *Stendhal*. Paris, 1948. 128 pp. (First published 1935.)

ALBÉRÈS, FRANCINE MARILL. *Stendhal*. Paris, 1959. 127 pp.

ANDRIEU, RENÉ. 'Soixante ans après *Lamiel, roman inédit*. Signification de Stendhal', *La Pensée*, no. 26 (1949), pp. 29–37.

ARAGON, LOUIS. *La Lumière de Stendhal*. Paris, 1954. 269 pp.

BLUM, LÉON. *Stendhal et le beylisme*. Paris, 1930. xiv+245 pp. (First published 1914.)

BOYLESVE, RENÉ. *Réflexions sur Stendhal*. Paris, 1929. 96 pp.

CARACCIO, ARMAND. *Stendhal, l'homme et l'œuvre*. Paris, 1951. 204 pp.

CLEWES, HOWARD. *Stendhal. An introduction to the novelist*. London, 1950. 128 pp.

CROCE, BENEDETTO. *Poesia e non poesia. Note sulla letteratura europea del secolo decimonono*. Bari, 1923. ('Stendhal', pp. 90–102.)

DAVID, MAURICE. *Stendhal — sa vie — son œuvre*. Paris, 1931. 71 pp.

DECOUR, JACQUES. 'Stendhal', *La Nef*, no. 3 (1944), pp. 8–16.

FERNANDEZ, RAMON. *Itinéraire français*. Paris, 1943. ('Stendhal', pp. 275–91.)

FINESHRIBER, WILLIAM H. *Stendhal, the romantic rationalist*. Princeton, 1932. ix+57 pp.

FRANCE, ANATOLE. *Stendhal*. Abbeville, 1920. 40 pp.

FRIEDRICH, HUGO. *Drei Klassiker des französischen Romans*. Frankfurt am Main, 1939. ('Stendhal (Henri Beyle)', pp. 37–85.)

GREEN, F. C. *Stendhal*. Cambridge, 1939. viii+336 pp.

HUNEKER, JAMES. *Egoists. A book of supermen*. London, 1909. ('A sentimental education. Henry Beyle—Stendhal', pp. 1–65.)

JACOUBET, HENRI. *A la gloire de ... Stendhal.* Paris, 1943. 221 pp.

JOURDA, PIERRE. *État présent des études stendhaliennes.* Paris, 1930. 122 pp.

—— *Stendhal, l'homme et l'œuvre.* Paris, 1934. 296 pp.

LACRETELLE, JACQUES DE. 'En relisant Stendhal', *Nouvelle N.R.F.*, vol. i (1953), pp. 446–57.

LEVIN, HARRY. *The Gates of Horn.* New York, 1963. ('Stendhal', pp. 84–149.)

LUKÁCS, GEORGE. *Studies in European Realism.* London, 1950. ('Balzac and Stendhal', pp. 65–84.)

MACCARTHY, DESMOND. 'Stendhal', *France Libre*, vol. iv (1942), pp. 16–23.

MARSAN, JULES. *Stendhal.* Paris, 1932. 289 pp.

MARTINEAU, HENRI. *L'Œuvre de Stendhal: histoire de ses livres et de sa pensée.* Paris, 1951. 638 pp.

—— and MICHEL, FRANÇOIS [and others]. *Nouvelles soirées du Stendhal Club.* Paris, 1950. 272 pp.

MARTINO, PIERRE. *Stendhal.* Paris, 1934. 318 pp. (First published 1914.)

MAURIAC, FRANÇOIS. *Petits essais de psychologie religieuse.* Paris, 1933. ('Henri Beyle et les revenants', pp. 105–54. The *revenants* are not ghosts, but the demobilized veterans of the First World War, Mauriac's essay having been written in 1920.)

NIMIER, ROGER. 'Le Gros Consul', *Nouvelle N.R.F.*, vol. v (1955), pp. 986–1002.

PRÉVOST, JEAN. *Les Épicuriens français.* Paris, 1931. ('Chemin de Stendhal', pp. 43–145.)

—— *La Création chez Stendhal. Essai sur le métier d'écrire et la psychologie de l'écrivain.* Paris, 1951. 406 pp. (An earlier war-time edition was published at Marseilles.)

PROUST, MARCEL. *Contre Sainte-Beuve.* Paris, 1954. ('Notes sur Stendhal', pp. 413–16.)

RICHARD, JEAN-PIERRE. *Littérature et sensation.* Paris, 1954. ('Connaissance et tendresse chez Stendhal', pp. 15–116.)

ROY, CLAUDE. *Stendhal par lui-même.* Paris, 1951. 192 pp.

SACKVILLE-WEST, EDWARD. *Inclinations.* London, 1949. ('Stendhal and Beyle', pp. 189–98.)

SAMUEL, HORACE B. 'Stendhal, the compleat intellectual', *Fortnightly Review*, vol. xciv (1913), pp. 69–81.

SCHWOB, RENÉ. 'Notes sur Stendhal', *Revue hebdomadaire*, 48ᵉ année (1939), no. 30, pp. 532–44.

STRACHEY, LYTTON. *Books and Characters French and English.* London, 1922. ('Henri Beyle', pp. 255–78.)

SUARÈS, ANDRÉ. *Portraits.* Paris, 1913. ('D'après Stendhal', pp. 183–274.)

SYMONS, ARTHUR. 'Stendhal', *English Review*, vol. xxv (1917), pp. 294–301.

THIBAUDET, ALBERT. *Stendhal.* Paris, 1931. 188 pp.

VALÉRY, PAUL. *Variétés II*. Paris, 1930. ('Stendhal', pp. 75–125.)

WAIS, KURT. *Französische Marksteine von Racine bis Saint-John Perse.* Berlin, 1958. ('Stendhal der Überwinder', pp. 97–128.)

D. SPECIAL STUDIES OF STENDHAL AS NOVELIST

ADAMS, ROBERT MARTIN. *Stendhal: notes on a novelist.* London, 1959. xxii+228 pp.

BARDÈCHE, MAURICE. *Stendhal romancier.* Paris, 1947. 473 pp.

BLIN, GEORGES. *Stendhal et les problèmes du roman.* Paris, 1954. 339 pp.

BONFANTINI, MARIO. *Stendhal e il realismo, saggio sul romanzo ottocentesco.* Milan, 1958. 220 pp.

BOURGET, PAUL. *Quelques témoignages.* Paris, 1928. ('L'art du roman chez Stendhal', pp. 41–55.)

BROMBERT, VICTOR. *Stendhal et la voie oblique: l'auteur devant son monde romanesque.* New Haven and Paris, 1954. 173 pp.

GIRARD, RENÉ. *Mensonge romantique et vérité romanesque.* Paris, 1961. 312 pp. (Five novelists are considered: Cervantes, Stendhal, Flaubert, Dostoevsky, and Proust.)

HYTIER, JEAN. *Les Romans de l'individu.* Paris, 1928. ('Stendhal et le roman', pp. 80–117.)

JACOUBET, HENRI. *Les Romans de Stendhal.* Grenoble, 1933. 207 pp.

MARTINEAU, HENRI. 'Stendhal et les origines du roman psychologique', *Causeries françaises*, 1ere année (1923), pp. 69–89.

O'CONNOR, FRANK. *The Mirror in the Roadway.* London, 1957. ('Stendhal. The flight from reality', pp. 42–57.)

TURNELL, MARTIN. *The Novel in France.* London, 1950. ('Stendhal', pp. 123–208.)

ZOLA, ÉMILE. *Les Romanciers naturalistes.* Paris, 1881. ('Stendhal', pp. 75–124.)

E. MONOGRAPHS ON PARTICULAR WORKS

1. *Armance*

BLIN, GEORGES. 'Étude sur *Armance*', pp. ix–lxxviii in Stendhal, *Armance*. Paris, Éditions de la Revue Fontaine, 1946.

GIDE, ANDRÉ. *Incidences.* Paris, 1924. ('Préface à *Armance*', pp. 175–89.)

HEMMINGS, F. W. J. 'Stendhal self-plagiarist', *L'Esprit créateur*, vol. ii (1962), pp. 19–25. (Reminiscences of *Armance* in Stendhal's later novels.)

HENRIOT, ÉMILE. *Livres et portraits, 3ᵉ série.* Paris, 1927. ('*Armance*, Olivier, Stendhal, Latouche et Mme de Duras', pp. 193–9.)

HOLST, C. V. 'Stendhal, l'auteur d'*Armance*', *Edda*, vol. xxxvii (1937), pp. 145–84.

HUXLEY, ALDOUS. *Music at Night and other essays*. London, 1931. ('Obstacle Race', pp. 157–73.)

IMBERT, HENRI-FRANÇOIS. 'A propos d'*Armance*', *Le Divan*, no. 287 (1953), pp. 183–4.

LUPPÉ, MARQUIS DE. 'Autour de l'*Armance* de Stendhal. L'*Olivier* de la duchesse de Duras', *Le Divan*, no. 250 (1944), pp. 263–8.

MARANINI, LORENZA. *Visione e personaggio secondo Flaubert ed altri studi francesi*. Padua, 1959. ('Monologo interiore e movimenti stilistici nel primo romanzo di Stendhal', pp. 91–118.)

MARTINEAU, HENRI. 'Stendhal et Henri de Latouche', *Le Divan*, no. 114 (1925), pp. 596–600.

—— 'Stendhal et H. de Latouche', *Le Divan*, no. 174 (1931), pp. 463–9.

MICHEL, FRANÇOIS. *Études stendhaliennes*. Paris, 1958. ('Armance de Zohiloff', pp. 217–25.)

MORAND, PAUL. *L'Eau sous les ponts*. Paris, 1954. ('Armance ne rime peut-être pas avec impuissance', pp. 73–80.)

MULLER, DANIEL. '*Armance* et la critique', *Le Divan*, no. 114 (1925), pp. 592–6.

TURNELL, MARTIN. *The Art of French Fiction*. London, 1959. ('Stendhal's first novel', pp. 61–90.)

VERMALE, FRANÇOIS. 'Les Sources d'*Armance*. M. de Beyle et les "complots" de Talleyrand en 1813', *Le Divan*, no. 218 (1938), pp. 97–108.

2. Le Rouge et le Noir

ALCIATORE, JULES C. 'Une source possible du deuil de Mathilde de La Mole', *Le Divan*, no. 288 (1953), pp. 250–2.

—— 'Pourquoi "Amanda" Binet?', *Le Divan*, no. 304 (1957), pp. 232–6. (Influence of Picard on *Le Rouge et le Noir*.)

—— 'Stendhal, Grimm, et une méditation de Julien Sorel', *French Review*, vol. xxxii (1959), pp. 366–7.

—— 'Stendhal, Shakespeare, et deux épigraphes du *Rouge et Noir*', *Stendhal Club*, no. 6 (1960), pp. 185–8.

—— 'Stendhal lecteur de *la Pucelle*' and 'Stendhal et les romans de Voltaire', *Stendhal Club*, no. 8 (1960), pp. 325–34, and no. 10 (1961), pp. 15–23. (Reminiscences of Voltaire in *Le Rouge et le Noir* particularly.)

AUERBACH, ERICH. *Mimesis. Dargestellte Wirklichkeit in der abendländischen Literatur*. Bern, 1946. ('Im Hôtel de La Mole', pp. 400–38.)

BAUER, ROGER. 'Julie et Julien, ou le problème du bonheur chez J. J. Rousseau et Stendhal', *Romanische Forschungen*, vol. lxv (1954), pp. 378–91.

BIBAS, HENRIETTE. 'Le double dénouement et la morale du *Rouge*', *Revue d'Histoire Littéraire de la France*, 49ᵉ année (1949), pp. 21–36.

BORGERHOFF, E. B. O. 'The Anagram in *Le Rouge et le Noir*', *Modern Language Notes*, vol. lxviii (1953), pp. 383–6.

BRUNET, GABRIEL. 'Un héros stendhalien', *Quo Vadis*, nos. 74–76 (1954), pp. 13–27. (Julien Sorel.)

CASTEX, PIERRE-GEORGES. 'Quelques cadres d'étude pour *le Rouge et le Noir*', *Information littéraire*, 2e année, no. 2 (1950), pp. 67–77.

DAMIEN, JEAN. 'Julien Sorel ou le complexe de David', *Stendhal Club*, no. 4 (1959), pp. 308–10.

DEL LITTO, VITTORIO. 'En marge de *Rouge et Noir*. L'affaire Berthet racontée par une petite-nièce de Louis Michoud de la Tour', *Stendhal Club*, no. 14 (1962), pp. 148–63.

DU BOS, CHARLES. *Approximations* (*deuxième série*). Paris, 1927. ('En lisant *le Rouge et le Noir*', pp. 1–8.)

DUMOLARD, HENRY, *Pages stendhaliennes*. Grenoble, 1928. ('Le véritable Julien Sorel', pp. 39–94; 'Le Casino de Verrières', pp. 95–101.)

—— *Autour de Stendhal*. Grenoble, 1932. ('En marge de *Le Rouge et le Noir*', pp. 125–52.)

FORNAIRON, ERNEST. 'Le véritable Julien Sorel', *Les Œuvres libres*, 2e série, no. 141 (1958), pp. 121–54.

GRANT, RICHARD B. 'The Death of Julien Sorel', *L'Esprit créateur*, vol. ii (1962), pp. 26–30.

HASTIER, LOUIS, *Vieilles histoires, étranges énigmes*, 5e série. Paris, 1961. ('*Le Rouge et le Noir*, ses personnages originaux', pp. 105–262.)

HEMMINGS, F. W. J. 'Deux débuts de Julien Sorel', *Stendhal Club*, no. 12 (1961), pp. 151–6.

—— 'Julien Sorel and Julian the Apostate', *French Studies*, vol. xvi (1962), pp. 229–44.

HENRIOT, ÉMILE. *Livres et portraits*, 2e série. Paris, 1925. ('Les dessous de Julien Sorel', pp. 215–21.)

HUGO, HOWARD E. 'Two strange interviews: Rousseau's *Confessions* and Stendhal's *Le Rouge et le Noir*', *French Review*, vol. xxv (1952), pp. 164–72.

JACOUBET, HENRI. *Variétés d'histoire littéraire, de méthodologie et de critique d'humeur*. Paris, 1935. ('Les fonds de réalité et l'invention romanesque dans *le Rouge et le Noir*', pp. 207–66.)

—— 'Autour du titre "Le Rouge et le Noir"', *Revue d'Histoire Littéraire de la France*, 40e année (1933), pp. 103–8.

JOHANNET, RENÉ. 'Sur la signification du titre "Le Rouge et le Noir"', *Le Divan*, no. 159 (1930), pp. 226–7.

JOURDA, PIERRE. 'Le Modèle de Mathilde de La Mole', *Le Divan*, no. 151 (1929), pp. 332–40.

—— 'Un Centenaire romantique: *le Rouge et le Noir*', *Revue des Cours et Conférences*, 32e année (1931), pp. 305–15, 428–36.

—— 'Toujours Mathilde de La Mole', *Le Divan*, no. 203 (1936), pp. 297–8.

Le Breton, André. *'Le Rouge et le Noir' de Stendhal. Étude et analyse.* Paris, 1934. 326 pp.

Liprandi, Claude. *Stendhal, le 'bord de l'eau' et la 'note secrète'.* Avignon, 1949. 221 pp.

—— *Sur un personnage du 'Rouge et Noir': la maréchale de Fervaques.* Lausanne, 1959. 74 pp.

—— *Au cœur du 'Rouge'. L'affaire Lafargue et 'le Rouge et le Noir'.* Lausanne, 1961. 368 pp.

—— 'Sur un épisode du *Rouge et Noir*: un roi à Bray-le-Haut', *Revue des Sciences Humaines*, fasc. 59 (1950), pp. 141–60.

—— 'Un Roi à Verrières', *Le Divan*, no. 275 (1950), pp. 390–8.

—— 'Sur un épisode du *Rouge et Noir*: les plaisirs de la campagne', *Revue des Sciences humaines*, fasc. 68 (1952), pp. 295–313.

—— 'Sur un personnage du *Rouge et Noir*: Monsieur Descoulis', *Le Divan*, no. 290 (1954), pp. 362–70.

—— 'Sur un épisode du *Rouge et Noir*: le bal du duc de Retz', *Revue des Sciences humaines*, fasc. 76 (1954), pp. 403–17.

—— 'Monsieur Appert à Verrières', *Stendhal Club*, no. 2 (1959), pp. 115–18.

—— 'Trois notes sur *le Rouge et le Noir*', *Stendhal Club*, no. 15 (1962), pp. 261–4.

Malraux, Clara. 'Les Grandes Sœurs de Mathilde de La Mole', *Confluences*, no. 30 (1944), pp. 262–4.

Martineau, Henri. 'La Chronologie du *Rouge et Noir*', *Le Divan*, no. 227 (1939), pp. 81–86.

—— and Vermale, François. 'La Prison de Julien Sorel', *Le Divan*, no. 261 (1947), pp. 15–22.

Parturier, Maurice. 'La Fin du *Rouge* et le problème de Mary', *Le Divan*, no. 192 (1935), pp. 455–9.

Reizov, Boris. 'Pourquoi Stendhal a-t-il intitulé son roman "le Rouge et le Noir"?' *La Littérature soviétique*, no. 1 (1957), pp. 173–8.

Royer, Louis. 'Madame Derville de *Rouge et Noir*', *Mercure de France*, vol. ccxxxix (1932), pp. 722–6.

Sacy, S. de. 'Stendhal et la *note secrète*', *Mercure de France*, vol. cccviii (1950), pp. 353–6.

Serrurier, C. 'Julien Sorel, une réincarnation du picaro', pp. 272–83 in *Mélanges de philologie offerts à Jean-Jacques Salverda de Grave*. Groningen and The Hague, 1933.

Vermale, François. 'Le dossier maçonnique de M. de Beyle', *Le Divan*, no. 209 (1937), pp. 145–53. (The final section of this study is entitled 'Souvenirs maçonniques dans le Rouge et le Noir'.)

—— 'Le vrai M. Valenod', *Le Divan*, no. 242 (1942), pp. 164–9.

VERMALE, FRANÇOIS. 'Le Philippe Vane du *Rouge et Noir*', *Le Divan*, no. 266 (1948), pp. 325–8.

—— 'Autour du *Rouge et Noir*', *Revue d'Histoire Littéraire de la France*, 51ᵉ année (1951), pp. 37–51.

VIGNERON, ROBERT. 'Stendhal en Espagne', *Modern Philology*, vol. xxxii (1934), pp. 55–66. (Establishes the exact date on which Stendhal decided to write *Le Rouge et le Noir*.)

3. *Lucien Leuwen*

COLESANTI, MASSIMO. '*Lucien Leuwen* o della nostalgia', *Galleria*, anno XI (1961), pp. 89–107.

DUMOLARD, HENRY. *Autour de Stendhal*. Grenoble, 1932. ('Un personnage de *Lucien Leuwen*: le véritable docteur Du Poirier', pp. 93–121.)

DURAND, GILBERT. 'Lucien Leuwen ou l'héroïsme à l'envers', *Stendhal Club*, no. 3 (1959), pp. 201–25.

GIRAUD, RAYMOND. *The Unheroic Hero in the Novels of Stendhal, Balzac, and Flaubert*. New Brunswick, 1957. ('Stendhal—the bridge and the gap between two centuries', pp. 53–92.)

MARANINI, LORENZA. *Visione e personaggio secondo Flaubert ed altri studi francesi*. Padua, 1959. ('Il privilegio contro l'uomo nel *Lucien Leuwen* di Stendhal', pp. 119–51.)

PRITCHETT, V. S. *Books in General*. London, 1953. ('A Political Novel', pp. 123–9.)

ROUSSEAUX, ANDRÉ. *Le Monde classique*. Paris, 1941. ('Au cœur de Stendhal', pp. 144–51.)

ROY, CLAUDE. *Descriptions critiques. L'Homme en question*. Paris, 1960. ('Stendhal et *Lucien Leuwen*', pp. 103–22.)

WAGNER, R. L. 'Les Valeurs de l'italique. Notes de lecture sur *Lucien Leuwen* de Stendhal', pp. 381–90 in *Mélanges d'histoire littéraire et de bibliographie offerts à Jean Bonnerot*. Paris, 1954.

4. *La Chartreuse de Parme*

ALCIATORE, JULES C. 'Stendhal, Scott, et une singulière cachette', *Le Divan*, no. 281 (1952), pp. 324–5.

—— 'Conjectures sur une maxime de l'abbé Blanès', *Le Divan*, no. 292 (1954), pp. 537–8.

—— 'Stendhal et *la Princesse de Clèves*', *Stendhal Club*, no. 4 (1959), pp. 281–94. (In particular, reminiscences of Mme de Lafayette's novel in *La Chartreuse de Parme*.)

—— 'Plutarque et Shakespeare. Sources possibles de deux présages stendhaliens', *Modern Language Notes*, vol. lxxvii (1962), pp. 309–10.

ARBELET, PAUL. 'Les Origines de *la Chartreuse de Parme*', *Revue de Paris*, 29ᵉ année (1922), tome II, pp. 356–79.

BALZAC, HONORÉ DE. *Œuvres diverses*, ed. M. Bouteron and H. Longnon, vol. iii. Paris, 1940. ('Études sur M. Beyle', pp. 371–405. This is the famous review of *La Chartreuse de Parme*, originally published in *La Revue parisienne*, 25 Sept. 1840.)

BARRÈS, MAURICE. *Du sang, de la volupté et de la mort*. Paris, 1895. ('L'automne à Parme', pp. 209–16.)

BENEDETTO, LUIGI FOSCOLO. *La Chartreuse noire: comment naquit 'la Chartreuse de Parme'*. Florence, 1947. 38 pp.

—— *La Parma di Stendhal*. Florence, 1950. 552 pp.

BONFANTINI, MARIO. 'Stendhal e il paesaggio italiano', *Aurea Parma*, anno XXXIV, fasc. II (1950), pp. 15–19.

BORNECQUE, JACQUES-HENRY. 'Dans la chambre noire de *la Chartreuse de Parme*', *Information littéraire*, 2ᵉ année, no. 3 (1950), pp. 90–101.

CORDIÉ, CARLO. *Sull'arte della 'Chartreuse de Parme'*. Florence, 1936. 61 pp.

DECOUR, JACQUES. 'Le Centenaire de *la Chartreuse de Parme*: France–Italie', *Commune*, no. 69 (1939), pp. 567–71.

DÉDÉYAN, CHARLES. 'Stendhal et le Risorgimento dans *la Chartreuse de Parme*', *Revue de Littérature Comparée*, 26ᵉ année (1952), pp. 168–82.

—— 'Une hypothèse sur le duc Sanseverina-Taxis de *la Chartreuse*', *Revue d'Histoire Littéraire de la France*, 54ᵉ année (1954), pp. 201–3.

DURAND, GILBERT. *Le Décor mythique de 'la Chartreuse de Parme': contribution à l'esthétique du romanesque*. Paris, 1961. 251 pp.

HAZARD, PAUL. 'La Couleur dans *la Chartreuse de Parme*', *Le Divan*, no. 242 (1942), pp. 64–74.

HEMMINGS, F. W. J. 'A Note on the origins of *La Chartreuse de Parme*', *Modern Language Review*, vol. lviii (1963), pp. 392–5.

HENRIOT, ÉMILE. *Stendhaliana*. Paris, 1924. ('*La Chartreuse de Parme* corrigée par Stendhal', pp. 77–104.)

HUBERT, J. D. 'Note sur la dévaluation du réel dans *la Chartreuse de Parme*', *Stendhal Club*, no. 5 (1959), pp. 47–53.

JACOUBET, HENRI. *Curiosités et récréations littéraires*. Paris, 1942. ('Les Atmosphères de *la Chartreuse de Parme*', pp. 120–56.)

JAMES, DAVID. 'The Harmonic Structure of *La Chartreuse de Parme*', *French Review*, vol. xxiv (1950), pp. 119–24.

JOURDA, PIERRE. 'L'Évasion de Fabrice', *Le Divan*, no. 179 (1932), pp. 221–3.

—— 'Les Corrections de *la Chartreuse de Parme*', *Revue d'Histoire Littéraire de la France*, 42ᵉ année (1935), pp. 77–89.

—— 'Le Paysage dans *la Chartreuse de Parme*', *Ausonia*, 6ᵉ année (1941), pp. 12–28.

LA VARENDE. 'En lisant *la Chartreuse*', *Revue de Paris*, 57ᵉ année (1950), pp. 39–46.

LEVIN, HARRY. 'La Citadelle de Parme : Stendhal et Benvenuto Cellini', *Revue de Littérature Comparée*, 18ᵉ année (1938), pp. 346–50.

MACCHIA, GIOVANNI. *Il paradiso della ragione: studi letterari sulla Francia*. Bari, 1960. ('*La Chartreuse de Parme* e il romanzo puro', pp. 295–306.)

MAGNANI, LUIGI. 'L'idea della *Chartreuse*', *Paragone*, no. 38 (1953), pp. 5–27.

MARTINO, PIERRE. 'La Parme de Stendhal', *Le Divan*, no. 242 (1942), pp. 75–86.

MÉLIA, JEAN. 'Stendhal, Parme, et J.-L. Boccheciampe', *Mercure de France*, vol. cccv (1949), pp. 480–94.

MICHEL, FRANÇOIS. *Études stendhaliennes*. Paris, 1958. ('Les Superstitions de Fabrice del Dongo', pp. 226–54; 'De Brunswick à Parme. Le Fiscal Rassi dans *La Chartreuse*', pp. 255–68; 'Un souvenir de Stendhal amoureux dans *la Chartreuse de Parme*', pp. 269–73.)

MOMIGLIANO, ATTILIO. *Studi di poesia*. Bari, 1938. ('*La Chartreuse de Parme*', pp. 5–11.)

MORAND, PAUL. '*La Chartreuse de Parme*', *Nouvelle Revue Française*, 10ᵉ année (1962), pp. 250–60.

PELLEGRINI, CARLO. 'L'Idylle de Fabrice del Dongo', *Stendhal Club*, no. 1 (1958), pp. 15–22.

ROYER, LOUIS. 'Le Lieutenant Robert de *la Chartreuse de Parme*', *Ausonia*, 2ᵉ année (1937), pp. 1–6.

SELLS, A. LYTTON. 'Boccaccio, Chaucer and Stendhal', *Rivista di Letterature Moderne*, anno II (1947), pp. 237–48. (The Fabrice–Clélia episode in *La Chartreuse* inspired by a story in the *Teseida* of Boccaccio.)

—— '*La Chartreuse de Parme*. The problem of style', and '*La Chartreuse de Parme*. The problem of composition', *Modern Language Quarterly*, vol. xi (1950), pp. 486–91, and vol. xii (1951), pp. 204–15.

STEPHAN, PHILIP. 'Count Mosca's role in *La Chartreuse de Parme*', *L'Esprit créateur*, vol. ii (1962), pp. 38–42.

TEMMER, MARK. 'Comedy in the *Charterhouse of Parma*', *Yale French Studies*, no. 23 (1959), pp. 92–99.

THIBAULT, RENÉ. '*La Chartreuse de Parme*: portrait du héros', *France Libre*, vol. ii (1941), pp. 329–32.

THOMAS, JEAN. 'Le Centenaire de *la Chartreuse*', *Annales politiques et littéraires*, 56ᵉ année (1939), pp. 467–70.

ULLMANN, STEPHEN. *Style in the French Novel*. Cambridge, 1957. ('Portrayal of a foreign milieu. Italy—Stendhal, *La Chartreuse de Parme*', pp. 44–52.)

VERMALE, FRANÇOIS. 'Le côté espagnol de *la Chartreuse de Parme*', *Le Divan*, no. 256 (1945), pp. 213–15.

VERMALE, FRANÇOIS. 'Fabrice prédicateur', *Le Divan*, no. 259 (1946), pp. 391–4.

WARDMAN, H. W. '*La Chartreuse de Parme*: ironical ambiguity', *Kenyon Review*, vol. xvii (1955), pp. 449–71.

WAYNE-CONNER, J. 'L'Arbre de Fabrice et l'abbé Blanès', *Le Divan*, no. 292 (1954), pp. 493–500.

5. Minor Fictional Works

DEBRAYE, HENRY. 'La Méthode de composition de Stendhal. A propos d'une ébauche de roman inédit: *Une Position sociale*', *Mercure de France*, vol. cvi (1913), pp. 705–17.

DÉDÉYAN, CHARLES. *Stendhal et les 'Chroniques italiennes'*. Paris, 1956. 104 pp.

DEL LITTO, VITTORIO. '*Lamiel*. Pages inédites', *Stendhal Club*, no. 1 (1958), pp. 3–8.

GIDE, ANDRÉ. 'En relisant *Lamiel*', pp. 9–36 in *Lamiel, roman de Stendhal*. Paris, Éditions du Livre Français, 1947.

JOURDA, PIERRE. 'L'art du récit dans les *Chroniques italiennes*', pp. 157–65 in *Journées stendhaliennes internationales de Grenoble*. Paris, 1956.

MARTINO, PIERRE. 'Stendhal et Lesage', *Le Divan*, no. 279 (1951), pp. 190–1. (Source of Stendhal's short story *Le Chevalier de Saint-Ismier*.)

—— 'Le Premier Écrit romanesque de Stendhal? *Les Souvenirs d'un gentilhomme italien*', *Le Divan*, no. 286 (1953), pp. 74–82.

PRÉVOST, JEAN. *Essai sur les sources de 'Lamiel'. Les Amazones de Stendhal*. Lyons, 1942. 42 pp.

ROYER, LOUIS. 'Stendhal imitateur de Scarron', *Mercure de France*, vol. cclv (1934), pp. 251–68. (Source of *Le Philtre*.)

F. STYLE, THEMES, AND MISCELLANEOUS ASPECTS OF THE NOVELIST'S WORK

ALBÉRÈS, FRANCINE MARILL. *Le Naturel chez Stendhal*. Paris, 1956. 470 pp.

—— *Stendhal et le sentiment religieux*. Paris, 1956. 228 pp.

ALCIATORE, JULES C. 'Un trait de caractère de l'héroïne stendhalienne: une sensibilité vive cachée sous une froideur apparente', *Le Bayou*, no. 58 (1954), pp. 78–81.

AMER, HENRY. 'Amour, prison et temps chez Stendhal', *Nouvelle Revue Française*, 10ᵉ année (1962), pp. 483–90.

BARRÈRE, JEAN-BERTRAND. 'Stendhal et le chinois', *Revue des Sciences Humaines*, fasc. 92 (1958), pp. 437–61. (On the cleavage between the hero in Stendhal and the rest of the world.)

BEAUVOIR, SIMONE DE. *Le Deuxième Sexe. I. Les faits et les mythes.* Paris, 1949. ('Stendhal et le romanesque du vrai', pp. 364–77.)

BONFANTINI, MARIO. 'A propos de "réalisme" stendhalien. Stendhal a-t-il été le maître de Balzac?', pp. 75–82 in *Journées stendhaliennes internationales de Grenoble.* Paris, 1956.

BRAUCHLIN, DORA. *Das Motiv des 'Ennui' bei Stendhal.* Strassburg, 1930. 94 pp.

BROMBERT, VICTOR. 'Stendhal: creation and self-knowledge', *Romanic Review*, vol. xliii (1952), pp. 190–7.

—— 'Stendhal, analyst or amorist?', *Yale French Studies*, no. 11 (1953), pp. 39–48.

CARACCIO, ARMAND. 'La Leçon de Stendhal', pp. 96–102 in *Studi sulla letteratura dell'Ottocento in onore di P. P. Trompeo.* Naples, 1959.

COOK, ALBERT. 'Stendhal's irony', *Essays in Criticism*, vol. viii (1958), pp. 355–69.

DELACROIX, HENRI. *La Psychologie de Stendhal.* Paris, 1918. 286 pp.

DEL LITTO, VITTORIO. *La Vie intellectuelle de Stendhal. Genèse et évolution de ses idées (1802–1821).* Paris, 1959. 730 pp.

EHRENBURG, ILYA. *Cahiers français.* Paris, 1961. ('Les enseignements de Stendhal', pp. 131–78.)

FERNANDEZ, RAMON. *Messages, 1ère série.* Paris, 1926. ('L'autobiographie et le roman. L'exemple de Stendhal', pp. 78–109.)

GARCIN, PHILIPPE. 'Arrigo Beyle, milanese', *Nouvelle Revue Française*, 8e année (1960), pp. 275–96, 457–74.

GILBERT, PIERRE. *La Forêt des cippes. Essais de critique.* Paris, 1918. ('Le style de Stendhal', vol. i, pp. 151–61.)

GOURMONT, REMY DE. *Promenades littéraires, 5e série.* Paris, 1913. ('Le style et l'art de Stendhal', pp. 105–14.)

HOOG, ARMAND. *Littérature en Silésie.* Paris, 1944. ('Stendhal ou le combat sur la frontière', pp. 87–150.)

LALO, CHARLES. *L'Art et la vie. I. L'art près de la vie.* Paris, 1946. ('L'art pour l'auto-excitation: Stendhal', pp. 41–57.)

MARTINO, PIERRE. 'Quelques thèmes de roman chez Stendhal', *Le Divan*, no. 249 (1944), pp. 198–219.

MAUROIS, ANDRÉ. *Cinq visages de l'amour.* New York, 1942. ('Les Héroïnes de Stendhal', pp. 89–127.)

MORIER, HENRI. *La Psychologie des styles.* Geneva, 1959. ('Le style Code Civil', pp. 336–44.)

NATOLI, GLAUCO. 'La Peinture italienne et les personnages de Stendhal', pp. 191–7 in *Journées stendhaliennes internationales de Grenoble.* Paris, 1956.

NAUMANN, MANFRED. 'Stendhals Bemühung um die Wirklichkeit', *Sinn und Form*, vol. xi (1959), pp. 110–39.

ORTEGA Y GASSET. *On Love. Aspects of a single theme.* London, 1959. ('Love in Stendhal', pp. 23–82.)

PICHOIS, CLAUDE. 'Sur quelques épigraphes de Stendhal', *Le Divan,* no. 285 (1953), pp. 32–36.

POULET, GEORGES. 'Stendhal et le temps', *Revue Internationale de Philosophie,* 16ᵉ année (1962), pp. 395–412.

RICHARD, JEAN-PIERRE. 'Thèmes romantiques chez Stendhal', *Revue des Sciences Humaines,* fasc. 62–63 (1951), pp. 201–10.

ROBERTAZZI, MARIO. *Poesia e realtà.* Modena, 1934. ('Il tema della prigione nello Stendhal', pp. 77–88.)

SACY, S. DE. 'Le Miroir sur la grande route. Les romans de Stendhal et le roman picaresque', *Mercure de France,* vol. cccvi (1949), pp. 64–80.

SAGNE, JULIETTE. *Le Sentiment de la nature dans l'œuvre de Stendhal.* Strassburg, 1932. 95 pp.

SOULAIROL, JEAN. 'La Poésie de Stendhal', *Le Divan,* no. 242 (1942), pp. 102–19.

STAROBINSKI, JEAN. *L'Œil vivant.* Paris, 1961. ('Stendhal pseudonyme', pp. 191–244.)

VALERI, DIEGO. *Da Racine a Picasso: nuovi studi francesi.* Florence, 1956. ('L'arte di Stendhal', pp. 69–92.)

VIGNERON, ROBERT. 'Beylisme, romanticisme, réalisme', *Modern Philology,* vol. lvi (1958), pp. 98–117.

WANDRUSZKA, M. 'Zum Stil Stendhals', *Zeitschrift für französische Sprache und Literatur,* vol. lxii (1939), pp. 429–36.

WICKE, BERTA. *Stilprobleme bei Stendhal.* Lucerne, 1936. 66 pp.

INDEX

PRINTED IN GREAT BRITAIN
AT THE UNIVERSITY PRESS, OXFORD
BY VIVIAN RIDLER
PRINTER TO THE UNIVERSITY